Hannes Werthner
Martin Bichler (eds.)

Lectures in E-Commerce

SpringerWienNewYork

Prof. Dr. Hannes Werthner
University of Trento and ITC-irst
via Sommarive
I-38050 Povo-Trento
Italy

Dr. Martin Bichler
25 South Dutcher Street (2nd floor)
Irvington, NY 10533
USA

Printing was supported by Bundesministerium für Bildung, Wissenschaft
und Kultur

Typesetting: Data conversion by Graphik Rödl, A-2486 Pottendorf
Printing: Manz Crossmedia, A-1051 Wien
SPIN: 10798427

CIP data applied for

With numerous Figures

ISBN 3-211-83623-3 Springer-Verlag Wien New York

Preface

We are witnessing a phenomenal change, one may even call it a revolution, in business and society primarily due to information technology and the resulting rapid emergence of electronic commerce (e-commerce). Commercial activities such as information gathering, shopping, trading, brokering, collaboration, and distribution are changing in top gear adopting an entire set of new technologies. This affects every aspect of how business is conducted, changing internal processes as well as external relationships, modifying and restructuring entire economic sectors. The Internet tends to increase the power of consumers who are redefining their buying patterns as the Web has also extended the reach of co-operations – integrating all different types of stakeholders. In this context businesses are analyzing new strategies to leverage both, the power of the next generation of information technologies as of potential new business models.

E-commerce developments can be described as an interaction between order and disorder – on the level of technologies and systems, services and industrial structures. The supply side tends to differentiate their products and services, whereas the demand side tries to harmonize, thus, creating permanently additional space for new services and players. Old value chains are "deconstructed", and new ones are created. New services tend to become commodities, where with increasing quality prices may decrease. At the same time the "classical" big players respond (with huge investments). This leads to a concentration process, which is, however, permanently challenged. Innovation happens much faster, time seems to be counted differently.

It does not come as a surprise that e-commerce – due to its "youth" and its turbulent development – is still missing a widely accepted definition. It has been described as "doing business electronically" or, more precisely, as sharing business information, maintaining business relationships, and conducting business transactions by means of open non-proprietary telecommunications networks, including also "dedicated infrastructure." We – and the authors – keep more with the second definition, which covers all transaction phases, and also refers to some layered architectural model – doing business needs infrastructure and software.

Numerous books have been published in the past few years which consider different aspects of e-commerce. Unlike previous technological developments, e-commerce is a particularly interdisciplinary field, involving managerial, economical, technological, legal and policy issues and no individual book can cover all relevant aspects. Based on a series of invited lectures at the Vienna University of Economics and Business Administration, Department of Information Systems, during the summer term 2000, we have selected contributions of leading researchers in the field, which illustrate the broad range of topics that need to be considered. The authors are renowned experts specializing in the various facets of e-commerce. This way the interested reader should be able to get an overview about important practical and theoretical questions in this fast moving field.

In this book we examine five salient topics, organized as five chapters. The first chapter is *E-Commerce and the E-Economy*. Paul Timmers, he is head of sector for e-commerce in the European Commission's Information Society Directorate-General where he is involved in e-commerce policy and program development, addresses with his article "Measurement, Policy and Research Issues of a New Phenomenon" some of the characteristics of the emerging e-economy with a view to future research, such as new business models, dynamic business networking, and the balance of global versus local.

The second topic is *Impacts of E-Commerce on Industry Structures*. Financial services and tourism are two of the industries, where e-commerce fundamentally changes the underlying business processes and industry structures. "IT-enabled Sophistication Banking" by Hans Ulrich Buhl, Dennis Kundisch, Andreas Leinfelder, and Werner Steck from the University of Augsburg, Germany, assesses the status of the financial services industry and outlines potential opportunities for future development. Alina M. Chircu and Robert J. Kauffman from the University of Minnesota, USA, describe "A Framework for Performance and Value Assessment of E-Business Systems in Corporate Travel Distribution". The authors lay out the corporate travel e-commerce system solutions value life cycle. Finally, in "Defining Internet Readiness for the Tourism Industry: Concepts and Case Study" Ulrike Gretzel and Daniel R. Fesenmaier from the University of Urbana Champaign, USA, propose a measurement model of Internet Readiness that incorporates the concepts of stages in effective technology use and organizational capacity to change.

The third chapter deals with *New Ways of Pricing and Deal Making* and analyzes how new technologies impact the way prices are set for products and services and how markets can be designed. In a thorough analysis named "Aggregation and Disaggregation of Information Goods" Yannis Bakos (New York University) and Erik Brynjolfsson (MIT) describe new pricing strategies for digital information goods. For instance, bundling, site licensing, and subscription pricing can be analyzed as strategies that aggregate consumer utilities across different goods, different consumers, or different time periods, respectively. Rudolf Müller from the University of Maastricht, The Netherlands, is then focusing on auctions, a trading mechanism that has gained considerable importance during the past few years. In his article "Auctions – The Big Winner among Trading Mechanisms for the Internet Economy" he introduces the basic literature on auction theory and outlines the research challenges in the field of multi-item auctions.

The next topic focuses on *Enabling Technologies*. Among the variety of techniques needed to implement e-commerce applications, we have picked two technological areas that are highly relevant, namely network security and electronic data interchange. The Internet is inherently an insecure network, although this is improving. Günter Müller from the University of Freiburg, Germany, describes basic concepts of security and trust and introduces the notion of multilateral security in his paper "Security in E-Commerce". Afterwards, Peter Buxmann from the Technical University of Freiberg, Germany, demonstrates with the case study "XML@work: The Case of a Next-Generation EDI Solution" how XML-based EDI can open communication networks and shape the way businesses can interact.

Finally, we tackle the topic of *Education for the New Economy*. New information technologies are probably one of the biggest challenges for universities and education in general. On the one hand information technology changes the way people are taught. On the other hand the educational sector has to meet the fast changing requirements and the high demand for IT-skilled people. In their paper "E-Commerce/E-Business Education: Pedagogy or New Product Development?" Paula M.C. Swatman from the University of Koblenz-Landau, Germany, and Elsie S.K. Chan from the Deakin University, Australia, look at the motivations prompting universities to engage in the flurry of new programs in e-commerce. And they also classify existing (and planned) programs, based on an extensive research.

Two important characteristics that are underlying all of the above topics are globalization and speed – these factors have also profound impact on ourselves. Although we organized the lectures in the summer term 2000, during our time at the Vienna University of Economics and Business Administration, Austria, we both have moved meanwhile. Hannes Werthner is now in Italy, at the University of Trento and the irst Research Center; Martin Bichler is working at the IBM T. J. Watson Research Center in New York.

When starting the project, we knew about the workload of the authors. All the more we really want to thank our colleagues for their contributions and the time they dedicated to this project. The book would not have been possible without the support of the colleagues at our previous home institution, the Department of Information Systems at the Vienna University of Economics and Business Administration, especially Barbara Sporn. We would like to recognize the financial support of the Austrian Ministries of Transport, Innovation and Technology as well as of Education, Science and Culture, and the Austrian Computer Society. We hope that the selected papers provide an interesting survey of recent trends in e-commerce and that they may serve as valuable sources for both, scholars and practitioners.

Hannes Werthner, Trento, Italy
Martin Bichler, New York, USA

Contents

E-Commerce and the E-Economy

Timmers, P.: Measurement, Policy and Research Issues of a New
Phenomena 1

Impacts of E-Commerce on Industry Structures

Buhl, H. U., Kundisch, D., Leinfelder, A., Steck, W.: Strategies for the
Financial Services Industry in the Internet Age 27

Chircu, A. M., Kauffman, R. J.: A Framework for Performance and Value
Assessment of E-Business Systems in Corporate Travel Distribution 47

Gretzel, U., Fesenmaier, D. R.: Defining Internet Readiness for the
Tourism Industry: Concepts and Case Study 77

New Ways of Pricing and Deal Making

Bakos, Y., Brynjolfsson, E.: Aggregation and Disaggregation of
Information Goods: Implications for Bundling, Site Licensing, and
Micropayment Systems 103

Müller, R.: Auctions – the Big Winner Among Trading Mechanisms
for the Internet Economy 123

Enabling Technologies

Müller, G.: Security in E-Commerce 149

Buxmann, P.: XML@work: The Case of a Next-Generation EDI Solution . 163

Education for the New Economy

Swatman, P. M. C., Chan, E. S. K.: E-Commerce/E-Business Education:
Pedagogy or New Product Development? 177

Measurement, Policy and Research Issues of a New Phenomena*

P. Timmers

Directorate-General Information Society, European Commission, Brussels, Belgium

paul.timmers@cec.eu.int

Abstract
This paper firstly sets out to provide a broad overview of the development of electronic commerce, addressing the current state of the market and the history and current status of policy development, in particular in Europe. Secondly, it addresses some of the characteristics of the emerging e-economy with a view to indicating directions for future research, such as into new business models, dynamic business networking, and the balance of global versus local, in e-business as well as in e-policy development.

1. Introduction

The subtitle of this paper could have been 'The Times They Are A'Changing', after the famous song of Bob Dylan. Indeed, electronic commerce does seem to introduce profound changes in the way business is being done, at the company level and at the level of business networks and industry sectors as a whole. E-commerce is also leading to a blurring of boundaries between sectors. Moreover, new economic structures are being created such as e-markets involving tens of thousands of companies and dispute settlement systems that span whole industries. We are on our way to the e-economy, a new economy of which we cannot yet precisely define the shape. This paper addresses policy and business aspects of these developments,

---

* Opinions expressed here are the author's and do not necessarily represent the opinions of the European Commission

reviewing the state-of-play, and raising a number of research questions for e-economy policy, business strategy and technology development.

The first section presents the state of electronic commerce, focusing in particular on the relative importance of business-to-business versus business-to-consumer electronic commerce, and on the attitudes of large versus small companies.

The second section addresses the question whether we actually know what the subject of our study is: what is the definition of electronic commerce and which metrics can reliably be used. As it will be shown, the task of defining and measuring has only very partially been completed.

The third section addresses e-policy, that is, policy development related to electronic commerce in terms of history, themes and achievements. Although these policy developments are put in international perspective, the details provided mostly relate to the situation in the European Union.

The e-economy, or at least some of its characteristics is the subject of the fourth section. Innovation on the basis of new business models, the changing nature of collaboration and competition in dynamic business networks, and the challenge to balance global and local in electronic commerce and in e-policy are amongst these characteristics.

The paper is concluded with an indication of the breadth of research issues that emerge at all levels, from society, organization, and process to technology and people issues.

2. Facts and Figures

Internet electronic commerce or e-business includes electronic trading of physical goods and of intangibles such as information. This encompasses all the trading steps such as online marketing, ordering, payment, and support for delivery. Electronic commerce includes the electronic provision of services, such as after-sales support or online legal advice. Internet electronic commerce also includes electronic support for collaboration between companies, such as collaborative on-line design and engineering, or virtual business consultancy teams. Electronic commerce can be between businesses and consumers (B2C), business-to-business (B2B), business-to-administrations (B2A, or B2G business to governments) and consumer-to-consumer (C2C).

The wide range of forms of e-commerce or e-business illustrates that it makes little sense to come up with a restrictive definition of electronic commerce but also that there is likely not to be a single unique definition. In this context we will work with a broad understanding of what the information economy or electronic commerce is about, namely "doing business electronically"[2].

---

[2] For this definition and a comparison of traditional and electronic commerce, see chapter 1 of the European Initiative in Electronic Commerce, European Commission, April 1997, http://www.cordis.lu/esprit/src/ecomcom.htm; as well as related publications at http://www.ispo.cec.be/Ecommerce/

Access to the Internet and the World Wide Web, the fundamental technologies of e-commerce, are growing at an explosive rate. As of September 2000 there were an estimated 378 million people online worldwide, up from 210 million just one year before, of which 161 million in North America and 106 million in Europe, see Table 1. The number in 1999 was roughly double that of 1998, as 2000 roughly doubles from 1999. The trend to double is expected to continue, in other words, in a few years time there will be 1 billion Internet users. Growth from 1999–2000 has been fastest outside the USA and Canada.

Table 1. Number of Internet users, September 2000 (millions), source NUA[3]

World Total	378
Canada & USA	161
Europe	106
Asia/Pacific	90
Latin America	15
Africa	3
Middle East	2

Electronic commerce is likewise booming. Predictions of market researchers, which often tend to be optimistic, have even been surpassed[4]. A Texas A&M survey in the USA showed that e-commerce was larger than the telecoms and airline industry in 1999. It will be larger than publishing and healthcare in 2003. E-commerce was growing by 130% from '98 to '99. In '99 there were an estimated 2.3 million Internet-related jobs in the USA. 400,000 of these were created by electronic commerce.

It is clear that electronic commerce will become pervasive. The Report on Electronic Commerce (1998) expected that Internet connectivity in business would grow from 10% in 1997 to an impressive 90% in 2001[5]. Eurobarometer's March 2000 survey in Europe seems to confirm this, finding average SME connectivity to the Internet in Europe to be 70%.

The Internet and e-commerce are also leading to a surge in new company creation. One-third of the Internet-related companies did not exist prior to 1996, according to the aforementioned Texas A&M survey. The companies of the e-economy experience a tremendous interest from stock markets. Capitalisation of Internet electronic commerce companies, that is those providing the hardware, software, services and content of the information economy such as Vodafone,

3   www.nua.com
4   According to the US Department of Commerce in its report of June 1999 The Emerging Digital Economy II, US Department of Commerce, June 1999, http://www.ecommerce.gov/ede/ede2.pdf
5   The Report on Electronic Commerce, Vol. 5, No. 4, 24 Feb, 1998

Nokia, Microsoft, Cisco, IBM, AOL+Time Warner and others far exceeds that of traditional industrial enterprises, even despite the stock market crises of this year. The mood of the stock market goes through huge swings trying to assess whether the dotcoms and their technology providers will live up to the promise.

Business-to-business electronic commerce is by far most important, representing about 80% of all e-commerce. The potential of B2B electronic commerce is huge, since products are traded multiple times in intermediate form between companies.

Forrester's 1997 forecast[6] was that B2B electronic commerce would grow to $ 327 billion in the year 2002 – that is the value of goods and services traded via the Internet. This excludes the value of the hardware, software and services that are needed to perform electronic commerce, whose value is estimated at several hundred billions of dollars likewise. It also excludes the value of other forms of electronic commerce mentioned before such as collaborative design and engineering or non-Internet electronic trading as in financial markets. In its 1998 survey Forrester expected B2B electronic commerce to jump to $ 1.3 trillion in the US by 2003, in line with the expectation of the abovementioned Texas study. More recent forecasts from the Boston Consulting Group even predict B2B to become as large as $ 3 trillion in 2003 in the USA. Others predict that the figure will further grow to 30% of the world economy in 2010 (Pecaut et al., 2000).

B2B electronic commerce is developing very rapidly – it is already becoming a true revolution in business. The recent flood of electronic marketplaces, e-markets or exchanges, cover very many sectors (automotive, aerospace, chemicals, utilities, MRO – maintenance, repair, operations, marketing & design, etc) and add up to hundreds of billions of euros in B2B trade. It is clear why industry rushes into these marketplaces: Goldman Sachs calculated purchasing cost savings in the order of 10–40% for many of these sectors[7]. No business will forego these immediate cost savings.

In B2C the pattern of development is more of an evolution. Consumer habits do not change so rapidly and language and cultural barriers are of more importance. In Europe credit card payments and efficient small package delivery is not as widespread as in the USA, which explains to some extent why European consumers significantly lag behind the USA in adopting online buying. The most important sectors for B2C in Europe are computer products and online travel ticket sales.

Hopes are high though that the widespread use of mobile phones in Europe is the basis for a breakthrough of B2C electronic commerce within just a few years time. The reasoning is that the GSM standard, being followed up now and over the coming years by the GPRS, EDGE (the $2^{1}/_{2}$ generation) and UMTS standards (third-generation, or 3G) will evolve mobile telephony into mobile Internet with permanent-on "phones" (or whatever we will call the devices by that time) that have standard Internet access. One of the protocols to deliver Internet content onto those mobile phones is called Wireless Access Protocol (WAP), another is i-mode as used

---

6   http://www.forrester.com
7   Goldman Sachs, 'B2B: 2B or not 2B', www.gs.com

in Japan (they may merge in due time). Mobile phones have become a fashion item, with replacement in as little as 18 months.

The estimates are that there will be one billion mobile phone users in 2003, up from 400 million today. No less than 65% of all Europeans will have a mobile phone by 2003. 85% of these third-generation phones will be Internet-enabled. It is likely that a flood of new services will be offered to the many newcomers on the Internet and that many of today's PC-based information and online shopping services will move onto mobile phones and personal digital assistants. Europe is well placed to profit from this opening of the floodgates onto the Internet. Mobile e-commerce turnover in Europe is expected to surge to? 24 billion in 2003.

Widespread and always-on access to the Internet via the mobile phone invites new business models to be developed, in particular those that overcome the limited screen 'real estate' of the mobile phone and that combine the tangible (handset, smart card) and intangible aspect (content, service, relationship) of the mobile phone. New applications will also exploit the location-aspect of the mobile phone, enabling location-dependent and personalised services, such as a single call taxi service throughout Europe. The combination of location and mobility opens up exciting possibilities for partnerships between local information providers and global infrastructure providers. The European Commission supports active experimentation with new business models and applications for mobile commerce in areas such as tourism, health, entertainment, and logistics.

Mobile electronic commerce or m-commerce also requires an assessment of the legal and self-regulatory framework for electronic commerce. For example, there are some open questions regarding liability and crime-prevention that need to be addressed with the help of technology and perhaps by reinforcing the legal safety net. It will also be very interesting to see how competition and collaboration in the industry develops in view of the future competitive structure of the e-economy.

Few data exists about business-to-administrations electronic commerce, such as electronic procurement by governments. They hardly seem to show up in the statistics. Where in many of our economies the government is the single largest buyer, it should be the leading e-commerce user. But it probably still is not!

According to Andersen Consulting's surveys interest of the larger firms in Europe in e-commerce increased rapidly from 1998 to 1999, a trend that was reinforced in 1999–2000. Electronic commerce is now firmly on the management agenda of large enterprises. The Andersen Consulting (2000) survey found that 97% of the firms interviewed were using e-commerce in one form or another and that 70% had an e-commerce strategy.

Despite the emerging positive attitude even large companies are still much pre-occupied by worries about internal acceptance, a management culture of relatively slow decision-making compared to the speed of Internet developments and difficult integration with existing systems. The large companies thus see more internal rather than external barriers. It is also noteworthy that the main driver for them to adopt e-commerce is fear of competition – and this is no longer so much fear of dotcoms, but rather fear of their traditional, 'old economy' competitors within the same sector or powerhouse outsiders those that reach out into their sector.

Small companies, and especially the enterprises with less than 10 employees, although now getting online *en masse*, are still hesitant about electronic commerce. Only 25% of the 70% of SMEs that are connected are selling online (Eurobarometer, March 2000). SMEs are concerned about costs and do not see the appropriate business model. Small companies in Europe worry more than their counterparts in the USA about the validity of the concept of doing business electronically and about the interest of consumers and about legal frameworks. In other words, they rather see external barriers and are struggling with the concept of e-commerce.

The Internet and electronic commerce are not a guarantee that old geographical differences disappear. Europe remains a collection of diverse markets. Certain highly advanced smaller countries and regions in Europe can be characterized as early adopters. Some are even ahead of the USA.

Some large countries can be called 'awakening giants' (Pecaut et al., 2000). They have a lot of potential in terms of market size and current growth rate. Also, recent reports from both Forrester and ECATT indicate for PC-based Internet access a North-South gap in Europe. This gap does not seem to be shrinking. However, the tremendous interest for mobile phones in Southern Europe, which will soon be Internet-enabled, is an encouraging indicator that the potential exists to bridge the gap.

3. Defining and Measuring the E-Economy

Electronic commerce can be seen to go through a succession of phases (see Fig. 1). The first phase is about achieving widespread adoption and critical mass. The second phase is about developing the best practice or 'proper' use of electronic commerce in the existing business organization. The third phase is about adapting and transforming the business to reap the full benefits of electronic commerce, while the fourth

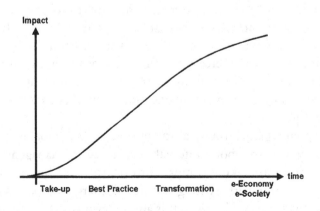

Fig. 1. E-commerce phases

phase is characterized by changes in economic structures at large. It is important to take into account that new technology continuously enters the market and initiates its own sequence of diffusion and transformation waves. The phases are explained in more detail here.

First Phase – Widespread Take-Up

Electronic commerce is moving from hype to reality. It is becoming part of everyday economic life in Europe, notably in B2B purchasing and procurement and for information gathering on the Web by consumers and businesses. Much is achieved in creating awareness, experimenting with new business models, and creating predictable and stable conditions for doing business electronically by adapting legal and self-regulatory frameworks. Nevertheless, take-up is still far from universal, especially amongst small companies and citizens.

Second Phase – Best Practice in Current Business

The second phase of electronic commerce is for businesses and consumers to develop 'best practice' over the coming years. An example would be a broad adoption of electronic signatures with the help of smart cards and strong consumer and privacy protection via widespread implementation of codes of conduct and cross-border dispute resolution.

Third Phase – Business Transformation

The third phase in electronic commerce is about widespread business transformation and adoption of new business models. This phase has already started today but is still limited to early adopters and innovative start-ups. The challenge is to innovate the processes of value creation and delivery by means of Internet technologies and to deliver new forms of value, meeting new customer needs, for example based on personalisation and localisation.

This impacts not only the way business is being done, but also how work is being organised, including 'e-work' within companies and with self-employed persons. It also pertains to governments themselves as both providers of services to businesses and in its role of public procurer.

Fourth Phase – E-Economy / E-Society

Finally, we already start to see the first indications that electronic commerce is about more than increasing efficiency in buying and selling and even about more than transforming individual companies. The many smaller and larger advances in the take-up of electronic commerce no longer add up to quantitative changes only. Instead they seem to lead to a qualitative change, affecting the very structure of the economy and driving structural changes in society at large.

Electronic commerce will profoundly transform competitive structures in industry and services and significantly change patterns of employment. This larger scale transformation of the economy towards the *e-economy* can be seen as the fourth phase of electronic commerce. Moreover, the e-economy and the future *e-society* are intimately linked.

In order to better characterize the phases of e-commerce and of the e-economy we need relevant, measurable and comparable metrics. While many market researchers publish statistics, they often follow somewhat different definitions and measurement approaches, which makes them difficult to compare. Moreover, most data are about the early phases of e-commerce, such as Internet access and e-commerce turnover, rather than about characteristics of the more advanced phases such as new business models and new ways of working, for which even fewer clear and comparable metrics exist.

The OECD (2000) seeks to come up with better metrics and measurements for the e-commerce and the e-economy. It defines three types of metrics: those that address readiness such as access to the Internet, those that are about intensity of use such as e-commerce turnover, and those that describes impact, such as new business models (see Fig. 2, modified on the basis of the OECD work). Altogether though they may not yet capture the picture of what the new economy or the e-economy is about.

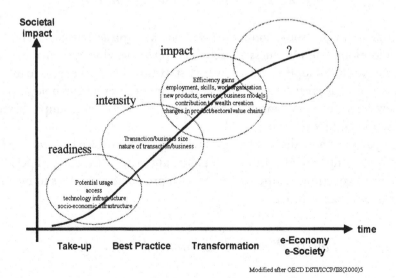

Modified after OECD DSTI/ICCP/IIS(2000)5

Fig. 2. Measuring the e-commerce and the e-economy

Further research is needed into precise definitions of especially the metrics for the transformation phase and the e-economy / e-society phase. For example, while the impression is that new economic structures are being created such as e-markets, there is as of today no classification of such economic structures, let alone a systematic measurement.

4. E-Policy

The 1995 Global Information Society Conference launched eleven international projects to promote and explore the information society. Electronic commerce for small- and medium sized enterprises (SMEs) was one of those. This "G7 Global Marketplace for SMEs" Project[8] enabled the European Commission to investigate the state of play and to draw up an inventory of key themes, and establish many links to national level policy making. This was an important step towards the 1997 European Initiative in Electronic Commerce[9], the framework policy document for much of the later more specific European Union (EU) e-commerce policy, or e-policy work. It initiated and promoted initiatives in areas such as R&D, self-regulation and the adaptation of the legal framework for the EU Internal Market. At the same time US President Clinton had established a taskforce for Internet commerce, led by Ira Magaziner. This resulted in the White House Framework for Global Electronic Commerce[10], which was officially published shortly after the EU policy paper. Similarly the Japanese governments, both the MITI and MPT Ministries, were producing policy documents, Towards the Age of the Digital Economy[11] and Vision 21 for Infocommunications[12] respectively.

Soon the discussions and policy documents moved beyond the national and regional (EU) level. International organizations got into the play, in particular the OECD. Stimulated by the flood of activities at international level national governments from all over the world started develop their own policy for e-commerce, often as part of a national information society policy. Generally they identified the same themes and proposed a similar overall to tackling the issues.

Today the European Commission, Council of Ministers, and European Parliament as well as each Member State of the European Union individually are all very active in policy and programmes for electronic commerce. The same holds for all other industrialized countries, most developing countries and many international organizations such as the OECD, the WTO and APEC.

---

8 http://www.ispo.cec.be/ecommerce/g8/g8pp.html
9 COM(97)157, April 1997; for these and other references to European Commission papers and activities in electronic commerce see http://www.ispo.cec.be/ecommerce, unless otherwise mentioned
10 http://www.whitehouse.gov/WH/New/Commerce/
11 http://www.miti.go.jp/intro-e/a228101e.html
12 http://www.mpt.go.jp/policyreports/english/telecouncil/v21-9706/info21-outline-e.html

In parallel to government-led initiatives business-led approaches have emerged such as the Global Business Dialogue for electronic commerce GBDe[13], the Global Information Infrastructure Commission[14], and many others. While these initiatives also provide input to the legal process, their main focus is the definition and promotion of codes of conducts, guidelines, trustmarks, and dispute settlement systems, that is, they pursue largely a self-regulatory approach.

A core element of the EU approach was (and still is) to take account of the interplay between technology, legislation and self-regulation, and business/consumer economic behaviour. In practice this includes active consultation with and between parties that bring in expertise and views about these constituent factors as well as support for studies and research, for example in the EU Information Society Technologies R&D programme which co-finances techno-legal and techno-self-regulatory projects[15]. The basic principles for adapting the legal framework were formulated in 1997: no regulation for regulation's sake (that is, minimal legislation); any regulation must take account of business realities; and any regulation must meet general interest objectives effectively and efficiently. For the EU, reinforcing the Single Market freedoms is also central to its approach: the free movement of goods, persons, services and capital together with the freedom of establishment.

Identifying most of the key themes for e-policy was a relatively easy first step, which happened during 1996–97. These themes include privacy, direct and indirect taxation, security, intellectual property protection, etc. Subsequently over the past years a lot of progress has been made within governments and industry addressing questions from the perspectives of law, self-regulation such as codes of conduct and dispute settlement schemes, and technology. One of the trends that have emerged is a shift towards co-regulation in the sense of industry-led initiatives with governments as discussion partner and provider of (non-binding) guidelines or underpinning legislation, leading to self-regulation with government support. The current status of the key themes at EU level is summarized in Table 2. It is noted that this is by necessity a highly condensed and simplified representation of the rich and complex set of developments in the legal and self-regulatory domain!

The challenge for the coming years will be to establish effective self-regulation ('with teeth') which is, with technology, the indispensable partner to the legal framework in order to provide the flexibility needed for this fast-moving economy. Some initiatives are already arising for example in trust labeling, money-back guarantees, and soon out-of-court and other alternative fast-track dispute settlement systems for consumers (ADR).

A research issue will be to establish the economics of trust schemes: when do they become a 'hygiene factor' rather than a motivator, to paraphrase Herzberg (1968),

---

[13]   For the work of the GBDe, see http://www.gbde.org
[14]   http://www.giic.org
[15]   An example of a techno-legal project are ECLIP and ECLIP-II, http://www.jura.uni-muenster.de/eclip/

Table 2. Status legal/self-regulatory framework at EU level

Policy theme	Legal/self-regulatory status (EU level)
Data protection/ privacy	EU Directive came in force October 98, 'Safe Harbour' accepted July 2000 Codes of conduct, e.g. in direct marketing, supported by R&D into privacy-enhancing technologies
Taxation	VAT principles (neutrality, simplicity, …), update 6th VAT Directive proposed May 2000; direct taxation follows OECD
Customs	WTO – 'duty free Internet' standstill expired – to become agreement?
Security	Authentication: EU Directive on Electronic Signatures Jan 2000; large scale R&D and standardisation support (IST, EESSI); Digital Signature laws in several Member States; Encryption: dual use regulation, September 2000.
Intellectual property/ copyrights	WIPO ratification; digital content delivery R&D in IST; Directive proposed May 2000.
Internal market	E-commerce Directive: Internal Market related, addressing establishment, commercial communications, electronic contracts, liability, redress, adopted June 2000 (country of origin principle but derogation related to consumer protection and promoting self-regulation) Codes of conduct at national and industry sector level
Harmful content	Self-regulation; Internet action plan & projects
Cybercrime	Communication in preparation; Dependability Initiative
Domain names	Support for private sector organisation ICANN; Proposal to introduce .eu domain in 2000/2001.
E-payments, financial services	Rules for e-money issuing institutions; draft Directive on distance marketing of consumer financial services
Consumer protection/ jurisdiction	Discussion on Regulation incorporating updated Brussels convention; codes of conduct; alternative & online dispute resolution, e-Confidence Forum March 2000
Competition	Individual cases
Telecommunications	Comprehensive Telecoms Regulatory Review (2000/2001), unbundling local loop adopted October 2000.

and correspondingly what are the costs and benefits associated with them and how can they be priced or charged for? Another research question is to what extent these schemes can be effective and what the effect will be of non-compliance by some fraction of market operators on overall trust. Related to this are the questions formulated by Lessig (2000) about the type and desirability of control and the system of norms that is introduced by such trust schemes. As he argues, such systems make part of the 'architecture' of Internet commerce, the 'code' that explicitly or implicitly constrains certain kinds of activities and promotes others. The research challenge is in particular on the implicit effects, which do not have to be the same in the virtual world as they are in the physical world.

In the legal framework there are also still some unresolved issues, such as taxation, and the protection of software and business methods by patents. Developing global legal and self-regulatory solutions is another challenge. While hopes are high that ADRs can bridge differences between legal systems, they still need to be developed for the larger part and be put to the test of real life practice.

New technology will also pose new challenges. New technologies may well force us to review the legal and/or self-regulatory framework for electronic commerce in a few years time. Examples are in nano-technology, the new version of the Internet protocols IPv6, quantum-encryption, peer-to-peer Internet, business networking software to create dynamic virtual business networks.

Future e-policy and e-strategy development are challenged to be:

1. *Pro-active, anticipatory, evolutionary:* anticipation of the future of technology, business, markets and society and flexibility to adapt is to be an integral part of policy making and strategy development, in order to cope with the intrinsic unpredictability and turbulence of the e-economy. In line with current thinking in strategy development, emergent processes and a market-driven, evolutionary approach has to be followed to seeking the 'best' solution (Fig. 3).
2. *Cross-disciplinary and inclusive:* policy-making for the e-economy is not the preserve of a select group of policy-makers, but instead needs to put all heads together, bringing many experiences and disciplines around the table, and develop a new way of integrative and inclusive thinking.
3. *Global:* policy-making is to be global in mindset and principles, because of the nature of the e-economy itself.

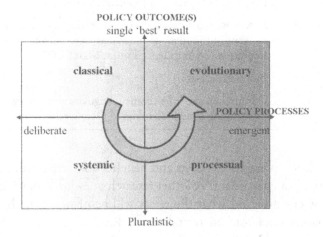

Fig. 3. Policy-making for the e-economy: from planned to evolutionary [modified after Whittington (1993)]

A recent major policy initiative is *e*Europe, which defines ambitious and concrete targets to bring the benefits of the information society within reach of all in Europe[16]. It can be considered the successor of the broad information society initiatives taken in 1994–1995 such as the Bangemann Initiative and the G7 Global Information Society Conference, and of the European Initiative in Electronic Commerce of 1997. EU leaders at the Feira European Council on 19–20 June 2000 endorsed the *e*Europe Action Plan. The Action Plan sets out a strategy to address key barriers to the uptake of the Internet in Europe and ensure that the conditions are set for a decisive move towards the new economy. It proposes that Member States and the Commission bind themselves to achieving the following three objectives quickly: a cheaper, faster, more secure Internet; investing in people's skills and access; and stimulating the use of the Internet. The thrust of the plan is to accelerate legislation, roll out infrastructure and services across Europe and open co-ordination between Member States – including benchmarking activities by the Commission.

The EU Member States and all other public and private actors concerned have a challenging task in ensuring its full and timely implementation by 2002. Also the preparation of longer-term perspectives for a knowledge-based economy encouraging inclusion in the Information Society and closing the numeracy gap is foreseen. The initiative already has delivered achievements: the unbundling of the local loop was agreed upon in October 2000. This should bring down the cost of accessing the Internet in particular from the home and small business.

The theme 'Accelerating Electronic Commerce' of the Action Plan contains actions to complete the internal market framework for electronic commerce, which was largely realised by the end of 2000, to promote e-procurement by governments during the next few years, to support self-regulation including the setting up of online and alternative dispute resolution in Europe, also during the coming years, to help SMEs go digital, which is expected to run until 2002, and to set up an '.eu' toplevel domain name, which is to be realised by 2001.

The EU Information Society Technologies R&D and pilot programme is one of the means to support *e*Europe. The IST Programme supports with a budget of about 550 million Euro over 4 years a range of projects in e-commerce and e-work, within the so-called Key Action II. The year 2000 topics of interest in Key Action II are indicated in Fig. 4. The diagram shows the action lines in the IST programme for which proposals could be submitted in the year 2000[17]. These action lines cover subjects such as knowledge management, mobile and ubiquitous e-commerce, sustainable forms of e-work, work in secure infrastructures for e-business, and dynamic value constellations. The latter addresses advanced approaches to dynamic business partnerships based on Internet market mechanisms and aiming to create forms of value for customers that can only be realised in such dynamic collaboration.

---

[16] For eEurope see http://www.ispo.cec.be/policy/i_europe.html
[17] The workprogramme of the IST programme is revised on a yearly basis and can be found at www.cordis.lu/ist

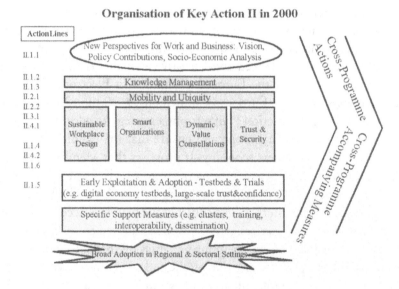

Fig. 4. E-commerce and e-work in the IST Programme in 2000

5. E-Economy

The new economy or e-economy is characterized by continued and sustainable productivity growth, low inflation and total employment. In short, an ideal picture … It is generally believed that pervasive take-up of ICT and the ample availability of risk capital are to a large extent responsible for these macro-economic effects, but how exactly this is brought about is not really known. Some of the characteristics in terms of business behavior of the e-economy are:

– New business models
– Business transformation
– Transaction cost theory in practice
– Dynamic business collaboration
– Global and local challenges

These features are briefly addressed in the following sections.

In addition there are other characteristics, which are not further discussed here, including winner-take-all and network effects and the transformation of marketing in many respects.

New Business Models and Business Transformation

Electronic commerce makes it possible to experiment with many new business models (Timmers, 1999, 2000).

A business model is the architecture of product/service, information and money flows, and of the business actors involved, their roles and benefits. A business model together with the companies' marketing strategies enables to assess the commercial viability of the business model and to answer questions like: how is competitive advantage being built, what is the positioning, what is the marketing mix, which product-market strategy is being followed.

In principle very many new business models can be conceived by breaking down the value chain or the set of business processes that make up a business, followed by re-constructing the value chain again using electronic commerce technologies to build up the business operation. In practice a limited number only is being realized in Internet electronic commerce as qualitatively presented in Fig. 5. The dimensions in this mapping are the degree of innovation relative to the non-electronic way of doing business, and the degree of integration of business functions. Also indicated in that diagram are the business models that individually or in combination are the basis of e-markets today.

The various business models are briefly detailed here (see also Timmers, 1998):

- *e-shop:* Often the entry point in electronic commerce is setting up a fairly straightforward e-shop, which is essentially the online version of the company brochure and logo. This already can bring significant savings in marketing costs. Potentially, however, an e-shop can be the visible part of a more extensive electronic commerce system, which is integrated throughout the company with the objective to improve quality, reduce time-to-market, and gain access to new markets.
- *e-procurement:* Where an e-shop is about selling, is e-procurement about buying. In e-procurement calls for tender are published on the Web, possibly accompa-

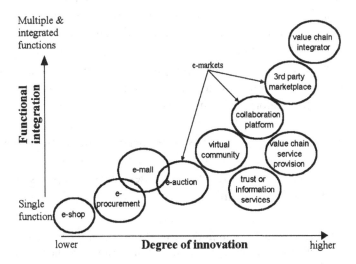

Fig. 5. Electronic commerce business models

nied by electronic submission of bids. Here too most often the objective is cost saving. In practice, e-procurement in the private sector is often restricted to a selected set of suppliers and therefore usually not visible on the public Internet, contrary to public e-procurement.

— *e-malls:* Electronic malls are in their basic form no more than a collection of e-shops, accessible from a common entry point on the Internet. E-mall providers can add value by common branding and e-shop presentation, possibly adding quality guarantees, an attractive presentation of the shops in the mall. E-shop hosting fees are one of the sources of revenue.

— *e-auctions:* Electronic auctions receive much attention, especially B2C auctions such as eBay in the USA and UK's QXL. However, B2B auctions have at least as much potential, especially where spare capacity and surplus stocks are concerned. Here too the prime objective is increased efficiency, reduced wastage and overall cost-reduction. Transaction fees provide the income for the auction operator, next to possibly advertising and trust services such as credit insurance.

— *virtual communities:* Virtual communities are both a business model and a facility that can be added to almost any other business model. The concept is to gather participants around an area of common interest and to let *themselves* contribute to the information base, inciting them to make public their experience. The business model is often based on advertising revenues and membership fees. However, in this business model as in many of the others advertising is not an easy proposition: there is far more advertising space on the Internet than that there are advertisers[18].

— *collaboration platforms:* Collaboration platforms support for example collaborative design or construction, collaborative virtual consultancy, collaborative export marketing, etc. Technology and standards support the collaboration (such as common databases, project management, search tools, etc). The platform must support integration of several functions such as market research, contact management, negotiation, contracting, IPR management, possibly payments, etc. Service, software license, hosting, and membership fees are all sources of revenues.

— *third party marketplaces:* A very important business model is the third party marketplace (TPM). The provider of a TPM puts the catalogues of suppliers online, and offers catalogue search, ordering and payment facilities in a secure environment to purchasers. The TPM provider can add branding, 1:1 marketing support, and even logistics, as well as more advanced functions such as pre- and post-financing, risk management and insurance, tax/customs handling, and product bundling. In short, the TPM provider relieves suppliers and buyers of much of the burden to go online.

---

[18] There are very many virtual communities, e.g. eGroups.com (now part of Yahoo) alone hosts more than 300,000 such groups, although of course not all of them are relevant for or interested in advertisers

The business model is based on a combination of subscription fees, transaction fees and service fees. This approach is so important as it is particularly suited for volume trading of routine supplies between businesses. These supplies are often called MRO goods – maintenance, repair and operations. The MRO market is estimated to be 50% of all electronic commerce.

A TPM that bases its revenue model on transaction fees only may soon find that these do not provide enough differentiation. Therefore TPMs can be expected to move into value added services[19].

– *value chain integration:* Value chain integrators focus on integrating multiple steps of the value chain, with the potential to exploit the information flow between those steps for further added value. Tight value chain integration is close to 'traditional' supply chain management, where a limited number of qualified suppliers are involved in deep information sharing and information systems integration. Revenues can come from many services, including stock management and production planning services, training, design assistance, etc. (see e.g. Rodin and Hartman, 1999).

– *value chain service provision:* Value chain service providers specialize on a specific function for the value chain, such as electronic payments or logistics, with the intention to make that into their distinct competitive advantage.

– *trust and specialized information services:* Finally amongst the innovative specialized functions and services that business and consumers need, are trust services (revenues e.g. from the issuing of certificates) and specialized information brokerage (revenues from information products or from advertising).

Invariably the experience is that electronic commerce ultimately is about re-thinking the business strategy and the very business organisation. Electronic commerce more often than not leads to business transformation. While this starts with changing one or two business processes internally in the company in order to achieve cost-reduction and more efficiency, soon it leads to more ambitious goals such as quality improvement and reduced time-to-market. This cannot be achieved without integrating electronic commerce all throughout the company and the supply chain. Goals may become more ambitious under the pressure of competition. Companies are challenged to offer customers individualised products and services and access to new markets. It then becomes necessary to re-think the network of business partners and how information technology can be deployed to achieve the necessary dynamics, flexibility and integration of information along the value chain. And finally companies discover through their much closer interaction with customers that there are completely new needs to be met. Companies then start to exploit value innovation and may ultimately even transform themselves into a completely different company.

---

[19] The Standard reported that some marketplace operators already offer free transaction support for free; see 'B-to-B's Broken Models', 30 October 2000, http://www.thestandard.com/

Venkatraman (1994) developed this thinking before the age of the Internet. However, it still remains applicable today and is reinforced by the Internet. In particular the step of business network redesign can be seen in a new perspective, as the Internet has created many more possibilities to engage in dynamic relationships with business partners, be it suppliers, customers, intermediaries, third party providers, etc. Such possibilities include e-auctions, virtual communities, affiliate schemes and catalogue schemes.

Transaction Cost Theory in Practice and Dynamic Business Collaboration

Business network design also fits closely with transaction cost theory thinking (Williamson, 1985, 1986). In the quest for efficiency and agility companies constantly need to re-assess what is core to their activities, which relationships are strategic, and in which markets they need to be active. Companies need to consider re-arranging their cost structure, trading off production that is organised in-house against sourcing from the market or partners. That is, they apply transaction cost theory in practice. Also other competitive factors need to be considered such as time-to-market, access to markets and market share, building of a strong brand, and others.

These considerations lead to re-thinking how business processes should be organised, that is, both inside the company as well as in relationship to other companies and to the market. In fact, all processes that add to value creation should be analysed to assess their intrinsic efficiency and the appropriate position inside the organisation or external to it, whether in a value network or in a dynamic market configuration.

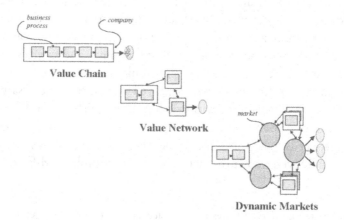

Fig. 6. From value chain to value network to dynamic market

A value network is defined as a multi-enterprise set of relationships focused on integration of information flows to exploit information and knowledge in the value network for strategic business objectives. A dynamic market configuration is defined as a market-mediated set of relationships focused on increasing flexibility and opportunity for strategic business objectives. Value networks and dynamic markets are about breaking up the traditional value chain, with different choices for the degree of dynamics. Value networks are based on the premise of strategic and long-term business relationships, with a high level of investment per relationship. Dynamic market configurations or dynamic value constellations seek flexibility in relationships in order to create value that fits with a dynamically occurring market opportunity. Consequently they have to be designed to cope with multiple and short-term variable relationships.

Both value networks, that are closer to the stream of thinking around virtual enterprises, and dynamic value constellations or dynamic market configurations are the subject of intense R&D in the IST programme. Value networks and dynamic value constellations raise many research issues, such as:

— *Standardization and interoperability:* what are minimal interoperability requirements and specifications for such arrangements to achieve sufficient 'breadth' (choice of partners) as well as sufficient 'depth' (information integration for added value)
— *Ownership and intellectual property rights:* who owns the intermediate and final results of the collaboration, especially where joint designs are concerned?
— *Control / network integration / network effects:* who will be able to control the business partnership and be the spider in the web? Will such control be based on financial power or on critical technology or standards with network externalities?
— *Trust and risk taking / future versus current opportunities:* which form of risk assessment can underpin business strategy to answer the question whether the business should invest in building long-term trust for future opportunities or rather pursue – at a greater risk – current opportunities?
— *Exposure to financial risk and liability:* who takes the financial risk and liability in a dynamic business network:
— *Lifecycle management:* who owns the information about product and customer that enables lifetime value management around product-customer? And who takes the obligation of maintenance and recycling when the lifetime of the product is longer than the lifetime of the business partnership?
— *Opportunities for SMEs versus large companies / structure of network:* are small companies the ones that will most benefit from dynamic partnerships as they are likely to demand specialized skills and agility? Or is the role of trust so important that large companies will always be present and indeed the networks will become dominant player centred?
— *From business process towards market process engineering:* how will companies transform themselves in order to reap the benefits of increased flexibility through

Internet market mechanisms (such as affiliate schemes, auctions, e-markets, peer-to-peer)?

In transaction cost theory there are three dimensions to consider in the buyer-supplier relationship: frequency of the transaction (from ad-hoc to regularly recurring), uncertainty in the relationship, and investment specificity, that is the extent of specific investment the supplier is requested to make. Where on one extreme paperclips require no specific investment and even the future buyer is not known, is on the other extreme the purchase of a battleship associated with unique investment for the buyer.

Most of today's B2B e-markets focus on MRO goods, that is indirect or non-production or non-strategic items, that often come straight out of an industry catalogue. These fall in the category of non-specific and recurrent purchases. In transaction cost analysis there is therefore a whole white space uncovered, of ad-hoc purchases, and of purchases that are customer-specific to some degree as far as investment is concerned. It is exactly in such dimensions that one can understand the evolution towards the new value-added services that are characteristic of future e-markets. E.g. customer profiling based on e-market transaction data will be used to provide customer-specific transaction services. E-markets will attempt to open up to lower-volume / ad-hoc buyers in order to increase liquidity. And some e-markets will invest in purchaser-specific variants in order to increase value (or simply to sign up critically needed customers), be it at the expense of future liquidity.

Global and Local

Electronic commerce is said to be 'born global'. It is a phenomenon without borders. It gives immediate access to markets internationally although competitors also get immediate access to the market that used to be your protected backyard. Most of the business models discussed before have the potential to 'go global'.

However, in reality international e-commerce is probably still fairly limited. Data are particularly sparse on international e-commerce. A survey by Forrester in September 1999 in the USA found that 85% of companies turned all international orders away. A Boston Consulting Group survey in February 2000 into online retail in Europe found that 93% (!) of all revenues were generated in the national market, with only 2% from exports outside Europe. On the other hand, US companies with a pan-European approach were serving already 20% of the European online retail market. Notably the small companies still make little use of the global nature of the Internet until now, with 90% of electronic commerce done by them still not crossing national borders.

E-commerce can also be a tool to do better business locally. Examples are now emerging which demonstrate that electronic business can excellently be combined with local physical presence. Local and vernacular content is the fastest growing segment of Websites, which is encouraging for a multi-cultural continent.

The question whether e-commerce is the means *par excellence* for global business or is rather more suited for doing local business better is being debated since a few years in the electronic commerce research community[20, 21]. There is not yet a decisive answer since evidence is anecdotal rather than systematic as the sparse data above show.

Recently this debate has been further stimulated by the emergence of large B2B e-markets, which generally combine several business models (e-auction, catalogue based third party marketplace, collaborative platform, see Fig. 5). Many of them seem well placed to become global electronic trading environments. Questions then arise about the opportunities for growing such e-markets globally and about barriers and marketing strategies.

There are several barriers to creating global business models such as:

1. Inadequate global delivery and fulfillment systems
2. Differences in culture, language, commercial practice
3. Fragmented global legal/ self-regulatory framework
4. Fragmentation in the industry
5. Barriers specific to small companies.

The first three of these are obvious barriers to global e-commerce. The fourth barrier, fragmentation in the industry, means that there is a difficulty to reaching sufficient scale globally as the choice of global partners is not obvious and most partners are relatively small. Examples are the health sector and construction industry. Barriers specific to small companies are next to their limited resources also their lack of international skills, and probably even more important, a locally oriented mindset that may not see global competitive threats coming that are enabled by the Internet.

Companies that wish to pursue global e-commerce will exploit their assets globally in view of the business opportunity and at the same time need to overcome the barriers in the business environment mentioned above, where these occur in their business, as well as address their own internal weaknesses. Marketing strategies to go global in e-commerce include:

1. Focusing on a global product-market;
2. Partnering in a global supply-chain;
3. Offering multiple language / culture support;
4. Setting up global networked franchising;
5. Internet presence on top of global physical presence;
6. Global mergers and acquisitions.

---

[20] See for example the proceedings of the Bled 1998 and 1999 conferences, P. Timmers in the World Market Research Centre Business Briefing on Electronic Commerce, September 1999, and the International Journal of Electronic Markets, Vol. 9, No. 1&2, June 1999

[21] A more detailed analysis can be found in Timmers P (2000) 'Global and Local in Electronic Commerce', UN/ECE report on electronic commerce and transition economies, published by WMRC, June 2000, see also http://www.wmrc.com

Such strategies lead to currently to the following approaches to global e-markets[22]:

A. *Intrinsically global e-markets*, that deal with global products, customers, and suppliers, e.g. MRO or automotive;
B. *Globally replicated local markets*, e.g. auctions of perishable products;
C. *Local markets with a global infrastructure*, e.g. location-dependent m-commerce;
D. *Export-oriented e-markets or e-ports*, where products are exported globally by a collaboration of producers.

This classification is no more than a first *Ansatz* to analysing the potential and conditions for e-markets to become truly global.

The question of global versus local in e-commerce can also be analysed from the perspective of e-policy development.

The global dimension of e-commerce increasingly becomes manifest in the various themes such as consumer protection, privacy, e-signatures etc. Where regions and countries did not wait for global solutions to be agreed upon, we are now faced with a rich variety of approaches that are not always mutually compatible. In certain areas there is little expectation of reaching international agreements that can be captured in law. Rather, as stated before, the hope is that alternative mechanisms, instead of law, will be able to bridge international differences. For example, for consumer protection currently ADRs, alternative dispute resolution, are all in the spotlight. They are expected to fill the gap between different legal systems, and moreover, offer a much more rapid and flexible and low-cost approach to solving problems, rather than having to resort to law and court. However, already ADRs are proliferating, so the question about their mutual recognition is being raised too. It is not yet sure whether mutual recognition or harmonisation of ADRs will go through the same lengthy consensus building processes as self-regulation (or legislation for that matter).

The issues that e-policy has to deal with can be analyzed on two dimensions: to what extent do they have a global reach, and to what extent do they have to deal with a legacy of established rules, whether of a formal nature such as laws or codes of conduct or informal practices.

Some are 'green field' issues that could at a first stage be dealt with at national/regional level and where relatively few rules already existed and where the role of legislation was fairly clear: e.g. electronic signatures (obviously requiring legal recognition) and illegal/harmful content (general agreement that regulation was not going to be practical). Here fairly quickly progress could be achieved.

Others were national/regional issues that required updating a legacy of rules: e.g. the EU Internal Market rules for establishment of a business, or the rules for issuing money; or public procurement rules. Here too fairly quickly progress at least at

---

[22] Timmers, P., (2000) 'Global and Local in Electronic Commerce'. In: Bauknecht, K., et al. (eds.) Proceedings EC-WEB 2000 conference, September 2000, Greenwich. Springer, Berlin Heidelberg New York Tokyo

national or regional could be achieved or seems within reach. However, the international or global dimension of these issues was always present in the background and will come to the foreground sooner or later.

In other cases already a legacy of national/regional rules existed, which were clearly becoming of international concern, e.g. encryption export, privacy; here progress was much more difficult as international compatibility needed to be achieved. This group of issues is going to expand, as increasingly working with a set of national/regional rules is becoming too complicated for business and consumers.

Then there are global issues that are already part of international agreements, which, however, do not seem fully adequate for e-commerce. An example is intellectual property protection. Progress is particular difficult because of conceptual problems to reconcile the existing set of rules with the intrinsic characteristics of the Internet and digital technology.

Finally there are issues of global nature for which rules did not yet exist or had little established tradition, such as the management of domain names.

A simplified picture is given in Fig. 7. This is clearly a time-dependent snapshot. Many issues will ultimately move towards the global/legacy upper corner.

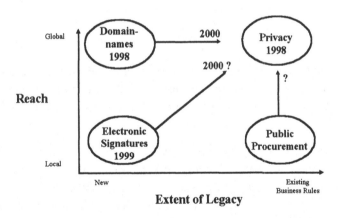

Fig. 7. E-policy issues (1998–2000): legacy vs global/local reach

The continuously changing legal/self-regulatory landscape poses many interesting research issues for political and other social scientists, such as the validity and feasibility of the trend towards global governance (cf. ICANN), the economic efficiency of the various choices to create 'regulability' (Lessig, 2000). As indicated in Table 3 the tool-set for creating rules that govern the e-economy is wide and varied, although further research is needed to provide criteria to policy-makers which mix of tools to select for which purpose.

Table 3. Toolset for e-economy rule-making

Means	Examples
Law, conventions, int'l agreements	EU Directives, UNCITRAL, …
Mandated Authority	OFTEL, WIPO, ICANN-URDP, court conclusions
Co-regulation	ADRs
Self-Regulation	*Direct marketing code of conduct, Webtrader trustmark, …*
Standardization – formal/semi-formal	ISO, CEN, W3C, IETF, …
Market: de facto standard technology or behavioral norms – *alliance* – *dominant player* – *community*	 – RosettaNet – Microsoft Explorer – Advertising best practice, Linux and other open source
Technology	Public key infrastructure to impose non-repudiation

6. Conclusions

We are only at the beginning of exploring e-commerce and the future e-economy. A plethora of new research issues is arising from the early indications. These new issues manifest themselves at the level of society, organization, processes, technologies and people:

- *Society:* as argued before new challenges are coming up in terms of policy, economics, values and norms. A 'fourth phase' of e-commerce has been suggested, where for example, many of the issues such as privacy or consumer protection that until now could be dealt with at a local level will ultimately have to be resolved in a global framework. Such 'globalisation' challenges existing policies and values and norms. Questions of economic nature come up around the giant e-marketplaces that have been described before. The study of economic and social issues is still severely hampered by a lack of definitions and measurements of the phenomena.
- *Organization:* new business models extend beyond the boundary of the firm into a networked arrangement of companies where mediation happens amongst others through various market mechanisms. Companies are challenged to re-think their business organisation and indeed to engage at the same time in 'market process engineering' in order to exploit the opportunities of a much more dynamic ways of doing business. The organisational challenge also extends to

policy making institutions (private and public) and to the management of the rules of the game, i.e. to governance in the e-economy.

- *Processes:* the new business models and dynamic ways of business collaboration raise plenty of questions about marketing in e-commerce, or e-marketing. Examples have been given of new ways of marketing in e-shops, virtual communities, and collaboration platforms. Likewise supply chain management in e-business, or e-SCM, is to be rethought. Online markets are like to move into SCM but are perhaps limited in their growth by the same problems that traditional SCM faces. Third party marketplaces as well as some of the marketplaces that aim to go global through global SCM have been indicated as focal points where the issues will come up first. In terms of processes also the way the policy debate is being carried out is being challenged. This goes back to the very principles formulated for policy development in Internet commerce, such as the interplay between technology, law and self-regulation and economic/social behaviour, which are inherently difficult to follow through in practice.
- *Technologies:* some of the business concepts such as dynamic value constellations are ahead of technology development and will require new market and business network management systems and tools. In other cases it is exactly the new technology that challenges to come up with viable business approaches, such as the greatly enhanced possibilities for customer interaction (as illustrated in some of the business models such as e-shops and virtual communities). And while new technologies increase security and thereby potentially raise the level of trust in e-commerce, it has also been demonstrated that trustworthy e-commerce may require new settlement mechanisms for which scalable and efficient technology still needs to become available.
- *People:* finally, although not made very explicit in this paper, many research challenges are directly related to how people perceive trust, how they are willing to engage in online interaction, and ultimately how they make sense of the new business models, the new technologies, the new interaction processes.

In conclusion, the e-commerce and e-economy research agenda is rich in themes and variety, reflecting that, indeed, 'The Times They Are A'Changing ...'

References

Andersen Consulting (2000) eEurope 2000: Connecting the Dots? http://www.ac.com

Herzberg, F. (1968) One More Time: How Do You Motivate Employees. Harvard Business Review 46: 53–62

Lesssig, L. (2000) Code and Other Laws of Cyberspace. Basic Books, New York

OECD (2000) Defining and Measuring Electronic Commerce. OECD, DSTI/ICCP/IIS(2000)5

Pecaut, D., Hansen, M., Forth, P. (2000) The Race for On-line Riches: E-Retailing in Europe. Boston Consulting Group, Feb 2000, http://www.bcg.com

Rodin, R., Hartman, C. (1999) Free, Perfect, and Now. Simon & Schuster, New York

Timmers, P. (1998) Business Models for Electronic Markets. Int J Electronic Markets 98 (2)
    http://www.electronicmarkets.org/
Timmers, P. (1999, 2000) Electronic Commerce: Strategies and Models for Business-to-
    Business Trading. Wiley, Chichester (hardcover 1999, paperback 2000)
Venkatraman, N. (1994) IT-Enabled Business Transformation: From Automation to Business
    Scope Redefinition. Sloan Management Review 35 (2), Winter 1994
Whittington, R. (1993) What is Strategy – and does it matter? Routledge, London
Williamson, O. E. (1985) The Economic Institutions of Capitalism. Free Press, New York
Williamson, O. E. (1986) Economic Organisation: Firms, Markets and Policy Control.
    Harvester Press, Hassocks

Paul Timmers
Head of sector for electronic-commerce in the European Commission's Information Society
Directorate-General where he is involved in e-commerce policy and programme development.
He previously held management positions in product marketing and software development at
Philips and co-founded a software start-up. He holds a PhD in theoretical physics (University
of Nijmegen, NL) and an MBA (Warwick Business School, UK) and is visiting professor at a
number of universities.

Strategies for the Financial Services Industry in the Internet Age*

H. U. Buhl, D. Kundisch, A. Leinfelder, and W. Steck

Department of Information Systems, University of Augsburg,
Federal Republic of Germany

{hans-ulrich.buhl|dennis.kundisch|werner.steck}@wiso.uni-augsburg.de
andreas.leinfelder@accenture.com

Abstract

Globalization of financial markets resulting from both IT (particularly Internet standards) and increasing homogeneity of regulation has strongly affected the environment, financial services companies are operating in. Given these changes on the market, innovation is not a choice, but a necessity to survive. Observable today, however, are defensive strategies and poor service quality. In this paper based on investments in trust relationships with customers we propose Sophistication (fit) Banking enabled by IT and qualified staff and show first steps towards the implementation of a sophistication banking strategy. While traditional markets are characterized by shrinking margins and declining shareholder values, which can easily be explained considering the digital character of financial products, new intermediaries for customer-centered Sophistication (fit) Banking have the opportunity of becoming spiders in the web and increasing shareholder values constantly.

1. Introduction

The market for financial services is undergoing a major shift towards the end of the second millenium. Mainly driven by information technology (IT) development, the

---

* This is an extended reprint of: *IT-Enabled Sophistication Banking.* In: Hansen, H.-R., Bichler, M., Mahrer H. (eds.) Proceedings of the 8th European Conference on Information Systems ECIS 2000, Wien, Österreich, Vol. 2, pp. 789–795. The reprint is approved by the editors

market has seen a wave of mergers, competition has intensified and working patterns are changing dramatically. In this setting it is more important than ever for incumbents to have the right strategy in order to generate an adequate value for their shareholders. The authors suggest and justify an IT enabled Sophistication Banking approach, which is illustrated in this paper.

The remainder of this paper is organized as follows. The mega-trends changing the environment of the firms operating in the financial services industry are described and the impacts of these mega-trends in this market are discussed (Section 2). Based on our research results of the last years and on our practical experience from projects with partners such as Advance Bank, Hypovereinsbank and Deutsche Bank, some predictions of future market developments are discussed and strategic options are identified on a qualitative level (Section 3). In Section 4 we justify why we think Sophistication Banking is a superior strategy and present an implementation design for it including examples of the potential of the new approach. In section 5 we will provide some of the conceptual steps to become a sophistication bank. The article concludes with a short summary in Section 6.

2. Mega-Trends in Financial Services

When discussing about mega-trends today there is no doubt that there is one development that will have the most impact on the financial services industry in the next centuries. "It is a power that is revolutionizing equities trading, a power likely to spread into core investment banking, in the process stripping away the inefficiencies previously integral to the financial system." (Euromoney, 1991) It is the rise of IT, especially of the Internet and its multimedial and interactive service, the world wide web (WWW). The authors first of all see three outstanding reasons for this, namely the new quality in communication, the change in (working) life circumstances and the ongoing deregulation in many economic sectors. Let us look at these in more detail in the following paragraphs.

New Quality in Communication

Picking-up the first reason, the Internet enables non-face-to-face communication not only adequate for "basic" financial services like managing a current account or a stock order. It also supports complex consultations in order to generate high-level solutions for financial problems like real estate financing (Advance Bank, 2001). At the same time a huge number of people – everyone who is connected to the Internet – can be reached at nearly no costs. "The rapid emergence of universal standards for communication (is) allowing everybody to communicate with everybody else at essentially zero cost" (Evans and Wurster, 1997). So with the Internet the former diversity between richness and reach of communication has vanished (see Fig. 1)

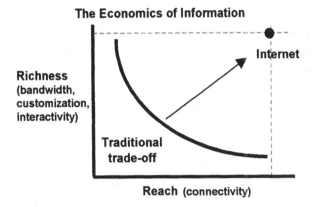

Fig. 1. Trade-off between richness and reach

(Evans and Wurster, 1997). Former barriers of entry like a set of branches or a big sales force that took years to establish were forced down by this to a few months and to much less investment.

Consequently a lot of new intermediaries used their chance to establish purely web-based and thus relatively cheap and competitive services in the financial service business like the so-called discount-brokers, e.g. e-trade or Consors, or founded completely virtual banks, e.g. the United States netbank. A sharp rise in competition, especially in the field of online-brokerage where costs were cut dramatically is the impressive result of the new possibilities described above. Not only in this area but in many fields of banking, web-based solutions have been established and turn past investments of traditional banks into expensive liabilities and by this to competitive disadvantages. In addition these web-based companies reduce returns for traditional banks by targeting only special and interesting customer segments. This switching of customers to the web based companies is supported by an astonishing lack of quality in consultation by the established players (Finanztest, 2000).

But there is another development that is forced by information technology. So it seems to be likely that the diminishing costs for communication "are forcing firms to become more flexible" (Economist, 1998).

Change in (Working) Life Circumstances

Because now (after the defeat of the traditional economics of information) temporary organizations formed by specialized units that are connected by standardized (Internet) communication channels have become possible. These virtual organizations are set together as parts of the former value chain creating new value networks by heavy use of (traditionally prohibitively expensive) communication (systems) and by this become able to better match the demand of the markets. The breakup of the hierarchical organizations brings firms both, opportunities and threats. It "foster(s) entrepreneurship and encourage(s) firms and individuals to exploit new opportunities and move into high value-added activities" (OECD, 1998). On the one hand the creation of virtual organizations or "hyperarchies" (Evans and Wurster, 1997) allows firms to react faster on market changes by recreating the virtual value networks. On the other hand there are impacts of this new organizational form on the ways of working and employment. There is a visible trend that a lot of the members of these virtual companies are freelancers (Abby, 1999) which are specialist in one or more parts of the value network.

The use of IT now offers the opportunity to coordinate these specialized parts and form a "best-of-everything" value network and by this enables to provide an improved solution for customers. The possibility of the fast exchange of the players in this network also allows a more flexible adaptation to changing market and customer needs. However, the income of this group might vary in a wide range. On the low-end there might be a group that is not even able to afford health insurance (Abby, 1999). On the high-end people will earn that much money that they are interested in large financial investments and possible tax savings. Still there is one thing that all of these freelancers have in common: They are not living in the world of regular income and constant cash flows any longer. In combination this means that in the future there will be an increasing number of customers that do not fit the standardized financial products and services of today, which are normally designed to fit to constant monthly income streams.

This trend towards an "income lifecycle" that is not corresponding to the income and asset growth of a lifetime typical after World War II is reinforced by another forseeable development. The number of people who will inherit a lot of money from their ancestors is growing tremendously. For example in Germany the value of money that will be shifted from one generation to the next will rise from 102 billion marks in 1987 to 415 billion marks in 2002. The average amount of money being shifted will increase from 199.100 marks in 1990 to 471.600 marks in 2002 (Spiegel, 1998). This means that there will be a lot of people facing the "problem" to decide at one time what to do with an amount of money they normally would have to work a long part of their life for. This also seems to indicate that there is a growing number of people who have a demand for financial services, that do not require constant income streams. Instead these people need sophisticated solutions that allow them to handle "unusual" amounts of money at one point in time.

Deregulation

Another development that is not enabled by information technology but has also great impact on the financial services sector is deregulation. By suspending the Glass-Steagall Act in 1999 the separation between commercial and investment-banking in the United States that was settled in 1933 has been abolished. In result the conditions for American financial services providers are now similar to the rest of the world. By this the entry in foreign markets for U.S. based companies as well as for the rest of the world in the U.S. is more likely and therefore competition will increase.

In summary, on the one hand the rapid development in modern information and communication technology, especially the Internet, has the consequence of increasing competition in the financial services industry that is also supported by deregulation. On the other hand there is a growing number of people who have no demand for traditional financial solutions, because their income situation does not match to the assumption of periodical income streams. In consequence a lot of innovative products that cover the needs of the described group of customers should be observable in the near future. Hence, in the third section we will have a closer look on the current developments in the financial services industry and the strategic options for financial services firms.

3. Strategic Options

Having discussed mega-trends of the financial services industry, we will now assess the strategic options for companies that operate in this dynamically changing business environment. In the end, it seems to come back to Porter (1985). The decision is whether to pursue to gain cost leadership or whether to differentiate the offered services from other competitors (Steffan, 1997). In the context of the booming Internet industries and the global information network, this has to be examined in more detail.

Mergers and Acquisitions

What we observe in the financial services industry is a splurge of mergers, mainly driven by the objective to lower costs and thus become more competitive in this global market. Some examples of 1999 are Unicredito and BCI (March 99), San Paolo IMI and Banca die Roma (March 99), Fleet and Bank Boston (March 99), HSBC and Repulic New York (Mai 99), Bank of Ireland and Leicester (June 99), and Banca Intesa and BCI (June 99) (see also ECB, 1999; De Swaan, 1999; Economist, 1999). Obviously, it is impossible to judge the success of a strategy upfront but the authors argue that merging is the wrong strategy basically because of two reasons.

– Firstly, it is a defensive reaction on market trends instead of an offensive action that influences and sets these trends.
– Secondly, in the long run cost leaders offering commodity products on net markets won't be able to generate shareholder value, because competition is driving prices and profit margins down (see e.g. Gölz and Göppl, 1999). This holds especially true with regard to web-based commodity markets (Kundisch, 2000).

Although the volume of mergers – especially in the financial services industry – has seen two record years in a row, there are in fact still lots of opportunities to combine the business of two or more financial services companies in order to cope with excess capacity. For instance, in the euro area the total number of credit institutions was 8,249 at the beginning of April 1999 (ECB, 1999) while many predictions claim that there is just place for a handful of players in the global battlefield. However, examining research about the success of mergers, there is an astonishingly consistent high number of failures. Though it is difficult to clearly define what a successful merger is, all studies – regardless of the chosen research method – show a failure rate well above 50% (see e.g. CSC, 1998a; AT Kearney, 1998; Bain and Company, 1999). This makes a merger in such a dynamic environment a high-risk-venture instead of giving the new company some relief. Moreover, the best employees are busy merging the company, that is, integrating the IT systems, training the employees in using the new systems, creating a new corporate identity and a shared vision, while the market is dynamically changing at a breathtaking pace. In addition, post-merger costs are often underestimated and the argument that bigger – merged – banks are safer than small ones is not necessarily true (BIS Quarterly Review, 1999).

Differentiation: Sophistication Banking

These disappointing results pose the question, why still so many financial services firms decide to merge. This might stay a miracle from a rationale point of view, especially since there is a choice: Differentiation. In the context of this article we mean by differentiation to become an innovative solution provider. The market for financial services is still dominated by a product and supply side view instead of a customer driven and solution oriented view. Because most financial services companies are organized around products, they have failed so far to fully leverage their relationships with customers and their superior knowledge of customers' lifecycle behavior.

In contrast to Porter's view that was based on the trade-off between flexibility and productivity, on net markets serving the mass market and pursuing differentiation are not mutually exclusive strategies (Piller and Schoder, 1999). Applying state of the art information technology in all business processes enables a company to pursue a hybrid strategy of mass customization – and the market for financial problems with innovative and financially sound solutions is definitely not just a niche, but a mass market with enormous potential. By sound solutions, we mean using Financial Engineering methods to create innovative and intelligent bundles of financial services that optimize a specific objective function

It is important to note the difference between a cost leader producing commodity banking products and a solution provider producing highly individualized and tailored solutions (Buhl and Wolfersberger, 2000a) to the customer. On the one hand, in the future the first one might not even have customer contact anymore and just serve as a "production bank" (Buhl and Wolfersberger, 2000b) for the solution provider delivering commodity banking products. In a competitive environment

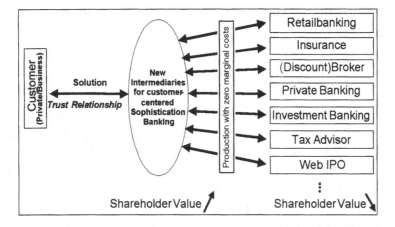

Fig. 2. New intermediaries and shareholder value implications

prices will be driven down to marginal costs. Obviously, banking products are digital products and their marginal costs are (close to) zero. Hence, we argue that in the long run most financial services companies pursuing a cost leader strategy will not be able to generate an adequate shareholder value. On the other hand, the solution provider (also: relationship manager) takes care of a highly valuable asset: The contact to the customer, that includes a lot of information about his preferences and objectives as well as his trust (see Fig. 2). Information can be gathered, formalized and processed in order to achieve a win-win-situation for the customer as well as for the solution provider, since particularly tailored solutions can be offered by Data Warehouse and Data Mining techniques.

It is vital for a solution provider to be as independent as possible from the "production banks", since regulative, legal, institutional and other settings may change quickly. In result, the ingredients (i.e. products) of solutions may change at the same pace. These changes should not force the customer to switch to a new supplier, instead a sophisticated solution provider should be able to adjust its process of finding a solution and eventually find new cost leading "production banks" that deliver the needed products at the best price. How a relationship manager should leverage its customer relation best, will be discussed in the next section.

4. Is IT-Enabled Sophistication Banking a Superior Strategy?

As outlined above in the traditional financial services markets we observe poor quality of consultation and service (not only for retail customers, but also for high end customers in private (investor) banking (Buhl et al., 2000) and for small/mid-size corporations), increasing customer willingness to switch banking affiliations and thus strong pressure on margins. At the same time financial services firms are facing increasing risk from (also IT-driven) continuously increasing volatile global markets. Thus, according to Drucker (1999) they only have two options, namely to either innovate or die.

Concentrating on "High Net-Worth Individuals"?

So far, in addition to cost-oriented merger strategies discussed above banking firms on the marketing side have been trying to concentrate on "high net-worth individuals". These are usually defined as having high income, high property or both. In many cases, for instance in the early years of Germany's Advance Bank this strategy has failed due to low willingness of these high-end customers to switch banking affiliations. Thus for the entrant per capita acquisition costs were quite high. Other income/property based segmentation strategies have also failed due to the fact that (because of lack of consultation service) interesting customers could not be retained. In contrast, successful exceptions on the financial services markets such as MLP AG concentrate on potentially interesting customers such as students of business administration, computer science and engineering, invest heavily in winning them early and accompanying them along their (often freelancer) career with increasingly sophisticated (and profit generating) financial products and services. Using IT as enabler and pursuing such a lifecycle-oriented strategy of [mass-individualized (see e.g. Hansen, 1995a, b; Hansen and Scharl, 1998)] sophistication banking seems promising to us for the following reasons:

– Particularly (potentially) interesting customers are often convenience-oriented and prefer (given a trust-relationship) financial services bundled by one sophistication supplier instead of spending their scarce time with shopping around and coordinating multiple suppliers.
– Financial services firms pursuing a strategy of investing in long-run trust relationships with (potentially) interesting customers are facing lower costs, because it is much cheaper to sell additional products to existing customers along their lifecycle instead of winning new interesting customers.
– Appropriately individualized bundles of financial services are usually advantageous for both the supplier and the customers for reasons of taxation and diversification as we have shown in a number of studies (see e.g. Buhl et al., 1999a, b; Buhl and Wolfersberger, 2000b).

Financial services firms from the US are often both short-term- and big deal-oriented. Thus such a long-run strategy applied to customers becoming interesting tomorrow seems promising for European financial services firms as a differentiation strategy on global markets. Moreover, German/European banking firms are in a good starting position of establishing the necessary trust-relationships with their customers: Investigations such as (CSC, 1998b) show that customers are trusting them much more than, for instance, insurance companies: "Bankers are rated by consumers as the most trusted financial advisor twice as often as brokers and three times as often as insurance agents." From the customer's point of view such a trust-relationship is required because the customer cannot (or does not want to spend effort to) monitor the quality of financial products and services.

IT Implementation Design

For mass individualization of financial services firms have to replace their traditional segmentation strategies.

Figure 3 shows a traditional situation where data about customers are extensively available but cannot be used appropriately to target customers with the appropriate services. Thus, financial services firms usually define a small number of different customer segments and allocate their customers to these segments. As a result, customers get (really) fitting services just by chance since they may have completely different preferences with respect to the different products which cannot be reflected in these segments. For instance imagine a customer who is very cost sensitive with regard to a current account but may be very convenience oriented with respect to mortgages.

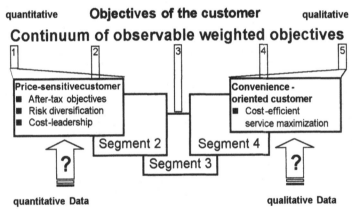

Fig. 3. Traditional segmentation approach

Thus, as Fig. 3 indicates, such a segmentation approach (if at all) only fits a small part of the customers. In addition, most financial services companies so far have not been able to utilize the valuable data of their customers: This is true for reasons of the (terabyte) data volume in their operational legacy systems. And it is particularly the case for the qualitative data available from customers' web usage and from personal communication with staff in call centers and branch offices.

IT allows (see Fig. 4) for a much better approach. Using Internet/Intranet-technologies as integration platform for all the channels to the customer (see Fig. 5), relevant customer information can be obtained via Data-Warehouse- and Data-

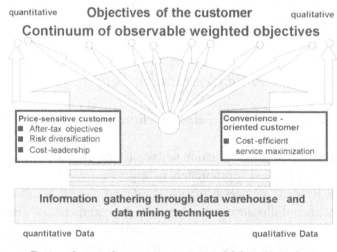

Fig. 4. Customer objectives and available data

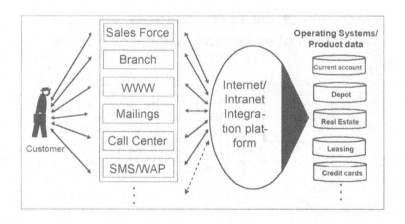

Fig. 5. Multi-channel approach with an integration platform

Mining-Technologies by analyzing both quantitative (hard) operational data and qualitative (soft) customer data e.g. from web tracking. Based on that IT application one-to-one-relationships can be established taking account of the specific (convex combination of) quantitative and qualitative customer objectives. In this area our research group is cooperating both with scientific partners from finance, information systems, computer science and economics in Augsburg and Nuernberg and with a leading German bank in Frankfurt.

If the financial services firm succeeds in replacing usual segmentation strategies by a potential-oriented strategy ensuring that competence of its consultants fits to the customer, individualized sophistication banking is feasible: for competent customers and complex financial problems along their lifecycle sophisticated solutions with substantial advantages for both the customer and the financial intermediary can be provided.

Superior Financial Engineering Solutions: Examples

For instance, in (Buhl and Wolfersberger, 2000a) we have shown that via sophisticated financial engineering the net present value of payments necessary for financing an office building of a small corporate compared to traditional financing can be reduced by some 70% via an appropriate combination of leasing with upfront one-time-payment, loan financing and zerobond investment. If instead of the zerobond a life insurance contract is employed and it is assumed that its present tax exemption holds in the future, a tax paradoxon can be constructed where the small corporate can use the office building for free. Of course such outstanding opportunities often do not last very long. Legal or institutional changes as well as reactions of competitors require to adapt quickly to changing market conditions. Customer-centered intermediaries can quickly react and reconfigure their value network by either dropping or picking up new providers of financial products – without affecting the trust-relationship to the customer.

For private banking customers we have shown in (Buhl et al., 1999) that the net present value of residential property financing can be reduced by some 30%. Briefly described, the financial engineering solution is constructed on the following observations and ideas: If the private banking customer finances his residential property traditionally, neither depreciations nor interest payments are tax-deductible in Germany. If, however, a leasing company is the (tax) owner of the house, first there are tax advantages from depreciation. In addition by optimizing the financial contracts between the leasing company and the customer additional advantages stemming from asymmetric taxation of both can be obtained. By simultaneous optimization of refinancing such businesses as described in (Schneider and Buhl, 1999) the leasing company can gain additional advantages from either factoring of leasing payments or constructing asset-backed-securities from these future payments sold to a funds company. The latter case is particularly interesting if the private banking customer is purchasing such funds shares for his retirement plan: He finally "repurchases" (part of) the depreciation of his own residential property. As a result the financial engineering solution has turned non tax-deductible payments into tax-deductible ones and provided considerable advantages for the customer, the leasing company, the fund and a refinancing banking firm. Such a solution is currently transferred into practical application also with a leading German universal bank and its subsidiaries.

While on traditional (mortgage financing) markets margins are driven to zero by competition, such individualized sophisticated solutions can generate substantial advantages. However, the pre-condition is a trust relationship with deep knowledge about the customer and sophistication fit with respect to competence, consultation, products, services and appropriate usage of (multi-)channels. Based on that the sophistication banking provider can generate on the one hand much larger profit/ shareholder value compared to traditional markets and on the other hand construct a network of brains with high-potential customers benefiting both the members of the network and the economy as a whole by solving better a number of problems being poorly (or not all) solved today in our society.

5. Tasks for the Sophistication Bank

Having described the advantages of sophistication banking, in the following we will provide some conceptual steps to become a sophistication bank, generating an increasing shareholder value by concentrating on trust relationships and offering adequate financial engineering solutions. Basically, there are three steps, that have to be considered. Firstly, customers have to be attracted. Secondly, (potentially) profitable customers have to be identified. Thirdly, the relationships to these customers have to be managed. Obviously, all steps are strongly interrelated and have to be seen as an ongoing (and often parallel) process.

Attracting Customers

Before we can start identifying (potentially) profitable customers and adequately servicing them, we have to attract them. Principally, two ways to attract customers may be distinguished: a passive and an active one.

Passively attracting customers can be performed by ensuring that a potential customer which is looking for financial services, will choose the sophistication bank on his own. Here, branding is one of the most important tasks that have to be carried out. Especially, since the basic building blocks of a financial engineering solution are standardized financial products, hence commodities, branding has to generate an emotional value (Eichelmann and Wild, 2000). According to a current survey by (Interbrand, 2000), a brand consultancy, just two corporations in the financial services markets were able to establish a brand ranking among the top 75 global brands (Citicorp as 16th and Amex as 19th). This gives at least some hints that financial services firms might have enormous potential to improve their situation.

Though branding and passively waiting for customers is one side of the coin, actively fighting for customer relationships is the other side. Certainly, branding should be an important part of a firms strategy so that customers affiliate positive characteristics, like security or sophisticated solutions, with a brand name in the financial services industry. However, branding is very expensive and the (short-term) success of a branding campaign can hardly be measured monetarily. Often a lot of money will be wasted just to reach a comparably small group of target customers. Hence, actively trying hard to build customer relationships seems to be a very promising – if not necessary – approach as well. The question has to be raised, when in the lifecycle it is a good time to target a potential customer. We argue that companies should not wait until post graduates apply for their first jobs after their studies to approach them with appropriate services.

- Firstly, it is quite difficult to approach post graduates since the university as a communication and networking platform cannot be utilized anymore.
- Secondly, a majority of post graduates will already have at least one relationship to a financial services firm due to their jobs during their studies. If they made good experiences with their current firm, they might be at least reluctant to switch. Thus, acquisition cost will be much higher for these relationships.

Therefore, firms should approach (high) potential customers as early as it is adequate to build a relationship. Here, the university and chairs in particular, lend themselves preeminently as a communication and networking platform. This holds true not only for recruiting purposes, where the struggle for the best brains gets also harder every day, but also for building long-term customer relationships. From the experience at our chair, we are strengthened in our view. We successfully built up a network of partner firms and high potential students that generates a win-win relationship for all participants of the network. Another example is the (so far) very successful approach of MLP, a German financial intermediary, that focuses its marketing efforts mainly on graduates.

An issue that is strongly related with fighting for customer relationships, is the question of profitability or potential of prospective customers. Profitability should not only be a concern with respect to existing customer relationships but it makes a lot of sense to think about the potential profitability of customer target groups – like specific graduate students to be considered in more detail later. Here, the concept of the customer lifetime value plays an increasingly important role: Companies try to determine the likely value of a customer relationship along the whole lifecycle of that customer.

Identifying Profitable Customers

The example of MLP AG shows that if you want to be successful in the financial services industry, you first of all have to identify and attract the valuable customers. But what does valuable mean regarding to our context?

A lot of companies try to value their customers based on the turnover they individually generate (Rieker, 1995). This typical behavior can be found in the financial services industry as well as in many other industries. A lot of banks tend to divide their customers into two or more groups based on their current fortune or income, e.g. Deutsche Bank AG that has its unit Deutsche Bank 24 for the standard customer and Deutsche Bank Private Banking for the more wealthy customer. The resulting two groups of customers are treated different in a way that the first group is served with standard products while the second group gets more individual treatment. This might be the right strategy for short term profitability improvement, but we think that if you want to get the most out of your customers in the long term you need not only to focus on the customers who seem to be interesting right now, but also on the ones who will very likely become interesting in the future. So in general what we think the focus – not only – in the financial services industry should be, is that customers need to be evaluated not only by what they are or have right now but by their future potential. In this case the view of the customer shifts toward being an opportunity in which you have to invest first in order to get out your paybacks in the future. In the best case banks take the whole lifetime of their customer relationship into consideration and therefore track the whole development of the relationship from its beginning to the end. This view is called *customer life time value* (see, e.g., Meffert, 1995). The question that still remains is how to separate the promising customers from the rest? MLP AG as one of the winners in the (German) financial services industry is doing this for example by targeting its clients to people with promising academic degrees such as business administration, computer science and engineering disciplines and so to the ones who will most likely have a very promising future with regard to their income. But for most banks this strategy might not be working. They need a way to identify the "valuable" customers from their customer base and then find a way to built a strong relationship over time with them. For this they first need new ways of measuring customer equity. This measures need to include more than the costs or turnover that is generated by an individual customer. They also need to take more qualitative factors into account, which allow an insight e.g. into the cross-selling-potential or the referential behavior of a customer. These factors become more and more important and the knowledge of them enables the companies to optimize their segmentation strategy. An optimized segmentation strategy combined with strong efforts to serve the customer with individualized products are not only a possible strategy existing parallel to a product-oriented strategy. It is the only way that enables companies to build strong relationships with their valuable customers. Otherwise these customers will use the new possibilities of comparison given by the Internet and switch their financial services provider within a short time. Therefore this step from "Inside Out": The Seller-Driven Enterprise to "Outside In": The Customer-Driven Enterprise (Renner, 2000) offers a lot of new opportunities. By successful relationship management it is not only possible to identify and select the most valuable customers, but also to increase margins, because of reduced costs for customer care and increasing selling numbers or prices (for individual products).

Customer Relationship Management

As we can see from the above it is not enough to identify the most valuable customers, but for a sophistication bank it is also important to give its customers the best financial solutions in response to their individual situation. This means to serve the customers perfectly regarding to their individual needs. Unfortunately, these needs are by no means static but changing over time – sometimes at a breathtaking pace. The question now is how it is possible to learn about the changing needs of the customers? The only way in our eyes again is to establish a intensive relationship between the financial services provider and the customer. This means to interact regularly with her to generate the information that is needed to engineer the solutions that perfectly fit for her individual needs.

In order to achieve the information that is needed we first of all have to think about the communication channels. In former times the customer primarily had one personal adviser that (if he did his job well) after a couple of years knew almost everything relevant about his customer and was able to generate good solutions. Today the situation has changed not only because of the mentioned changes in life circumstances that force the financial services providers to establish new communication channels like call-center or internet but also because the financial services providers can cut their costs by an intelligent mix and use of the different channels. However, it is very important and challenging, though, to preserve consistency between all these different channels. Just imagine a customer buys stocks using the call-center or the Internet channel and afterwards asks his personal adviser where to put his stop-loss limit. If the personal adviser has no clue about this stock purchase, customer satisfaction might suffer severely. Thus, there must be one database that serves every channel and is served by every channel itself. Getting back to the issue of cutting costs, a very popular example is that a money transfer the customer is directly doing by using the Internet channel offered by the financial services provider is very much cheaper compared to a money transfer that is done personally by a counter clerk in a branch.

But the new channels should not only be seen as passive reactions to changes in life circumstances or tools in order to reduce costs. Moreover, they can contribute to high level financial solutions by collecting information about the customer. We think that especially the WWW should be used as a source of information. This, because it has some special abilities like the following: You are able to collect information about the customers interests that is not influenced by an adviser. With the WWW the time between contacts with the customer can be reduced dramatically. If you identify changes in the customers interests you can react very fast and suggest financial solutions. All in all the WWW can be used as a high quality information source about the customer if the financial services providers are able to rise high value information. For this it is necessary to design and implement web-tracking systems that go far behind standard abilities like counting the number of page views or visits. Hence, to find out the customers interests you have to track not only the technical information mentioned before but also meta information about the content she is interested in, like "stocks; biotechnology; amgen". For this intelligent concepts for marking content with semantic based on XML or other meta-languages have to be developed.

In the following, we will present two conceptual models from our research on customer relationship management and one-to-one marketing. The first one deals with the customer model, i.e. the formal and machine readable presentation of customers' preferences. The second one is a model to formally describe finance related content as a prerequisite to individually provide customers with the appropriate content at the right time via the right channel.

Customer modeling is one possible solution for establishing a central repository, which can provide services for various sophistication banking applications. (Fridgen et al., 2000a) show that those generic customer models should include both, knowledge, e.g. about risk-affinity, attitude towards net present value and affinity towards special products, in the form of preferences, but also plain information, like age and know-how. Furthermore, they suggest an approach for one-to-one-banking, which, in a first step, completes customer models from given information and thereby lays ground for the ongoing step two, in which user specific actions are inferred.

Figure 6 summarizes this process: The preferences of a customer are deducted by an inference process (I_1) from the customer information base built up in (a) and (b). Domain specific and domain independent knowledge about building customer models is used for this deduction. Inference process I_2 is the actual consulting process, in which starting from an instance of the customer model, the adequate individualized action is determined. This process is supported by a domain specific and domain independent knowledge base built up for consulting processes as well (Fridgen et al., 2000a). It is important to note, though, that individualized goods and services are not advantageous at all costs. (Schackmann et al., 2000) and (Link and Schackmann, 2000) analyze conditions where CRM and individualized services should be preferred. Main advantages of the proposed approach compared to the state of the art one-step approach are the following (for a detailed discussion see Fridgen et al., 2000a):

– The complexity of the whole process is significantly reduced.
– The matching algorithm/inference process I_2 may be specified more precisely.
– The two different inference processes I_1 and I_2 can follow different paradigms.
– The two-step approach provides for more flexibility.
– The processes of knowledge generation can be traced more easily.

We should mention though that there is one major deficiency affiliated with this approach: Since the deducted knowledge about a customer (preferences base) is performed by a so-called pre-process (inference process I_1) the actual matching process (I_2) cannot take place in real-time.

While in (Fridgen et al., 2000a) the structure of the knowledge base is not discussed, (Fridgen et al., 2000b) propose a conceptual model that may serve to establish a central customer repository using a quasi-hierarchical graph to deduce knowledge. In particular, problems of inconsistency, changing needs over time, and explicating and deducing implicit knowledge are discussed there.

A profound customer model is a prerequisite to be able to offer individualized services on a broad scale, but also models to formally present finance related content and financial products have to be developed. With respect to the content model, (Kundisch et al., 2001) propose to describe finance related content with a standardized set of 11 attributes (see Table 1) as a basis for a matching with an instance of a

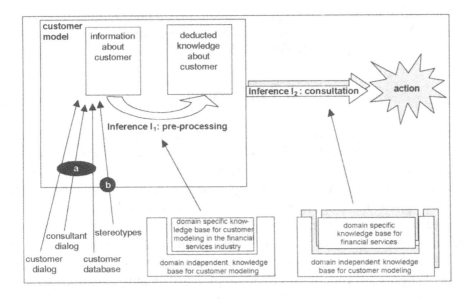

Fig. 6. Process of establishing customer models and deducting user-specifacctions

customer model. The overall objective is formulated as to individually provide a customer with the right content at the right time via the appropriate channel. Conveniently, the basic setup of the model is quite comparable to the customer model described in (Fridgen et al., 2000a). In the content model, there is also a two-step inference process. First, a knowledge base is built up using a pre-process. Meta information is mainly derived by an IT-enabled inference process and partly by human content managers. Consequently, the meta information about finance related content can be used in a second step for a matching with knowledge about customers. As a result, content may be individually provided based on the customer's preferences and according to market developments and the customer's current situation.

All this research has not just been done with the far vision to enable true one-to-one marketing and an optimal customer relationship management but – using current technology – vital parts of this vision have recently been realized and

Table 1. Relevant attributes to describe finance related content

Right Content	Author, Source, Subject Categories, Language, Release Date, Content Type, Recommendation Level, Specificity, Sophistication Level
Right Time	Subject Categories, Length, Sophistication Level
Right Channel	Subject Categories, Length, Content Style
Complete Attribute List	Author, Source, Subject Categories, Language, Release Date, Content Type, Recommendation Level, Specificity, Sophistication Level, Length, Content Style

implemented in a project with the private banking part of Frankfurt based Deutsche Bank AG. The discussion about conceptual models concludes the paper and we will now summarize our main findings.

6. Conclusions

We have illustrated the mega-trends affecting the financial services industry and discussed strategic options for the upcoming global and volatile markets. We have argued and justified why cost-oriented strategies such as mergers/acquisitions are not beneficial in the long run; using IT and people instead concentrating on the customer's problems along the lifecycle and becoming a Sophistication Banking intermediary seems much more promising: Offering the appropriate channel, product, service and advice for each specific customer/problem combination is superior with respect to convenience, cost, tax and diversification advantages. Financial engineering combining IT and people based on long-term trust relationships with customers is a strong element to succeed in future markets turning the mega-trends from threats into business opportunities.

References

Abby, E. (1999) A. Generation of Freelancers. The New York Times, Aug 15, Sec. 3: Money and Business/Financial Desk, p.13

AT Kearney (1998) Global PMI Survey

Advance Bank (2001) http://www.advancc-bank.dc. Use the section "Immobilien/Der Online-Berater", tested 1/2/2001

Bain & Company (1999) Fusionswelle im Bankenbereich

BIS Quarterly Review (1999) International Banking and Financial Market Developments, August

Buhl, H. U., Wolfersberger, P. (2000a) Neue Perspektiven im Online- und Multichannel Banking. In: Locarek-Junge, H., Walter, B. (Hrsg.) Banken im Wandel: Direktbanken und Direct Banking. Berlin-Verlag, Berlin, S. 247–268

Buhl, H. U., Wolfersberger, P. (2000b) One-to-one Banking. In: Riekeberg, M. v., Stenke, K. (Hrsg.) Banken 2000 – Projekte und Perspektiven. Gabler, Wiesbaden, S. 189–211

Buhl, H. U., Hinrichs, J.-W., Satzger, G., Schneider, J. (1999a) Leasing selbstgenutzter Wohnimmobilien. Die Betriebswirtschaft 59, 3: 316–331

Buhl, H. U., Sandbiller, K., Will, A., Wolfersberger, P. (1999b) Zur Vorteilhaftigkeit von Zerobonds. Zeitschrift für Betriebswirtschaft 69, 1: 83–114

Buhl, H. U., Huther, A., Reitwiesner, B., Schroeder, N., Schneider, J., Tretter, B. (2000) Performanceattribution im Private Banking. Die Bank 5: 318–323

CSC (1998a) Executing the successful merger: Smart Play in a High-Risk Game. CSC Index Research Report

CSC (1998b) Competing to Win in the New Marketspace, p.10

De Swaan, T. (1999) The Single Financial Market and the restructuring of European banks. Österreichisches Bankarchiv 9: 675

Drucker, P. (1999) Drucker on financial services: Innovate or die. The Economist, September 25th: 27–34

ECB (1999) Banking in the euro area: structural features and trends. ECB Monthly Bulletin, April: 41–53

Economist (1998) Finance and economics: Economic focus: The end of jobs for life? The Economist, 21st February: 96

Economist (1999) The bank-merger splurge. The Economist, 28th August: 13–14

Eichelmann, Th., Wild, A. (2000) Banken müssen emotionalen Mehrwert bieten. Die Bank 12: 840–844

Euromoney (1991) The new battleground. Euromoney, September: 53

Evans, P. B., Wurster, T. S. (1997) Strategy and the New Economics of Information. Harvard Business Review, Sept./Oct.: 71–82

Finanztest (2000) For a survey about the quality of consultation in the German market see Finanztest, no. 5

Fridgen, M., Schackmann, J., Volkert, S. (2000a) Preference Based Customer Models for Electronic Banking. In: Hansen, H.-R., Bichler, M., Mahrer H. (eds.), Proceedings of the 8th European Conference on Information Systems ECIS 2000, Wien (Austria), Vol. 2, pp. 819–825

Fridgen, M., Volkert, S., Haarnagell, M., Marko, D., Zimmermann, S. (2000b) Kunden-modell für eCRM – Repräsentation individueller Einstellungen, accepted submission for: 3. FAN-Tagung 2000, Siegen (Germany)

Gölz, R., Göppl, F. (1999) Electronic Commerce: Entwicklungspfade und Differenzierungs-strategien. technologie & management 48, 5: 26–29

Hansen, R. (1995a) A Case Study of a Mass Information System. Information & Management 28, 2

Hansen, R. (1995b) Conceptual Framework and Guidelines for the Implementation of Mass Information Systems. Information & Management 28, 3

Hansen, R., Scharl A. (1998) Cooperative Development of Web-based Mass Information Systems. Proceedings of the 4th Americas Conference on Information Systems (AIS '98), Baltimore

Interbrand (2000) Interbrand's Annual Survey: The World's Most Valuable Brands 2000, available at http://www.interbrand.com/league_chart.html, tested 1/2/2001

Kundisch, D. (2000) Buyer Search Behavior in an Electronic Commodity Market: Consumer's Decision for a Sequential or Simultaneous Search Method. In: Kim, S. H. et al. (eds.) Proceedings of the 2nd International Conference on Electronic Commerce 2000 (ICEC2000), Seoul (Korea), pp. 88–93

Kundisch, D., Wolfersberger, P., Calaminus, D., Klöpfer, E. (2001) Enabling eCCRM: Content Model and Management for Financial eServices, accepted submission for 34th Annual Hawaii International Conference on System Sciences (HICSS) 2001, Maui (USA)

Link, H., Schackmann, J. (2000) Ein ökonomisches Modell für die Produktion individueller digitaler Produkte. In: Bodendorf, F., Grauer, G. (eds.) Proceedings of the Verbundtagung Wirtschaftsinformatik. Shaker, Aachen, S. 192–207

Meffert, H. (1995) Was versteht man unter dem Kundenwert? Welche Ansatzpunkte ergeben sich zur Verlängerung? In: Handelsblatt (Hrsg.) Special issue: Berufsinformationen und Stellenmarkt, pp. 7–8

OECD (1998) Industrial Performance and Competitiveness in an Era of Globalisation and Technological Change. The OECD Observer 210, Feb./March: 55

Piller, F., Schoder, D. (1999) Mass Customization und Electronic Commerce. Zeitschrift für Betriebswirtschaft 69: 1111–1136

Porter, M. (1985) Competitive Advantage: creating and sustaining superior performance. Free Press, New York

Renner, D. H. (2000) Focusing on Customer Equity – The Unrealized Asset. In: Defying the Limits: Reaching New Heights in Customer Relationship Management. Montgomery Research Inc., San Francisco, pp. 11–17

Rieker, S. A. (1995) Bedeutende Kunden: Analyse und Gestaltung von langfristigen Anbieter-Nachfrager-Beziehungen auf industriellen Märkten. Deutscher Universitätsverlag, Wiesbaden (Germany), p. 51

Schackmann, J., Steck, W., Hummel, S., Rödl, K. (2000) Eine ökonomische Betrachtung von Customer Relationship Management und individuellen Finanzdienstleistungen, accepted submission for: 3. FAN-Tagung 2000, Siegen (Germany)

Schneider, J., Buhl, H. U. (1999) Simultane Optimierung der Zahlungsströme von Leasingverträgen und deren Refinanzierung. Zeitschrift für Betriebswirtschaft 69, Ergänzungsheft 3: 19–39

Spiegel (1998) Das goldene Los. Der Spiegel 17: 78–96

Steffan, C. (1997) Entwicklung und Perspektiven des Investment Banking. Sparkasse 114, 4: 169–173

Hans U. Buhl

Holds two M.S. degrees in Industrial Engineering and Operations Research from the University of Karlsruhe, Germany and the UC Berkeley, CA and Ph.D. and PD Dr. habil. also from the University of Karlsruhe. After having worked for IBM Germany in the departments of finance, logistics, information systems, and financial marketing he was appointed full professor of Information Systems at the University of Augsburg, Germany as full professor of Financial Engineering and Information Systems. His research interests include electronic financial services and financial engineering.

Dennis O. Kundisch

Holds a Masters graduate degree in Business Administration from the University of Dayton, OH, and a diploma in Business Administration with majors in Financial Engineering, Information Systems and Economic/Business Policy from the University of Augsburg, Germany. Since 2000 he is working in the Information Systems department at the University of Augsburg's Business School as a doctoral student. His research interests include strategies on electronic markets, electronic financial services, and financial engineering. Mr Kundisch is presently involved in a multi-year project "Efficient Electronic Coordination in the Service Sector".

Andreas S. Leinfelder

Has studied Business Administration at the Universitiy of Augsburg, Germany and the Katz Graduate School of Business at the University of Pittsburgh, PA. He holds a diploma in Business Administration with majors in Financial Engineering, Information Systems and Organization/Management from the University of Augsburg, Germany. His research interests include strategies on electronic markets and customer relationship management. In January 2001 he has joined the Strategic Services Division of Accenture (formerly Andersen Consulting).

Werner Steck

Holds a diploma in Business Administration with majors in Information Systems, Organization/Management and Environmental Economics from the University of Augsburg, Germany. Since 1998 he is working in the Information Systems department at the University of Augsburg's Business School as a doctoral student. His research interests include strategies on electronic markets, electronic financial services and customer relationship management. Mr. Steck is presently involved in a multi-year project "Efficient Electronic Coordination in the Service Sector".

A Framework for Performance and Value Assessment of E-Business Systems in Corporate Travel Distribution*

A. M. Chircu[1] and R. J. Kauffman[2]

[1]Management Science and Information Systems, McCombs School of Business, University of Texas, Austin, U.S.A.
[2]Information and Decision Sciences, Carlson School of Management, University of Minnesota, Minneapolis, U.S.A.

amchircu@yahoo.com
rkauffman@csom.umn.edu

Abstract
This chapter proposes and illustrates a framework that the authors call the *value life cycle for e-commerce systems*. Based on recent research results that relate to technology investments in the corporate travel industry and related theoretical and empirical perspectives, the authors lay out the corporate travel e-commerce system solutions value life cycle. The perspective involves estimating the maximum value that that an organization can obtain by implementing an e-commerce system in a specific industry and competitive environment. It also considers multiple factors that act as value contingencies for the implementation process. These create barriers to value accrual and to post-implementation performance assessment. The analytical perspective emphasizes the importance of comparing the *expected value* from the evaluation stage with the *realized value* from actual system usage. The authors highlight a key finding for

* The findings that are presented in this chapter are based on a large corporate travel industry research project conducted through the MIS Research Center at the Carlson School of Management, University of Minnesota. A presentation related to this research was given by Robert J. Kauffman at Abteilung für Wirtschaftsinformatik, Wirtschaftuniversität Wien, Vienna, Austria, May 15, 2000. We thank the participants of that seminar for comments and suggestions on the specifics of that research

corporate travel procurement specialists: the value of e-commerce systems infrastructure is surprisingly dependent on a variety of factors in the implementation environment of the organization, and as a result, the authors suggest that investments in this kind of technology be made with considerable caution and a clear sense of the potential pitfalls that may lead to insufficient value accrual.

"Like an earthquake, deep within the earth, many of the forces reshaping business today are happening out of sight, and often don't register on corporate Richter scales until they erupt violently on the surface. The Internet is just such a force. The rapid emergence of e-commerce has shaken business to its core, forcing managers to streamline their processes ... expand the markets in which they compete ... and continually rethink their strategies"

From a speech by George H. Conrades,
Chairman, Akamai Technologies

1. Introduction

E-commerce (EC) technologies are hypothesized to impact business interactions at the individual, organizational and industry level in ways no other *information technology* (IT) application has done before. But industry leaders recognize that the focus of EC is not on simple implementation of Internet technologies, but instead, it is on the total transformation of traditional business processes into e-business processes. E-business, in this context, describes how EC technology starts to permeate all aspects of business interactions and creates new value.

One of the industries having a significant amount of experience with the challenges of implementing EC technologies and transforming traditional business-es into e-businesses is the corporate travel industry. EC innovations in this industry range from the first introduction of Internet-based travel reservation systems for business travel in the early days of Internet in 1995 to the very recent attempts to establish online B2B e-marketplaces that directly connect buyers and sellers of travel services. All players in the industry – including corporate travel buyers, travel services providers, and travel intermediaries – are attempting to implement EC technologies in a desire to streamline processes and reduce their costs. (The interested reader is encouraged to see Werthner and Klein (1999), who provide the fullest treatment of the IT issues in travel and tourism that we have seen to date.)

However, as it is often the case, not all industry players benefit from the same EC innovations the same way. Some established players – traditional business travel agencies and even powerful aggregators such as computerized reservation systems (CRSs, also called global distribution systems in the industry – GDS) – have witnessed their traditional sources of revenue drying up, and even have experienced the threat of being pushed out of their traditional market niches due to the introduction of EC innovations for corporate travel distribution.

Travel purchasing is particularly suitable for automation through EC technologies since information about travel services – and not a *physical* product – is what is handled through the industry value chain. Business travel currently represents about 40% of the entire travel market (Thompson, 1999), and is positioned, according to Forrester

Research, to experience the highest growth rate among business services predicted to move online by 2003 (Putnam et al., 1999). Harteveldt et al. (2000) predict that online business travel purchases will grow to $20.4 billion in sales by 2004. In spite of such predictions, the EC-enabled corporate travel industry transformation has really just begun. All industry players still experience the pressure of determining their e-business strategy when faced with ever-evolving technological standards, competitive conditions, and unexpected implementation and adoption problems. Managers making EC investment decisions still have no clear benchmarks for determining what EC technologies will ultimately be successful in the marketplace and deliver value.

Based on our previous research results with respect to technology investments in the corporate travel industry and related theoretical and empirical perspectives, we propose a more general yet integrated view of the *value life cycle for e-commerce systems*. This view describes the corporate travel EC system solutions value life cycle, from determining the maximum value of an EC system that an organization can obtain by implementing the system in a specific industry and competitive environment, to the contingencies of the implementation process that create *barriers* to value accrual, and to the post-implementation performance assessment that compares the *expected value* from the evaluation stage with the *realized value* from actual system usage.

In the next section, we provide a more detailed background on several major e-business system solutions in the corporate travel industry. We then introduce a new framework that can help us understand how e-business solutions provide value and what are the factors that impact this value. We continue by discussing the individual elements of the framework as they apply to the corporate travel industry, the theories that inform our understanding of each framework element, and the managerial recommendations stemming from our own research. Finally, we will end with a brief discussion of the contributions and implications for future research.

2. E-Business Systems Solutions in Corporate Travel Distribution

In this section, we discuss the traditional industry structure in corporate travel before the advent of e-commerce, the intermediation attempts made by EC system providers and the disintermediation threats they posed to traditional industry players, as well as the traditional players' efforts to reintermediate and strategize around the new technologies of the Internet.

Industry Background and the Systems Solution Setting

Business travel, the third largest controllable corporate operating expense, significantly impacts a company's bottom line (Johnston and Sherlock, 1998). Together with other operating resources such as office and computer supplies, and maintenance, repair and operations (MRO) supplies, business travel is often purchased by individual employees, on an *ad hoc* basis without the proper controls in place (Kalakota and Robinson, 1999). Operating resources can cost as much as 30% of total company spending, but the traditional phone and paper-based purchasing methods that are still used in the majority of companies make controlling these costs very difficult. In addition, many companies have difficulties preventing "maverick buying," where employees bypass the preferred suppliers and select their own purchasing outlets. This is especially true for business travel, and more and more, companies now attempt to reduce their travel costs through negotiations with preferred suppliers and corporate travel policies mandating the use of these suppliers and certain travel reservation rules (Hjermstad, 1999). To understand the forces shaping the EC-enabled transformation of the corporate travel industry, one must first understand the current structure of the business travel industry (see Fig. 1).

Traditionally, companies have used *corporate travel agencies* to purchase travel services from their preferred airline, hotel and car suppliers. These suppliers have listed, in exchange for a fee, their process and availability information in CRSs that any agency may access through dedicated connections. With the advent of e-commerce, however, *Internet-based electronic travel reservation systems* for corporate travel, also called *online booking* (or *self-booking*) *systems*, are expected to partially, or, in some cases, even totally replace the traditional travel agents. To obtain travel supplier information, these systems have initially established electronic connections to the traditional CRSs, and, more recently, to the actual suppliers through direct

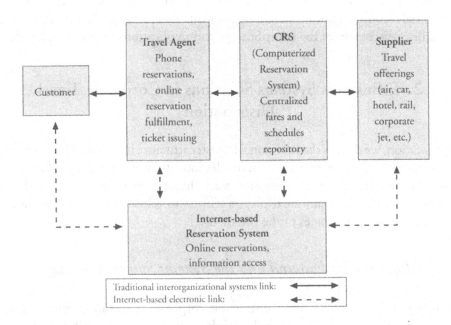

Fig. 1. Traditional and EC-enabled players in the corporate travel industry

connections. In general, after a firm's employees make reservations using these systems, the details are sent to that firm's corporate travel agency, which then fulfills the transaction by checking the quality of the reservation and issuing tickets.

Generally, companies pay their travel agencies either a transaction fee for every travel transaction, or a management fee that covers the cost of the travel agents and all the transactions performed by the company. Transaction fees have become increasingly popular among travel agencies lately, especially after the introduction of new kinds of fares. In exchange for these fees, the travel agency agrees to meet specific service levels both in terms of promptly responding to company employees' phone calls and providing the lowest available prices for their specific travel requests, based on the company's negotiated rates with suppliers. Table 1 presents a summary of the top 5 U.S. travel agencies whose revenues are primarily generated by business travel.

However, with the advent of electronic reservation systems for corporate travel such as GetThere.com (recently acquired by Sabre), Sabre BTS or e-Travel (now owned by Oracle), companies now have another, potentially less expensive, choice for corporate travel purchasing. Many third-party electronic travel reservation system providers exist, but few have managed to successfully capture major corporate customers and help them achieve high online adoption levels among their travelers (see Table 2). At present, all major travel agencies offer their customers the option of reserving travel online through third party or proprietary system implementations.

While many knowledgeable industry observers recognize that huge opportunities for online business travel purchases exist, they also point out that we are still witnessing the early stages of the EC-enabled industry transformation. The implementation of online systems is still fraught with problems, and the adopting companies soon realize that significant resources are required to enable successful implementations in light of complicated corporate travel policies, negotiated rates agreements, and traveler needs. Then there is the problem of system usage – without which the companies cannot start seeing the promised savings.

Indeed, the reader should note that the patterns emerging for online business travel reservations are very different from the ones for online leisure travel reservations. As Table 1 showed, two online leisure travel agencies are already ranked in the top 10 U.S. travel agencies, confirming a trend indicating that more leisure travelers than business travelers currently make their reservations online (Gartner Group, 2000).

Disintermediating Systems Solutions

The travel industry has been buffeted by a number of forces, affecting travel providers and traditional intermediaries (e.g. travel agents and CRSs) that characterize the industry marketplace (Clemons and Row, 1991a; Clemons and Hann, 1999; Chircu and Kauffman, 2000c).

Table 1. Top U. S. travel agencies (source: *Travel Weekly*, various issues in 2000)

Rank	Agency	US$ gross (in millions)		Locations	Business travel (as a percentage of total sales)	Online corporate travel reservation system
		1998	1999			
1	American Express	$11,950 (*Travel Weekly* estimate)	$13,700 (*Travel Weekly* estimate)	3,700	2,000 locations serve corporate customers; "business mix is dominated by corporate travel"	AXI, GetThere.com (under development); 272 corporate customers with 667,000 registered online users already use AXI
2	Carlson Wagonlit Travel	$11,000	$11,000	3,000	96%	SoloAct online booking solution powered by Sabre BTS, e-Travel, KDS; GetThere.com will be used for leisure travel only
3	World Travel Partners	$3,300	$4,300	1,632	84%	TRX's ResAssist recommended (but clients may use any online system); 7% of corporate clients use online reservation systems.
4	Rosenbluth International	$3,740	$4,200	N/D	96%	@Rosenbluth powered by XOL's XTRA On-Line; Biztravel.com, which Rosenbluth now owns, is targeted to unmanaged business travel
5	Navigant International	N/D	$3,300	1,150	88%	XOL's XTRA On-Line, Sabre BTS and Worldspan Trip Manager; 10% of corporate clients use these systems
6	Maritz Travel	$1,883	$1,740	367	94%	eCom Booking Solutions powered by Sabre BTS, GetThere.com and Worldspan Trip Manager; 24 clients are currently implementing these systems
7	Liberty Travel	$1,089	$1,200	198	2%	Agency has Internet-based reservation system for leisure clients

continued

Table 1. Continued

Rank	Agency	US$ gross (in millions)		Locations	Business travel (as a percentage of total sales)	Online corporate travel reservation system
		1998	1999			
8	Sato Travel	$1,089	$1,200	925	92%	Proprietary reservation request system integrated with agency's call center (Res By Web); 5% of reservations are currently made online
9	Travelo-city.com	$285	$1,200	Online only	Primarily leisure travel	Proprietary (www.travelocity.com)
10	Expedia, Inc.	$250	$832	Online only	Primarily leisure travel	Proprietary (www.expedia.com)

Table 2. Leading online reservation system providers for corporate travel (Sources: McNulty, 1999a; Rosen, 2000b; Rice, 2000; PhoCusWright, 2000)

Technology provider	On-line system	Customers and adoption levels	Most recent developments
Worldspan	Trip Manager	891 customers, Adoption: N/A	Automated quality control; wireless services
TRX	ResAssist	More than 600 customers, Adoption: N/A	Multi-lingual capabilities; direct connections with suppliers
GetThere.	GlobalManager, DirectCorporate (newly launched)	100 major corporations and travel providers (who license private label versions of Get-There.com's software) 1,000 small American Express customers, Adoption: N/A	Wireless services; direct connections with suppliers; acquired by Sabre in October 2000
Sabre	Sabre BTS	500 corporate customers, Adoption: 5% of customers book 90% of travel online, 95% of customers book 15–25% of travel online	Automated quality control; has acquired GetThere.com on 10/00
Microsoft	AXI	272 American Express corporate customers, Adoption: N/A	Exclusivity agreement with American Express ended June 1999; international versions
XOL	XTRA On-Line PowerTrip	200 corporations, Adoption: N/A	Combined fare rules and schedule listing; automated trip planning product
Oracle	e-Travel	9 major global corporations featured on e-Travel.com website, 200 customers, Adoption: generally 10–15%, in some cases 25–30%	XML-based release; direct connections to suppliers; wireless services

One of the most well accepted predictions regarding the impacts of EC on market structure, even though it not necessarily confirmed by practice, is *disintermediation*, or the replacement of established industry players with Internet-based systems. In the corporate travel industry, depending on the intermediaries replaced by Internet-based reservation systems, several types of disintermediation can occur: disintermediation of traditional travel agents only, disintermediation of traditional travel agents and CRSs, and disintermediation of CRSs only (see Fig. 2).

The *disintermediation of traditional travel agents* was triggered by the introduction of the first generation Internet-based travel reservation systems in late 1995, when the EC technology provider GetThere.com (then ITN, the Internet Travel

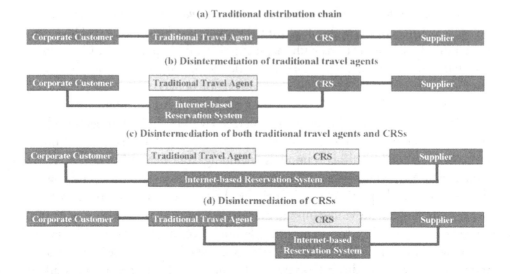

Fig. 2. EC disintermediation of the traditional distribution chain in corporate travel

Network) announced the first such product intended for the corporate travel market. Other system providers were soon to follow, and a whole range of electronic reservation system solutions offered by technology vendors (such as GetThere.com and e-Travel), CRSs (such as Sabre BTS) or travel agencies (such as American Express' AXI) later emerged. At the same time, the developers of business travel reservation systems were also focusing on the leisure market, where names such as Travelocity.com (offered by Sabre, the developer of Sabre BTS) or Expedia (offered by Microsoft, American Express' development partner for AXI) were starting to establish themselves as viable online travel services providers.

The Internet-based electronic travel reservation systems promised significant cost savings for the corporate customers through the replacement of traditional travel agency fees with much lower electronic travel reservation system fees, better travel policy enforcement, and better negotiations with suppliers. These savings are now possible due to the more prevalent use of *net/net* fare agreements, which enable companies to negotiate discounts from regular prices and receive these discounts at the time of purchase, without the involvement of the travel agency (National Business Travel Association, 1999). This replaces the old system of passing back the supplier rebates by the corporate travel agency, which used to offset the fees the corporation had to pay to the travel agency in exchange for its services. As a result of this fee reduction, Internet-based travel reservation systems pose a significant threat to established corporate travel agencies. They now see their travel information and reservation services being replaced by these automated systems, as potential savings on the transaction fees attract more of their customers.

The *disintermediation of traditional travel agents and CRSs* has been triggered by the latest attempts of EC technology providers such as e-Travel and GetThere.com to establish direct connections with major suppliers. By bypassing the CRSs, these providers hope to generate significant transaction fee savings for these suppliers, who now have to pay much lower fees for every reservation booked through the direct link as opposed to the CRS.

e-Travel pioneered the direct connection trend with its ETLink program, which became operational in March 1999 (McNulty, 1999a). ETLink enabled direct connections to just a handful of suppliers, including Continental Airlines and Hertz Corporation. Since then, e-Travel's supplier network has grown slowly, and now, in addition to its early participants, it includes Amtrak, Pegasus Solutions (a hotel distribution network providing links to more than 90 hotel brands with over 25,000 properties), and StarCite Inc. (a meeting planning electronic system). e-Travel also has connections to the CRSs Galileo/Apollo, Sabre and Worldspan. e-Travel's latest strategy is to encourage direct links by developing its system in Extensible Markup Language (XML), which will ensure a standard, cost-effective way of adding additional suppliers. GetThere.com has already attracted several major suppliers, as well as smaller ones, to connect directly to its B2B marketplace. As of June 2000, participants include United Airlines, Northwest Airlines, Trans World Airlines, British Airways, Accor Hotels, Marriott International, Radisson Hotels and Resorts, Starwood Hotels and Resorts, Micros Fidelio & Hotel Bank, Candlewood Hotels, Avis Rent a Car, Budget Rent a Car, and Hertz. GetThere.com's B2B marketplace now incorporates wireless access capabilities, and as a result, it exemplifies a combination of strategies that go well beyond simple disintermediation, based on aggregation of buyers, suppliers, and access options.

We further note that another CRS disintermediation scenario is also possible: the establishment of direct connections to suppliers by travel agencies (see Fig. 2 presented earlier). While this scenario has not been implemented yet by any travel agency, it is entirely possible that we will see it occurring more frequently in the future.

The reader should bear in mind that the leisure travel industry has also experienced similar disintermediation attempts of traditional travel agents, represented by the Internet-based reservation systems such as Expedia.com and Travelocity.com. However, disintermediation approaches specific to the leisure travel market have also occurred. For example, travel agency disintermediation approaches include the introduction of *supplier-specific systems* for travel reservations, such as NWA.com or Hilton.com, where travelers can make reservations without the involvement of a travel agency. They also include *reverse auction systems* for leisure travel, such as Priceline.com, or the online outlet for discount travel services, Hotwire.com. The interesting "twist" in Hotwire.com's business model is that it hides the identity of the supplier of the airline ticket and the times of the flight, like Priceline.com does, right up to the time the traveler makes a purchase, thereby enabling the airline to retain some market power by maintaining anonymity around its inventory of

supply. It is also interesting to note that the CRS disintermediation approaches for leisure travel have been promoted by different players than in the case of business travel: the suppliers. This, for example, is the case of the soon-to-be-launched airline website, Orbitz (www.orbitz.com), which promises to offer unbiased fare searches among all regular and Internet-only fares available at any time in an attempt to identify the lowest possible fares for any travel request.

Reintermediating Systems Solutions

Full disintermediation of either travel agencies or CRSs has not yet occurred, however, as only a small percentage of business travel transactions are now conducted online. It is in fact possible that full disintermediation will *never* happen as the established industry intermediaries find solutions to fight back and adopt the very EC systems that caused their disintermediation in the first place. These firms' *reintermediation* strategies are based on leveraging their long-standing industry position while taking advantage on the new developments in EC technologies.

Reintermediation of travel agencies is made possible by licensing agreements with EC technology providers that allow agencies to offer their clients the option to book either by phone, using traditional travel agency services, or on the Internet using electronic systems for making reservations, which are then checked for quality and ticketed by the traditional agency. Currently, all major corporate travel agencies offer such an arrangement, most often by providing a choice among several electronic reservation systems – a result of strong demand for Internet-based electronic reservation systems from these agencies' clients (see Table 1). Indeed, as a recent survey of the largest 100 corporate travel buyers shows, 67% of the respondents have already selected – independently or through their travel agency – an Internet-based travel reservation system provider, and the rest intend to follow within 1 year (Campbell, 2000a) (see Fig. 3).

This strategy, however, presents a number of challenges, related primarily to losing important revenue streams from reduced transaction fees for fulfilling online reservations, which, clients argue, are easier to handle than phone reservations and therefore require a lower fee. Still, the travel agency has to receive enough online reservations in order to make the fulfillment processes efficient. As a result, many travel agencies have established tiered pricing schemes, where transaction fees for online reservation fulfillment goes down only when online reservation volume reaches a reasonable threshold, which should be, by industry estimates, at least 20%, and even 35–40% in some cases (Welt, 1999).

Reintermediation is also made possible by the significant travel-specific expertise required to use Internet-based travel reservation systems effectively and effectively. Because of this, these systems may not always be so convenient for busy business travelers. Hal Rosenbluth, chairman of Rosenbluth International, put this into the proper perspective:

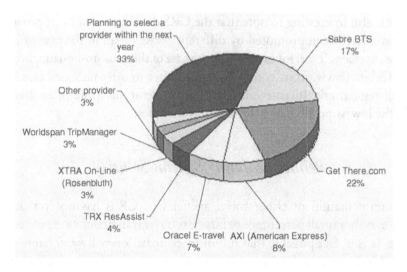

Fig. 3. Internet-based reservation system adoption among the largest 100 corporate travel customers in 2000 (Source: Campbell, 2000a)

"I believe that [Internet-based electronic reservation systems] will become more and more ubiquitous. [...] Where I begin to diverge a little bit is in the rate of intervention. It needs a human interface, whether it's GetThere, e-Travel, @Rosenbluth or Sabre BTS. [...] A lot of companies would rather take one minute speaking to an agent as opposed to taking 10 to 15 minutes doing something on their own." (Limone, 2000)

The CRSs' reintermediation attempts have just started to emerge, given that the disintermediation threat itself is fairly new. Some of the most powerful industry players have acted quickly by lowering suppliers fees pay for online reservations and by buying direct-connect technologies. Their reintermediation attempts present similar challenges for the traditional travel agencies: building (or acquiring) technology for direct connections is relatively easy. However, lowering the transaction fees is a hard decision, given that it is against the very business model of the CRSs. The first CRS to respond to the disintermediation threat is Sabre, which has recently completed the acquisition of GetThere.com.

3. A 'Value Life Cycle' Framework for Corporate Travel Systems

We next present a framework that conceptualizes our overall thinking about how different industry players can achieve high value outcomes from implementing such EC systems as we have discussed up to this point in this chapter. Although our focus is mainly on corporate customers, we will point out related examples and theoretical perspectives that relate to value realization for the other industry players, especially travel agencies, CRSs and suppliers.

As the reader can see from our industry analysis, Internet-based electronic reservation systems are the major force behind the recent corporate travel industry transformations. But some companies see immediate benefits from implementing such systems, while others take a longer path to realizing benefits (Spradling, 2000).

Based on our previous research on the corporate travel industry, as well as on the most recent results related to EC impacts on other industries, we propose a life cycle framework that describes how value from EC technology solutions for corporate travel is created and realized by firms implementing these technologies (see Fig. 4). The first step in determining the value of an EC technology is to perform an *investment evaluation of the system* (Box 1) that enables the identification of its core value propositions, and the projected favorable cost and revenue impacts associated with them. In this context, it is important for the corporate investor to identify the key sources of value, as well as the extent of the potential value that may be obtained

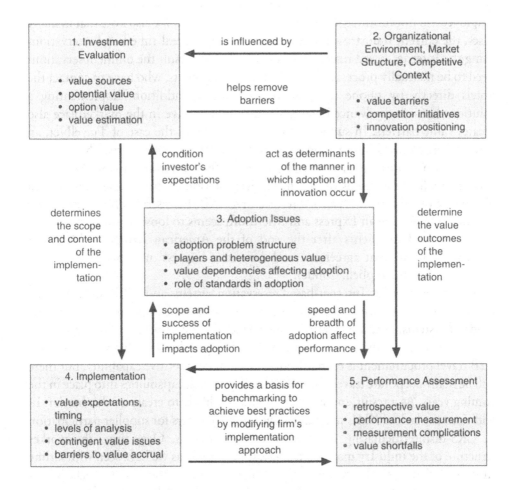

Fig. 4. A life cycle framework for understanding the value of e-commerce technologies

for the firm. Some value may come in a *direct form* (e.g., savings from the e-channel), or in a more *indirect form* (e.g., leverage for improved market share through business intelligence for better pricing). In both cases, however, the value flows will be tied to the implementation of the current technical infrastructure.

These projections depend on *value barriers* generated by the *organizational environment, market structure* and *industry competitive context* where the system is implemented, and also require background analysis (Box 2). For corporate customers, the organizational environment might prevent the successful implementation and adoption of an Internet-based reservation system because of specific processes that make travel automation difficult, such as complicated travel policies or requirements for special handling for international travel and complicated routes for many of the company's reservations. In addition, a company whose employees are not knowledgeable computer users or do not have easy access to the Internet is unlikely to have too much success with an Internet-based travel reservation system. Such a systems' wireless features may also be useless for a company whose employees do not routinely have wireless Internet access. We also note that in many cases, the current industry structure does not support real-time hotel reservations using the Internet-based reservation system, and as a result the online reservations need to be manually processed by traditional travel agents, who have to contact the hotels directly by phone to make reservations. In addition, implementing a solution that is not advanced enough and cannot survive in the marketplace also creates value barriers. In support of this issue we recall the case of TravelNet, an early Internet-based reservation system whose users had to switch to other providers when the company closed its doors in 1998 and thus have lost their initial investment (both in terms of system implementation costs and user training) in TravelNet (McNulty, 1998a). More recently, AXI, the reservation system jointly developed by American Express and Microsoft, seems to loose its support from its developers and its clients after the end of the American Express – Microsoft exclusive development agreement and American Express' new partnership with GetThere.com (Campbell, 2000c).

For travel agencies, Internet-based reservation systems and CRSs, the key issues that arise have to do with the fact that competitors may be implementing the same kinds of systems, creating external value barriers to the achievement of high value outcomes from the investment. For example, being early to market with a wireless B2B travel procurement is currently an important competitive capability, but there will be many corporate travel vendors that will put such capabilities into place in the coming years. As a result, industry competition is likely to create a value barrier. In addition, the lack of XML standards might create barriers for supplier participation in CRS-disintermediating Internet-reservation systems. Over time, the market structure of the industry may also change, for example, as we have seen with airline firms and their own DotCom business models to lure travelers to make direct bookings, dulling the prospects of the major Internet-based, but non-airline or travel agency affiliated airline reservation portals. Finally, the organizational environment of a firm may change, impacting the value of a systems investment for leisure and corporate travel booking. TravelBids.com, an early and innovative competitor that brought "on bundle" bidding for travel and hospitality services to the Internet, is one of the Internet-based travel reservation marketplaces that is no longer operational, despite the attractiveness of its original business model that forced travel agencies to bid against one another for leisure business. In its case, the industry structure and competitive environment changed considerably, rendering its business model ineffectual. Faced with such changes, numerous other firms in the DotCom patch – not just travel industry-related – have chosen to shift their business models in order to survive in the marketplace.

The market structure and competitive context also influence the organizational *adoption* of the system (Box 3) by corporate customers, and, if direct links are provided, by suppliers. Adoption also needs to be analyzed in terms of individual traveler usage within organizations implementing Internet-based reservation systems. The expected benefits of the EC systems are highly dependent on the adoption levels within the organization, after implementation is completed. Few such organizations can, or want to, mandate the use of the electronic system. Instead, many offer it as an alternative to phone reservations through traditional travel agents. They try to drive adoption through focused communication and training campaigns and by charging back the transaction fees to the individual department to which each traveler belongs, such that these departments have an incentive to encourage the less expensive online reservations.

The evaluation of the investment decision provides guidelines regarding the scope and content of the *implementation* (Box 4). During implementation, companies are usually faced with various problems, ranging from technical difficulties to lack of sufficient organizational resources. All these problems act as *value contingencies*, lengthening the time of the implementation and affecting its success. It is therefore important to assess the impact of all the factors that can limit the realization of all potential value that was estimated during the evaluation phase, and try to take action to maximize the realized value.

Performance assessment (Box 5) helps firms understand how successful their implementation has been, and establish benchmarks for improving implementation. This step should involve value measurements at the level of the reservation processes supported by the implemented systems, and *not* at the aggregate organizational level, since this is a mismatch for assessment the implementation. It should also compare pre-implementation and post-implementation value measurements. This is not a trivial step, however, as value from EC systems is multi-faceted, and monitoring of all hard and soft benefits will require additional effort that not every company is willing to make. What is important, though, is that senior managers pay attention to their *realized value estimates* and the characteristics of the reservation processes for which they are obtained. [For a fuller interpretation of this recommendation, the interested reader should see the first author's doctoral dissertation (Chircu, 2001)].

In the next several sections, we will provide more details about each framework element by highlighting specific issues and problems, the relevant theoretical perspective that can help us understand these issues, and managerial recommendations related to these issues.

4. Investment Evaluation

Investment evaluation is the first step corporations have to go through to determine the benefits of implementing Internet-based reservation systems. Industry reports show that investment costs are high, but also suggest significant benefits may exist (see Table 3).

Relevant Theoretical Perspectives

A number of theoretical frameworks can aid our conceptualization regarding the investment evaluation phase. For example, Davern and Kauffman (2000) show how firms can discover the *potential value* of a technology by looking at the maximum benefits the technology can generate and comparing them with the benefits obtained without using the technology. Chircu and Kauffman (2000b) propose that this potential value is created by generic *value flows* applied to the specific characteristics of the technology implementation environment. Value flows describe sources of value that are generally observed for a specific technology successfully implemented and used as expected. However, these *perfect* implementation and adoption conditions cannot be found in every company. Instead, existing organizational processes

Table 3. Internet-based corporate travel reservation systems: investments, potential savings

Investments	Potential savings
One-time costs: evaluation consulting fees of $10,000–$20,000, system cost of $30,000–$80,000 to $1–$5 million depending on vendor significant implementation costs (Chircu et al., forthcoming; McNulty, 1998b, c, 1999b)	Transaction cost savings: tiered pricing savings of 20–40% depending on adoption level agent headcount savings (Welt, 1999; Rosen, 2000a)
Recurring costs: annual license fees of $10,000–$50,000 depending on volume; transaction fees (50% or more lower than traditional transaction fees); maintenance and upgrade costs of 15%–20% of license fees; adoption costs (consultants, incentives) and system improvement costs (Chircu et al., forthcoming; Feldman, 1999; McNulty, 1998b, c, 1999a, b)	Lower price savings: more informed and responsible travelers and better enforcement of corporate travel policy, leading to lower prices chosen online among the set of available travel options (McNulty, 1998b, c; Rosen, 2000a)

or culture, the current level of technological infrastructure and standards adoption in the industry, and the actions of competitors all create *value barriers* that limit the value flows, resulting in firm and industry-specific technology potential value. Investment evaluation should therefore involve analyzing how these generic value sources apply to the specific organizational and industry context of the firm that makes the technology investment decision, what the value barriers are and how they can be overcome (if possible).

How can firms identify the general value flows that will occur for their EC technology investments? Existing theoretical and empirical studies suggest that these value flows occur primarily from two sources. *First, process-level value flows* will be observed, consisting of increased process efficiencies, that are reflected in cost savings and improved product quality (Barua et al., 1995; Brynjolfsson and Hitt, 1995; Srinivasan et al., 1994; Lee and Clark, 1996). *Second, market-level value flows* will also occur, based on the extent to which the business model offers sustainable competitive advantage (Clemons, 1991; Clemons and Row, 1991b; Teece, 1987). In some cases, another market-level value flow is generated by positive network externalities that increase the value of the technology for all of the firm's technology adopters, as more adopters join the network (Katz and Shapiro, 1986; Kauffman et al., 1999). The reader will recognize that this value flow applies, for example, to second-wave CRS-disintermediating EC solutions that we described earlier, such as GetThere.com and e-Travel.

A new approach to analyzing the value of investments, *real option pricing* (**ROV**) *methods*, has become increasingly popular during the past few years (Luehrman, 1998). The option value of a technology investment relates to the flexibility for future projects enabled by the current technology investment. In other words, firms create, through the current investment, the *option* (a right, but not an obligation) to make future investments as they gain valuable experience with the technology and improved knowledge of the industry and competitive environment. EC technologies are generally characterized by uncertainties that arise as these technologies are adopted in the marketplace, industry standards evolve and industry competition intensifies. Therefore, they are very well suited for real option pricing analysis (Benaroch and Kauffman, 1999). We need to point out, however, that in the special case of Internet-based reservation systems, real option pricing models are most suitable for evaluating the value that industry intermediaries can obtain from implementing such systems. For example, Sabre's acquisition of GetThere.com, or travel agencies' decisions to complement their traditional travel services with Internet-based reservation services all create future options for these firms.

Managerial Actions and Recommended Solutions

Given that investment evaluation bears significant costs as well – for example, the evaluation consulting fees alone can range from $10,000 to $20,000 – some companies are willing to skip the evaluation step and jump directly to implementation based on industry-wide estimates (see Table 3). This is probably the biggest mistake firms can make in implementing Internet-based travel reservation systems. Only firms that take this step seriously and thoroughly analyze their organization and industry affordances for the new technology achieve successful implementations (Chircu and Kauffman, 2000b).

Companies have to spend time analyzing the range of value sources for a specific investment decision, as well as the value barriers that impact them. For example, the value flows for a corporate customer using Internet-based reservation systems are less travel agents required to handle the company's phone reservations resulting in significantly reduced transaction fees, better compliance with travel policy, and more informed and responsible travelers. But various value barriers – which will be detailed in the next sections – can limit these value flows, as the reader will shortly see.

The investment evaluation should prompt an investigation of the advantages and disadvantages offered by a specific industry setting, as well as by existing organizational routines and resources that can limit potential value otherwise available to other firms. Taking into account all these issues during the investment evaluation stage can help identify real value and moderate overly optimistic estimates. In some cases, it is also possible that the investment decision will be delayed until market and organizational conditions allow the benefits to be realized. Most importantly, the investment evaluation phase can help companies plan accordingly to remove at least *some* of the barriers in order to streamline the implementation and encourage the adoption of the system among their travelers.

5. Organizational Setting, Market Structure and Competitive Context

As suggested by the theoretical perspectives presented in the previous section, barriers to value limit the technology value flows. These barriers depend on the specific organizational environment, market structure and competitive context where the technology implementation will eventually take place.

Relevant Theoretical Perspectives

There are a number of theoretical perspectives that explain the basis for the conditions that affect potential value in a specific organizational context and in a competitive marketplace, and what limits the success of the technology implementation. The existing industry structure and established relationships a firm already has within this industry structure can lead to different potential value estimates for different firms investing in the same technology. In addition, value barriers are also created at the market level by technological standards that may favor compatible technologies over incompatible technologies (Katz and Shapiro, 1994; Brynjolfsson and Kemerer, 1994). Another value barrier involves negative network externalities generated by non-standard technologies or technologies that increase competition (Bakos and Brynjolfsson, 1993; Riggins et al., 1994). Again, we note that most of these barriers become relevant for the online reservation system investment decisions of travel agencies, CRSs and suppliers.

At the organizational level, constraints a company must face in capturing value include unique organizational routines and human capital developed over time (see, for example, Brynjolfsson and Hitt, 1998; Chircu and Kauffman, 2000b; Clemons and Row, 1991b; Davern and Kauffman, 2000; Leonard-Barton, 1988; Teece, 1987) Recent theoretical perspectives on technology investments also point out that successful implementation requires firms to reengineer their processes to enable the new capabilities of the technology in which they invest (Barua et al., 1996; Brynjolfsson and Hitt, 1998; Lee and Clark, 1996).

Managerial Actions and Recommended Solutions

Our research also suggests that correct estimation of the valuation barriers enables companies to better assess the success of the IT investment. Firms, therefore, should proactively identify barriers created by their organizational environment, in conjunction with the market structure and industry competitive context, and then take steps to overcome them. In this context, value barriers for companies implementing Internet-based reservation systems can include company character-istics such as specific company travel mix and specific company travel reservation rules, negotiated rates restrictions, existing provider relationships, or travelers lacking time for or experience with online reservations. Barriers can also be generated by Internet-based reservation systems restrictions or limited search capabilities.

How can some of these barriers be eliminated? Some solutions include investing in implementation expertise and human capital, thorough analysis of company's travel reservation processes and rules and their reengineering to fit the Internet-based reservation system, and establishing special relationships with other industry partic-ipants that would leverage the technology investment. If the Internet-based reserva-tion system success depends on other industry players' "buying into" the system – such as in the case of direct connections solutions whose viability depends on how many suppliers join the system – the promoters of the system have to sponsor it until it becomes widely accepted by enough suppliers. It is also important that the corresponding cost be factored into the overall investment evaluation, when a firm aims to eliminate such barriers.

6. Adoption Issues

An important part of the investment evaluation for an online reservation system is determining the *realizable* adoption level for the system. Our experience with analyzing such investments indicates that individual user "buy in" of the new reservation technology is extremely important in realizing value from this investment. For example, even a perfectly implemented system will be unable to deliver much value, if the firm's employees do not view it as a viable alternative for booking travel. In addition, it turns out that despite the fact that they are promoted as an easy-to-use alternative to calling a traditional travel agent, Internet-based reservation systems have specific travel expertise requirements that hinder their adoption by individual users.

Relevant Theoretical Perspectives

The classical theory of the diffusion of technological innovations, proposed by Rogers (1983), focuses on individual perceptions of innovations in terms of relative advantage, compatibility, complexity, trialability and observability. Significant differences in users' levels of innovativeness exist, which makes them adopt the technology at different rates (Moore and Benbasat, 1991; Rogers, 1983). The *technology acceptance model* (Davis, 1989) shows how individual perceptions regarding technology ease of use and usefulness are important determinants of adoption intentions. Unfavorable perceptions regarding the various characteristics of technology will create barriers to adoption, and result in users choosing not to adopt (Davis, 1989; Moore and Benbasat, 1991; Rogers, 1983).

Technology complexity is important in understanding adoption as well, since complex technologies require new skills, that might be hard to learn because of knowledge barriers (Attewell, 1992). Such barriers describe the inability of a user to acquire new knowledge and use it effectively due to poorly developed *absorptive capacity* (Cohen and Levinthal, 1990). To accelerate adoption of new technologies among their employees, firms can use *change agents* (Rogers, 1983). For example, managers can communicate authority messages to influence adoption decision for employees with low tolerance for change and innovation (Leonard-Barton and Deschamps, 1988).

Managerial Actions and Recommended Solutions

Managers have to understand that high adoption levels are not always *sufficient* for the realization of benefits, though they often are necessary. It is important to keep in mind that, depending on a company's specific travel patterns, that not all reservations can be completed online. Complex travel requirements, including multiple stops and international travel, or last-minute travel, are best reserved by phone given the current capabilities of online reservation systems. For those reservations that can be performed online, however, adoption levels need to be monitored and encouraged. If the organizational culture does not afford mandating an Internet-based reservation system, managers should focus on improving these adoption levels through communication, training and incentive programs.

Training can be used to improve absorptive capacity and lower the knowledge barriers, by allowing employees to develop the necessary skills for using the system at least as efficiently as the traditional reservation method by phone. Communication programs can improve the perceptions employees have about the online systems, pointing out their relative advantage over phone calls. Incentive programs can also be used to overcome employees' initial resistance to using an unfamiliar technology and familiarize all employees – even those with low *innovativeness levels* – with the benefits of online reservations. Most importantly, companies have to continue providing training and advertising for the Internet-based reservation system until its use becomes routine. This often takes longer than most managers expect.

7. Implementation of Corporate Travel Systems Solutions

Companies that implement Internet-based travel reservation systems have to overcome a number of difficulties related to process re-engineering, seamless integration across the company, the traditional travel agency and the online system, and system performance. Among 20 companies that we interviewed in 1999 regarding their implementation of leading online systems, 30% complained that they lacked the resources to solve unforeseen implementation difficulties. Almost half of these companies have also discovered the automating travel reservations was more complex than expected. Finally, in 60% of the cases, companies were faced with technical problems and hard-to-remedy system errors (Chircu et al., forthcoming). It comes as no surprise, however, that the majority of these companies (40%) were in the pilot testing stage, and only very few (20%) were able to move to a full enterprise rollout (see Fig. 5).

Relevant Theoretical Perspectives

When business organizations implement systems, they aim to convert the potential value of the IT in which they have invested into *realized value* that is measurable (Davern and Kauffman, 2000). However, the implementation process is usually characterized by *conversion contingencies*, which describe the extent to which the

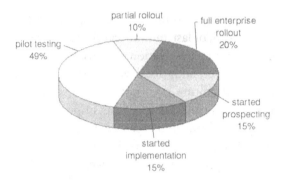

Fig. 5. Internet-based reservation systems implementation stages at 20 U.S. companies surveyed during 1999 (Chircu, 2001)

implementation goes as planned (Weill, 1990), and which affect conversion effectiveness of potential value into realized value (Chircu and Kauffman, 2000b; Davern and Kauffman, 2000; Lucas, 1999).

These contingencies limit the amount of potential value that the organization can realize from implementation. In general, contingencies occur due to the specific organizational environment and the market structure context where the technology is implemented, as we described earlier, and due to the inherent uncertainties embedded in technology implementation projects (Atler and Ginzberg, 1978).

In most cases, successful implementations require additional investments in specialized technology-supported industry relationships and new organizational processes. Developing or acquiring the requisite implementation expertise is also important (Grove et al., 1995; Thong et al., 1996). Moreover, top management support during the implementation process is important (Beath, 1991; Howell and Higgins, 1990; Thong et al., 1996), to ensure that the critical implementation uncertainties are actively managed (Alter and Ginzberg, 1978). When these factors are not taken into account, the implementation either is delayed or may fail, and the expected value that the technology can produce will be diminished accordingly.

Managerial Actions and Recommended Solutions

When it comes to implementation, managers have to proactively identify and manage implementation problems. Being aware of these potential problems from the beginning improves the chances of a successful implementation. However, ignoring them and not investing in specialized implementation expertise can lead in extreme cases to the failure of the implementation project. Implementation problems reported by companies implementing Internet-based reservation systems include lack of implementation knowledge, financial and personnel resources, unexpected system errors, and lack of a technology champion promoting the implementation.

To overcome these problems, managers can plan ahead and ensure they have adequate implementation support from their own IT departments or outside implementation specialists, and allocate sufficient financial resources to the project. Dynamic allocation of resources during the implementation and proactive problem solving are also crucial in dealing with implementation problems that cannot be predicted in advance. Most importantly, the implementation needs to be approached as a project yielding only long-term benefits while requiring significant short-term financial and human resources commitments. As a result, managers need to realize that the implementation of an Internet-based travel reservation system requires not only their company, but also their company's travel agency to reengineer their travel processes to seamlessly integrate phone-based and online reservation making. Commitments of time, resources and expertise from the company itself, its travel agency, and online reservation system vendor are thus essential for ensuring a smooth implementation.

8. Performance Assessment and Business Value

Many organizations that invest in IT struggle to adequately assess the business value of their investments. This occurs because technology investments are often intended to support business activities, and are less often the thing that directly produces the revenues. In the case of e-procurement systems, such as those we have discussed in the travel industry, the technology provides an *infrastructural utility* upon which to build a service delivery capability that enables a firm to leverage a new channel, the Internet. This is complicated by the fact that typically there are *multiple channels* through which the same services can be delivered, each with its own associated costs and benefits, and unique value proposition for the user. Moreover, such delivery systems also handle *heterogeneous transactions*, and these, as we have already argued, may be subject to different quality support (e.g., support for simple versus complex travel specifications). In this context, organizational estimates of savings can differ, depending on what type of comparison was performed (transaction fee savings or average ticket price savings) and on whether the heterogeneous transaction characteristics have been taken into account (see Table 4).

Relevant Theoretical Perspectives

Barua et al. (1995) suggest that the measurement of business value from technology applications has to be performed at the level of core business processes of the firm where the application is implemented. This perspective points out that the process

Table 4. Different comparisons of Internet-based and travel agent-based reservations (sources: Chircu and Kauffman, 2000a; Rosen, 2000a; Welt, 1999)

Basis of comparison	Savings estimate (electronic vs. phone)	Comments
Transaction fees	35–55%	Range of values reported in industry journals: 20–40% (starting at minimum 20% electronic reservation usage)
Average ticket price (ignoring ticket or traveler choice details, travel routes or seasonality)	11%	Range of values reported in industry journals: 15–20%
Average ticket price (accounting for travel routes and seasonality, ignoring ticket or traveler choice)	13%	Range of values reported in industry journals: 15–20%
Average ticket price (accounting for travel routes and seasonality, ticket details; ignoring traveler choice details)	0–2%	Range of values reported in industry journals: N/A
Average ticket price (accounting for travel routes and seasonality, ticket details, traveler choice details)	0% for brand-related choices (airline preference), 11–26% for non-brand-related choices (schedule preference)	Savings limited to small subset (10%) of company transactions for which the non-brand-related choices occur

level is the locus of true business value, where the impacts of technology accrue and are easily discernable.

Performance assessment of e-procurement technologies can focus on three types of performance measures. *First*, performance can be measured in terms of *transaction efficiency*, which, turn, can be expressed as transaction cost reductions (Lee and Clark, 1996; Malone et al., 1987; Srinivasan et al., 1994) and lower prices (Bakos, 1991, 1997, 1998). Lower prices can result from an increased ability to negotiate better prices with suppliers due to an increase in industry competition brought about by easier price identification using EC technologies (Bakos, 1991). Lower prices can also result from improvements in evaluation of available products and selection of the lowest price option (Barua et al., 1997; Degeratu et al., 1999; Lynch and Ariely, 2000; Shankar et al., 1999). *Second*, performance can be measured in terms of *transaction effectiveness*, or fit with the preferences regarding product attributes specified at the beginning of transaction (Clemons et al., 1998; Lee and Clark, 1996). *Third*, performance can be measured in term of *subjective benefits* such as less time spent searching, convenience, employee empowerment, and increased liquidity (Bakos, 1991, 1997, 1998).

Managerial Actions and Recommended Solutions

In the travel context, the key questions that need to be answered include the following: Do Internet-based travel reservation systems permit users to obtain better information, resulting in lower booked airline fares? Or do they support some kinds of reservations better than others, resulting in an uneven distribution of reductions in fares? And, to what extent is the extent of individual adoption of an Internet-based corporate travel reservation system a primary determinant of the system's value?

Managers have to recognize that although reductions in transaction costs for Internet-based electronic reservation systems are certainly an important source of savings, they can be achieved only when adoption levels for electronic transactions are relatively "high." By "high," we mean at least 20% and usually 35% to 40%, according to industry estimates (Welt, 1999). In addition, despite aggregate level estimates of a 15% to 20% reduction in prices due to better evaluation of alternatives and more informed buyers (McNulty, 1998b; Rosen, 2000a), more accurate process level estimates indicate that this reduction is an order of magnitude smaller than what is typically expected. Moreover, it occurs only for a small percentage of transactions (Chircu and Kauffman, 2000a) (see Table 4). Therefore, managers have to measure the price reduction benefits at the process level, and not at the aggregate firm level, by taking into account all situational factors.

Even if the expected transaction price reductions due to improved evaluation and selection capabilities are not as high as expected, managers should not discount the ability of the Internet-based travel reservation system to reduce overall ticket prices. Having access to centralized spending data through such a system can help corporations select the most appropriate suppliers and negotiate better volume-based discounts.

Managers also have to keep in mind that various Internet-based reservation systems will have different efficiency and effectiveness levels, mainly because they rate the importance of finding the lowest price or of finding the best fit with schedule and routing preferences in different ways which are implementation-specific. Rather than assuming that all system behave the same way, managers should evaluate the search efficiency and effectiveness of all available Internet-based travel reservation systems and select the one that works best for their company's goals.

Finally, because the implementation and adoption processes of Internet-based reservation systems are lengthy and problem-laden, managers need to establish realistic timelines for performance assessment, and recognize that they will have to incur significant short-term costs before being able to measure the true value of these systems.

9. Conclusions

The primary conclusions that we draw from our research relate to the surprisingly contingent value that is associated with the implementation of EC systems, and especially those in the corporate travel procurement area. In this chapter, we presented the findings of research that suggests caution to organizations that implement this kind of technology. Senior managers need to be aware of the extent to which business process change, user adoption, external factors, and a variety of other considerations may diminish the value that an organization can actually obtain from its EC technology investments, relative to the great promises of value that are typically offered by vendors and managed corporate travel services providers.

In closing, we recognize several important contributions from this research that should be useful for different audiences. *First,* for the *academic research audience,* we integrate a number of theoretical perspectives regarding value creation and accrual from EC technologies. We offer a new framework that can be a starting point for the establishment of a general and comprehensive assessment of the business value of such technologies. *Second,* for *industry professionals and executives* interested in justifying the value of their investments in EC technology solutions for corporate travel, we provide guidelines for investment evaluation, implementation and measurement, and managerial recommendations that can help maximize value in every stage of the EC technology life cycle. *Third,* for *MBA students,* we provide a framework for analyzing the corporate travel industry that is applicable to a wide range of technology investments, and show how theoretical perspectives can be used to explain real-world transformation fueled by EC technologies.

The research that we have discussed is a by-product of an industry-university collaboration that spans three years and has offered unique opportunities for case study, field survey and empirical research. Even though the range of new knowledge about e-procurement of travel services that we have produced has been significant, we are struck by how little we know about the value of e-business technologies. Indeed, our work sets the stage for additional research so that managers can obtain an even more refined understanding of the situational contingencies that deflate the value that can be achieved by the organizations that invest in them.

References

Alter, S., Ginzberg, M. (1978) Managing uncertainty in MIS implementation. Sloan Management Review 20 (1): 23–31

Attewell, P. (1992) Technology diffusion and organizational learning: The case of business computing. Organization Science 3 (1): 1–19

Bakos, J. Y. (1991) A strategic analysis of electronic marketplaces. MIS Quarterly 15 (4): 295–310

Bakos, J. Y. (1997) Reducing buyer search costs: Implications for electronic marketplaces. Management Science 43 (12): 1676–1692

Bakos, J. Y. (1998) The emerging role of electronic marketplaces on the Internet. Communications of the ACM 41 (8): 35–42

Bakos, J. Y., Brynjolfsson, E. (1993) From vendors to partners: Information technology and incomplete contracts in buyer-supplier relationships. J Organizational Computing 3 (3): 301–328

Barua, A., Kriebel, C. H., Mukhopadhyay, T. (1995) IT and business value: An analytic and empirical investigation. Information Systems Research 6 (1): 3–23

Barua, A., Lee, C. H. S., Whinston, A. B. (1996) The calculus of reengineering. Information Systems Research 7 (4): 409–428

Barua, A., Ravindran, R., Whinston, A. B. (1997) Efficient selection of suppliers over the Internet. J Management Information Systems 13 (4): 117–137

Beath, C. M. (1991) Supporting the information technology champion. MIS Quarterly 15 (3): 355–372

Benaroch, M., Kauffman, R. J. (1999) A case for using real options pricing analysis to evaluate information technology project investments. Information Systems Research 10 (1): 70–86

Brynjolfsson, E., Hitt, L. M. (1995) Information technology as a factor of production: The role of differences among firms. Economics of Innovation and New Technology 3 (4): 183–200

Brynjolfsson, E., Kemerer, C. F. (1996) Network externalities in microcomputer software: An econometric analysis of the spreadsheet market. Management Science 42 (12): 1627–1647

Brynjolfsson, E., Hitt, L. (1998) Beyond the productivity paradox. Communications of the ACM 41 (8): 149–55

BusinessWeek (January 17, 2000) B2B: The hottest net bet yet? Accessed via www.business-week.com/2000/00_03/b3664065.htm

Campbell, J. (September 4, 2000a) Sabre to get Get There. Business Travel News, accessed via www.btnonline.com/db_area/archives/2000/09/00090401.htm

Campbell, J. (June 12, 2000b) GetThere, e-Travel push bypass. Business Travel News, accessed via www.btnonline.com/db_area/archives/2000/06/00061210.htm

Campbell, J. (June 12, 2000c) Amex makes booking play. Business Travel News, accessed via www.btnonline.com/db_area/archives/2000/06/00061203.htm

Campbell, J., McNulty, M. A., Vallejo, M., Welt, S. (April 26, 1999) Big buyers benchmark. Business Travel News, accessed via www.btnonline.com/db_area/archives/1999/04/99042632.htm

Chircu, A. M. (2001) Intermediation in electronic commerce. Unpublished doctoral dissertation, Carlson School of Management, University of Minnesota, Minneapolis, MN

Chircu, A. M., Kauffman, R. J. (2000a) Comparing the business value of traditional and electronic B2B procurement systems. Presented at the 11th Workshop on Information Systems and Economics, Brisbane, Australia

Chircu, A. M. Kauffman, R. J. (2000b) Limits to value in electronic commerce-related IT investments. J Management Information Systems 17 (1): 61–82

Chircu, A. M., Kauffman, R. J. (2000c) Reintermediation strategies in business-to-business electronic commerce. International J Electronic Commerce 4 (4): 7–42

Chircu, A. M., Kauffman, R. J., Keskey, D. (forthcoming) Maximizing the value of Internet-based corporate travel reservation systems. Communications of the ACM

Clemons, E. K. (1991) Evaluation of strategic investments in information technology. Communications of the ACM 34 (1): 22–36

Clemons, E. K., Row, M. C. (1991a) Information technology at Rosenbluth Travel: Competitive advantage in a rapidly growing global service company. J Management Information Systems 8 (2): 53–79

Clemons, E. K., Row, M. C. (1991b) Sustaining IT advantage: The role of structural differences. MIS Quarterly 15 (3): 275–292

Clemons, E. K., Hann, I. (1999) Rosenbluth International: Strategic transformation of a successful enterprise. J Management Information Systems 16 (2): 9–28

Clemons, E., Hann, I., Hitt, L. (1998) The nature of competition in electronic markets: An empirical investigation of online travel agent offerings. Working paper, Wharton School of Business, University of Pennsylvania, Philadelphia, PA

Cohen, W. M., Levinthal, D. A. (1990) Absorptive capacity: A new perspective on learning and innovation. Administrative Science Quarterly 35 (1): 128–152

Conrades, G. H. (September 1, 2000) Managing on the fault line: Forces of change in the Internet economy. Vital Speeches of the Day 66 (22): 702–704

Davern, M. J., Kauffman, R. J. (2000) The value of decision technologies: Discovering potential and realizing payoff. J Management Information Systems 16 (4): 121–143

Davis, F. D. (1989) Perceived usefulness, perceived ease of use, and user acceptance of information technology. MIS Quarterly 13 (3): 319–341

Degeratu, A., Rangaswamy, A., Wu, J. (August 1999) Consumer choice behavior in online and traditional supermarkets: The effects of brand name, price, and other search attributes. Working paper 03-1999, eBusiness Research Center, Pennsylvania State University, College Park, PA

Feldman, J. M. (January 1999) Battle of the mouse clicks. Air Transport World 36 (1): 49–51

Gartner Group (February 28, 2000) Internet travel: Popular, and still more opportunity, accessed via www.gartner.com

Grover, V., Jeong, S. R., Kettinger, W. J., Teng, J. T. C. (1995) The implementation of business process reengineering. J Management Information Systems 12 (1): 109–144

Harteveldt, H. H., McQuivey, J. L., Bermont, B., DeMoulin, G. (March 2000) Online business travel's boost. Forrester Research Report, accessed via www.forrester.com

Hjermstad, M. (November 15, 1999) IATA survey: Corporate travelers heed policy when buying. Business Travel News, accessed via www.btnonline.com/db_area/archives/1999/11/99111513.htm

Howell, J. M., Higgins, C. A. (1990) Champions of technological innovation. Administrative Science Quarterly 35 (2): 317–341

Johnson, M. A., Sherlock, N. R. (1999) Business travel forecast. Business travel and corporate travel management: capitalizing on emerging trends. National Business Travel Association, accessed via www.nbta.org/basics/travelforecast.htm

Kalakota, R., Robinson, M. (1999) e-Business: Roadmap for success. Addison-Wesley, Reading, MA

Katz, M., Shapiro, C. (1986) Technology adoption in the presence of network externalities. J Political Economy 94 (4): 822–841

Katz, M., Shapiro, C. (1994) Systems competition and network effects. J Economic Perspectives 8 (2): 93–115

Kauffman, R. J., McAndrews, J., Wang, Y. (2000) Opening the 'black box' of network externalities in network adoption. Information Systems Research 11 (1): 61–82

Lee, H. G., Clark, T. H. (1996) Market process reengineering through electronic market systems: Opportunities and challenges. J Management Information Systems 13 (3): 113–136

Leonard-Barton, D. (1992) Core capabilities and core rigidities: A paradox in managing new product development. Strategic Management J 13: 111–125

Leonard-Barton, D., Deschamps, I. (1988) Managerial influence in the implementation of new technology. Management Science 34 (10): 1252–1265

Limone, J. (August 28, 2000) Rosenbluth Interntaional sticks to its theme of 'bucking trends.' Travel Weekly 49 (69): 23

Lucas, H. C., Jr. (1999) Information technology and the productivity paradox: Assessing the value of investing in IT. Oxford University Press, New York, NY

Luehrman, T. A. (1998) Investment opportunities as real options: Getting started on the numbers. Harvard Business Review 76 (4): 51–67

Lynch, J. G., Ariely, D. (2000) Wine online: Search costs and competition on price, quality and distribution. Marketing Science 19 (1): 83–103

Malone, T. W., Yates, J. Benjamin, R. I. (1987) Electronic markets and electronic hierarchies. Communications of the ACM 30 (6): 484–497

McNulty, M. A. (April 27, 1998a) TravelNet shuts its doors. Business Travel News, accessed via www.btnonline.com/db_area/archives/1998/04/98042752.htm

McNulty, M. A. (August 17, 1998b) Technology costs are high, but ROI is swift. Business Travel News, accessed via www.btnonline.com/db_area/archives/1998/08/98081701.htm

McNulty, M. A. (November 2, 1998c) For online booking, focus turns to usage. Business Travel News, accessed via www.btnonline.com/db_area/archives/1998/11/98110219.htm

McNulty, M. A. (March 22, 1999a) Oracle buys e-Travel. Business Travel News, accessed via www.btnonline.com/db_area/archives/1999/03/99032250.htm

McNulty, M. A. (June 7, 1999b) AXI hits open market. Business Travel News, accessed via www.btnonline.com/db_area/archives/1999/06/99060725.htm

Moore, G. C., Benbasat, I. (1991) Development of an instrument to measure the perceptions of adopting an information technology innovation. Information Systems Research 2 (3): 192–222

National Business Travel Association (December 14, 1999) Net fare white paper. Accessed via travelvault.nbta.org/pubs/netfares.htm

PhoCusWright (December 14, 1999) Sabre's big teeth are coming in. WebTravel News/The Insighter 3 (9): accessed via www.webtravelnews.com

Putnam, M., Dolberg, S., Sharrad, J., Lanpher, G. (January 1999) Business services on the net. Forrester Research Report, accessed via www.forrester.com

Rice, K. (August 7, 2000) Corporate travel booking sees major growth. WebTravelNews, accessed via www.webtravelnews.com/642.htm

Riggins, F. J., Kriebel, C. H., Mukhopadhyay, T. (1994) The growth of interorganizational systems in the presence of network externalities. Management Science 40 (8): 984–998

Rogers, E. M. (1983) Diffusion of innovations, 3rd edn. Free Press, New York, NY

Rosen, C. (February 21, 2000a) Online booking cuts prices 20%. Business Travel News, accessed via www.btnonline.com/db_area/archives/2000/02/00022116.htm

Rosen, C. (March 6, 2000b) Tech companies turning focus on integrating with outside systems. BusinessTravelNews, accessed via btnonline.com/db_area/archives/2000/03/00030621.htm

Shankar, V., Rangaswamy, A., Pusateri, M. (August 3, 1998) The online medium and customer price sensitivity. Working paper 04-1999, eBusiness Research Center, Pennsylvania State University, College Park, PA

Spradling, R. (August 3, 1998) Op-ed: Evaluating self-booking. Business Travel News, accessed via www.btnonline.com/db_area/archives/1998/08/98080329.htm

Spradling, R. (July 2000) What's the real bottom line on e-business in the travel industry? Senior Management Position Paper, Maritz Travel Company, accessed via www.maritztravel.com/mtc/feature/default.htm

Srinivasan, K., Kekre, S., Mukhopadhyay, T. (1994) Impact of electronic data interchange technology on JIT shipments. Management Science 40 (10): 1291–1304

Teece, D. J. (1987) Profiting from technological innovation: Implications for integration, collaboration, licensing and public policy. In: Teece, D. J. (ed.) The competitive challenge. Harper & Row, New York, pp.185–219

Thompson, M. J. (June 7, 1999) Corporate travel: An emerging killer app. The Industry Standard, accessed via www.thestandard.com/metrics/display/0,1283,903,00.html

Thong, J. Y. L., Yap, C.-S., Raman, K. S. (1996) Top management support, external expertise and information systems implementation in small businesses. Information Systems Research 7 (2): 248–267

Travel Weekly (June 23, 2000) The top 50, www.twcrossroads.com/news/newswrapper.asp?ArticleID=21662

Weill, P. (1990) Do computers pay off? ICIT Press, Washington, DC

Welt, S. (March 8, 1999) Tiered pricing gains foothold. Business Travel News, accessed via www.btnonline.com/db_area/archives/1999/03/99030815.htm
Werthner, H., Klein, S. (1999) Information technology and tourism: A challenging relationship. Springer, Wien New York

Alina M. Chircu

Assistant Professor, Management Science and Information Systems, McCombs School of Business, University of Texas at Austin. Her doctorate is from the Carlson School of Management, University of Minnesota. Her research interests focus on the IT business value, market structure and intermediation in e-commerce, and IT adoption. Her recent work explores these issues in the corporate travel industry in the context of a long-term sponsored research project. She has published related articles in the *International Journal of Electronic Commerce*, *Electronic Markets* and the *Journal of Management Information Systems*.

Robert J. Kauffman

Associate Professor and Department Chair, Information and Decision Sciences, Carlson School of Management, University of Minnesota. His doctorate is from the Graduate School of Administration, Carnegie Mellon University. He worked in international banking, and was a faculty member at NYU and University of Rochester. His current research emphasizes e-commerce, economic analysis of IS problems, and applications of technology in the financial services, travel and hospitality industries. He has published this work in *Information Systems Research*, *MIS Quarterly*, the *International Journal of Electronic Commerce*, *Organization Science* and elsewhere.

Defining Internet Readiness for the Tourism Industry: Concepts and Case Study

U. Gretzel and D. R. Fesenmaier

National Laboratory for Tourism and E-Commerce, University of Illinois, Urbana Champaign, U.S.A.

drfez@uiuc.edu

Abstract
Integrating emerging technologies into the organizational fabric is a prerequisite for capturing the full benefits of the new tourism e-economy. However, most tourism organizations are still struggling with the adoption of Internet technologies and are far from reaching a stage of highly effective technology use. This paper proposes a measurement model of Internet Readiness that incorporates the concepts of stages of effective technology use and organizational capacity to change. A case study conducted among American convention and visitors bureaus serves as a first empirical test of the model and provides management implications as well as directions for future research.

1. Introduction

For many tourism organizations Internet presence begins as some kind of experiment in order to extend their current marketing effort. However, the Internet is a different medium. It is a broadcast and narrowcast medium at the same time (Gretzel et al., 2000). The Internet blurs the trade-off between richness and reach and, thus, throws "the hierarchical structure of supply chains, the organizational pyramid, asymmetries of information, and the boundaries of the corporation itself" into question (Evans and Wurster, 1999). In such an environment it becomes increasingly difficult to create value based on traditional business models. Day (1998) stresses that the further we move towards strategies augmented with interactivity, or even fully interactive strategies, the greater the need for organizational transformation. Interactivity increases the speed with which business needs to be done. It calls for real-time decisions which cannot be realized unless technology and organizational strategies become integrated (Hanson, 2000). Modahl (2000) refers to this approach as the "whole view of technology management", as opposed to strategies where technology management is seen as "essentially separate from the conduct of *real* business." Today's technologies cannot lead to future competitive advantages if they are applied within yesterday's organizational structures. However, many organizations are still trying to maintain traditional business approaches instead of trying to reorganize themselves. Day (1998) predicts that these companies will become victims of organizations with a better alignment of strategy and structure. New competitive strategies have to focus on intelligent, innovative, and integrative ways of using technology.

New technologies can greatly support tourism organizations in addressing the challenges encountered in the new tourism *e*-conomy. There has always been a long-standing relationship between information technology and tourism; this interrelationship of IT and tourism is becoming increasingly intense and will probably reach a point where IT will be the strongest driving force for changes within the tourism industry (Werthner and Klein, 1999). Today, tourism is one of the most important users of the World Wide Web. Between 33 to 50 percent of Internet transactions are tourism based (Werthner and Klein, 1999). The emergence of the World Wide Web and Internet technologies opens up completely new perspectives for the tourism industry; yet, their potential remains largely untapped. Most tourism organizations have yet to grasp the full potential of information technologies (Baker et al., 1999). They usually see a need for investments in new technologies but typically only use IT to substitute old ways of doing business. They need to realize that the actual value of Internet technology lies in making the implementation of new business models possible, and not in facilitating old, established ways of doing business. Small convention and visitors bureaus are active IT users, for example, but they apply the technologies in a very basic and simplistic way and, thus, are not able to gain the full benefits (Yuan et al., 1999). It is often a lack of expertise and a lack of information about the benefits of IT that make organizations less likely to effectively use information technology (Sheldon, 1997). Other organizations have already realized that effective technology adoption can only be achieved if it is embedded in an organization-wide change concept and combined with the introduction of new informational strategies. The changes in the tourism industry call for new organizational concepts. The key strategic variables that will drive successful tourism organizations in the future are (Finerty, 1997):

- Direction – Organizations must have a picture of where they are heading to in the longer term but must also be flexible enough to modify they way in the short term.
- Form – Organizations can be distinguished by the way plans are translated into action.

- Communication – Success depends on the nature and extent of communication within the organization and with its environment.
- Adaptation – The organization's approach to learning and change determines its long-term chances for survival.

Huffington et al. (1997) formulate it in a slightly different and more specific way (see Table 1). Traditional structures and processes will soon become obsolete and a barrier to success. Successful organizations of the future will be characterized by learning, collaboration, flexibility, proactive change, and communication. Information regard and knowledge management have to become a business imperative for tourism organizations, because organizations that stop processing information and neglect the creation, dissemination, and use of knowledge cease to change and ultimately die (Adams and Adams, 1995).

Table 1. Future strategic orientation (adopted from Huffington et al., 1997)

Strategic emphasis and orientation	
Current	Future
Structure / Form	Virtual Organization
Expert / Facilitator	Learner / Developer
Emphasis on People	Emphasis on All
Long-term Change	On-going Change
Remedial	Preventative
Hierarchical Structure	Networks
Discontinuous	Continuous
Linear	Cyclical
Planning	Alignment
Start / Step	Flow
Communication	Dialogue
Values	Meaning
Existing	Being

This paper provides a definition of effective technology use and introduces the concept of stages as a way to assess an organization's current status along a path toward higher levels of effectiveness in technology use. Also, based on the above-mentioned need for continuous organizational reconfiguration, influences on the ability of organizations to adapt to changing environmental conditions are analyzed and integrated into a general "Capacity to Change" model. A case study among American convention and visitors bureaus is used to illustrate how the concepts of stages of effective technology use and capacity to change can be combined and used as a measure for Internet Readiness. Last, implications for increasing Internet Readiness in the tourism industry are discussed.

2. Assessing Effective Technology Use for the Tourism Industry

The tourism industry is highly fragmented, with small and medium-sized businesses dominating the industry landscape (Poon, 1993). Although technological change represents a challenge for all organizations, smaller businesses seem to especially struggle with the effective implementation of IT. Recently published studies (Dun and Bradstreet, 2000; Arthur Andersen Consulting, 2000) show that small US businesses are increasing their online presence, however, their IT use remains restricted to very basic levels. A growing number, currently 88 percent, of US small businesses have computers and 53 percent have their own Web sites; 71 percent use the Internet to send/receive emails while only 26 percent administer E-commerce transactions through their Web sites. Most importantly, only 3 percent consider e-commerce an integral part of their business and 42 percent indicate the Internet has no impact on their business (Arthur Andersen Consulting, 2000).

The relationship between IT spending and actual impacts/productivity gains has been the concern of researchers and managers for quite some time. Knowing the real benefits for productivity was named as one of the major challenges in dealing with information technology in the study conducted by Arthur Andersen. The gap between what companies spend on information technology and what benefits they get from it seems to stem from a combination of not seeing and not understanding the potential of IT. Another reason for this so-called productivity paradox is that wider organizational and management concerns are overlooked (Madnick, 1987). Brynjolfsson (1993) groups the various explanations for the productivity paradox into four categories: 1) Mismeasurement, 2) Learning lags, 3) Redistribution of profits, and 4) Mismanagement. Although mismeasurement is usually identified as the major cause for the productivity paradox at the aggregate industry level, it fails to explain all the productivity shortfalls occurring at the firm level. Thorp (1998) mentions learning lags as the most commonly observed productivity problem. He states that it can take a considerable amount of time before businesses can fully exploit the potential of new technologies. Learning lags are closely related to mismanagement issues because organizational structures, processes and cultures influence learning capabilities (Senge et al., 1999). "It is not enough to acquire technology, you also have to learn to apply it intelligently. New ways of thinking, managing and working are required" (Thorp, 1998). The information system to be adopted needs to fit into the organizational concept of strategy, culture and structure (Linder, 1985). This broader concept of effective technology use calls for evaluation strategies that are able to capture and assess problems that reach beyond the technology itself. Evaluation research has already moved away from system quality measures to user needs assessment, and more recently to social and situational influence models (Venkatesh and Davis, 2000; Wöber and Gretzel, 2000). Bruce and Rubin (1993) point out that new technology is often seen as sufficient by itself to create change although existing social systems are very unlikely to change simply because new practices are technically possible. Vandenbosch and Ginzberg (1997) argue that change depends on the "fit between the technology's underlying premise (e.g. collaboration) and the organization's structure, culture, and policies". Orlikowski et al. (1999) stress that, "however good the technology may be, it will not be effective unless the institutional and interpretive conditions facilitate its use" and opportunities and resources for improving technology use are consciously and carefully managed. However, the existing evaluation approaches do not sufficiently define the elements that may be used to measure organizational context and fail to reflect that impacts of technology use in early development stages may differ from outcomes and structuration processes in later stages.

Consulting companies have started to offer online tools that allow organizations to evaluate the effectiveness of their IT use. NetReady (Hartman and Sifonis, 2000), for example, evaluates organizations in terms of leadership, governance mechanisms, organizational competencies, and technology skills. The eBusiness Voyage (Forrester, 2000) uses organization & resources, technology & development, customer experience & service, and partnerships as the pillars of its assessment. However, both tools are based on consulting experience and appear to lack sound theoretical foundations. This article proposes an alternative evaluation model that widens the focus from productivity measures to what we refer to as Internet Readiness, a concept that incorporates the rich literature regarding stages of technology use and organizational context as defined by organizational capacity to change (see Fig. 1).

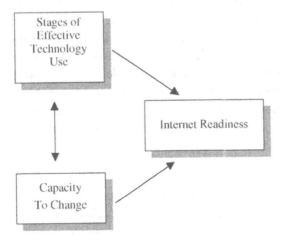

Fig. 1. Internet readiness

3. Stages of Technology Use

Technology adoption typically occurs in stages. Scott Morton (1991) describes the stages as 1) Automation, 2) Information, and 3) Transformation. Organizations usually invest in new technologies to achieve efficiencies and cost-savings. The emphasis lies in automating existing processes. In this initial stage of technology use, few technologies are employed, only obvious uses are realized (e.g. a Web page is used to simply display information), and only minimal organizational changes are required. In the second stage, the Information stage, new information is gained through the use of technology. This opens up new opportunities and new markets. The number of applications and functions used and the scope of organizational activities increase. Broad learning is realized based on the new information available through the technology. In the Transformation stage, technology is integrated into the organizational fabric. Organizational concepts and goals such as leadership, vision, and empowerment become the main focus. Technology use in this stage is extensive, complex, and leads to the development of new processes. Organizational learning that occurs in this stage is comprehensive and continuous. Basic efficiency gains are already possible in the earlier stages, but real productivity gains can only be achieved when an organization reaches the Transformation stage (see Thorp, 1998 for a detailed explanation of the connection between stages of technology use and the productivity paradox). The problem can also be seen from an Internet marketing perspective. According to Hanson (2000), Stage 1 Web sites (see Table 2) are pure "publishing sites" which only distribute data. There is limited dialogue between the Web site and the consumer because the Web is used like a traditional broadcast medium. Stage 2 Web sites concentrate on information. These sites are database-driven and allow for more specific retrievals and ask-respond interactions. Stage 3 sites are "personalized interaction sites" which stress relationship building. The concept of stages of technology use can also be applied to e-business models (see Timmers, 2000). Stage 1 models have low degrees of innovation and require little adjustment of organizational structures. Simple advertising strategies such as advertising banners and mass email fall into this category. Stage 2 models are more innovative and integrate more functions. Online auctions are one example for Stage 2 models. Stage 3 e-business models are highly innovative, multifaceted, and

Table 2. Internet marketing stages (adopted from Hanson, 2000)

Internet marketing stages	Description
STAGE 1: Publishing site	Limited dialogue between Web site and user
STAGE 2: Database retrieval	Ask-respond interaction
STAGE 3: Personalized Interaction	Relationship

integrated into the overall organizational framework. Virtual value chain integration and virtual communities are seen as models that have Stage 3-characteristics.

Contractor, Wasserman and Faust (1999) approach the issue from a communications perspective. They suggest that the adoption and diffusion of technology occurs in three stages: Substitution, Enlargement, and Reconfiguration (see Fig. 2). The productivity gains achieved vary extensively, depending on the stage of technology adoption a particular organization has reached. In the first stage, the Substitution phase, IT is adopted but only used for doing old things in a new manner, for example, replying to customer requests by email instead of sending letters. Organizations in the Substitution stage consider IT applications as viable substitutes *"to do the same with less effort"* (Contractor et al., 2000). This stage requires only limited knowledge, basic skills, little resources, and almost no change in organizational structures and processes. The criterion for evaluating success in this stage is increased efficiency and the focus is on IT as a tool. The use of technology leads to cost efficiencies and time savings and enables the organization to do more business of the same kind. This increase in volume leads the organization into the second phase of adoption, the Enlargement phase. In the Enlargement phase, organizations use technologies *"to do more with less effort"* (Contractor et al., 2000). The strategic emphasis is placed on efficiency and expansion. Companies in the Enlargement stage get more accustomed to the technologies and will use them in a more sophisticated way, but the real benefits of technological innovations can only be reaped when its use is accompanied by organizational changes (Van de Ven, 1991; Contractor et al., 1999). The technology-induced growth will sooner or later reach limitations, mainly organizational constraints. IT requires changes of organizational structures and practices, it requires reconfiguration. In this third stage of technology adoption and diffusion new things are done in new ways. The dictum of the Reconfiguration

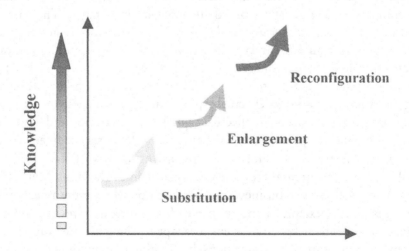

Fig. 2. Stages of technology adoption (adopted from Contractor et al., 1999)

phase, therefore, is *"to do more with different effort"* (Contractor et al., 2000), and even further, to implement innovative business models, i.e. to do different things with different effort. Organizations in the reconfiguration stage use technology extensively and innovatively. Also, reaching the reconfiguration stage requires a substantial amount of knowledge that needs to be carefully managed and translated into continuous learning.

The proposed model of Internet Readiness defines stages of effective technology use based on two important concepts: 1) the extent and sophistication of an organization's IT use, and 2) the extent to which knowledge management strategies and organizational learning have been successfully implemented. A recently conducted study of IT use among American convention and visitors bureaus indicates that tourism organizations differ substantially in terms of what information technologies they use, how long they have been using certain applications, the variety of applications adopted, the perceived usefulness of Internet technologies, and the perceived impacts of IT on organizational tasks and activities (Yuan et al., 2000). Only a small group of organizations, so-called Knowledge Adopters, have been found to use IT extensively and in more innovative ways. The study conducted by Arthur Andersen Consulting (2000) shows similar results: 71 percent of small and medium-sized enterprises (SMEs) use the Internet to send/receive business email, yet, only 32 percent establish and/or maintain relations with customers through the Internet. On average, 64 percent of SME employees have Internet access. For the Internet Readiness model, extent measures the "quantity" of use and includes concepts such as the number of applications used, percentage of employees with Internet access, and length of use. Sophistication refers to the "quality" of use. It is comprised of the functions used, an organization's overall IT strategy, the perceived barriers to technology use, and the perceived impact of technology on organizational processes.

In almost every organization, knowledge is the most important asset, but not many companies have already grasped its strategic importance. The increasing globalization and the accelerating speed with which environmental and technological changes occur require fast and effective strategies for sharing and expanding this corporate knowledge. The primary goal of knowledge management is to bring the intellectual capital of a firm to the individual knowledge workers. Knowledge management means treating intellectual capital as an asset that needs to be managed. Any company that depends on intellectual capital and the creation and flow of ideas has to choose a knowledge management strategy in order to stay competitive. Since the tourism industry is an information intensive industry (Poon, 1993), this rationale is especially important for tourism organizations. Davis and Meyer (1998) describe a knowledge-based business as an organization where every aspect of doing business has been re-examined and re-invented. Learning involves the creation of knowledge and, thus, helps any system to adapt to changing environmental demands by enabling it to make innovations, by assisting it in building capabilities to continuously improve itself, and by creating conditions which facilitate a radical

transformation of the system (Shukla, 1997). Learning is the key to identifying and exploiting opportunities more rapidly and completely than the competitors. Without learning, organizations simply repeat old practices and changes remain short-lived and cosmetic (Garvin, 1998). The Internet Readiness model incorporates measures that describe the extent to which a tourism organization: 1) considers knowledge a corporate asset, 2) has successfully implemented knowledge management mechanisms, 3) manages corporate learning systems, and 4) has created learning opportunities for employees.

4. Organizational Capacity to Change

Achieving high levels of Internet readiness takes more than sophisticated and leading-edge technologies (Greengard, 1998). Rather, it demands the change of organizational structures, cultures, and approaches. These are profound change tasks that cannot be accomplished easily. Organizations differ considerably in terms of their ability and willingness to change, evolve, and adapt to the need for continuous change better than the competition (Mariotti, 1997). They also differ regarding their understanding of the importance of such change efforts for their survival in a global and increasingly dynamic marketplace. Change-adept organizations anticipate, create, and respond effectively to change. They innovate, stress learning, and collaborate extensively with allies and partners (Kanter, 1998). Capacity to change or organizational adaptability, respectively, comprises three different aspects that have an influence on an organization's effectiveness (Denison, 1990):

1. Its ability to perceive and respond to the external environment
2. Its ability to respond to internal divisions and departments
3. Its ability to implement an adaptive response through restructuring and reinstitutionalizing a set of behaviors and processes.

An organization's capacity to change is an indicator of its ability to compete and, thus, the relationship between information technology and organizational change has become a vital concern for most organizations (Rossetti and DeZoort, 1989). Change is the talk of the moment but the concept of capacity to change has not yet been comprehensively analyzed and explained. Traditional literature on change and change management typically focuses on certain aspects of change management (e.g. resistance to change) or specific factors that determine an organization's ability to change (e.g. corporate culture), however, a comprehensive measurement model of organizational capacity to change has not yet been developed. Therefore, it is necessary to combine several theoretical concepts from different areas including technology adoption/diffusion, information dissemination, organizational communication, intellectual capital, knowledge management, network organization, learning organization, change management, leadership theory, and corporate culture in

order to gain a comprehensive theoretical understanding of the factors that determine an organization's capacity to change (see Fig. 3).

Five distinct independent constructs were identified as factors that have a theoretical impact on an organization's capacity to change: Environment, Leadership, Organizational Structure, Change Management, and Corporate Culture.

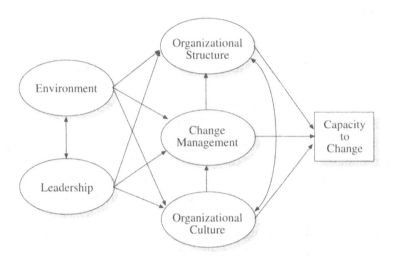

Fig. 3. Organizational capacity to change model

Environment

The conditions prevailing in the technological, economical, political, and legal environment of an organization have a strong influence on an organization's capacity to change. The change equation proposed by Huffington et al. (1997) can serve as a basic framework for explaining why environmental conditions have an influence on the number and extent of change projects accomplished by organizations. According to their findings, change efforts 'are only undertaken if the following equation holds true,

$$A \times B \times C > D$$

where A refers to the dissatisfaction with the status quo, B is the shared vision of a better future, C is the knowledge of the first practical steps, and D is the (psychological, financial, etc.) cost of making the change. Environmental conditions shape the status quo of a firm. Companies that belong to a stable industry where high profits are realized and high entry barriers exist are probably very satisfied with their situation

and are less likely to see a need for change. The higher the cost of change and the lower the cost of not changing, the higher the risk of change, and, as a consequence, the smaller the likelihood that a need for change will be perceived and translated into change action. Organizations in a highly competitive industry are forced to continuously adapt to new situations, thus, see a greater need for change, and, as a consequence, have probably already achieved a higher flexibility and greater capacity to change than companies in stable, less competitive environments. Also, information relevant to a market can be expected to spread across all players in this market, but diffusion will occur more quickly for certain organizations (Burt, 1998). It is the industry structure that determines how information circulates within and between industry groups and individual companies. Depending on the relationships with other industry players, a company will be more or less likely to change. For example, if one of the major partners uses a certain technology, the company will be very likely to get to know about the technology, will have an incentive to implement it, too, and may even get assistance from the partner in the adoption and implementation process.

The technological, economical and legal environment an organization has to face does not only depend on the industry it is part of, but also on what stage of the value chain it belongs to, and what markets it deals with. Different types of businesses typically face different business cycles. Organizations also have a distinct history of technology use and act within discrete legal frameworks. It is necessary to include the markets a company deals. The type of market, the political, legal and economic situation in the various countries and their technology status influence an organization's need to implement information technology.

Leadership

Leadership defines what succeeds and thus determines to a great extent the culture and structure of an organization as well as its approach towards change management. Leadership is "human (symbolic) communication which modifies the attitudes and behaviors of others in order to meet shared group goals and needs" (Hackman and Johnson, 1996). Effective leaders provide strategic directives, encourage learning, and facilitate the creation of mechanisms to transfer knowledge across divisions and organizational boundaries (Prokesch, 1997). Managers produce results, leaders produce change (Hackman and Johnson, 1996). Leadership refers to the leader's attitude towards change, his/her power and respect and entrepreneurial spirit, especially in terms of technology adoption. In addition to its influence on organizational variables, leadership also has an influence on the organization's position within the industry. It is often the leader's network of personal contacts that shapes the organization's interaction with other organizations within or across industries. Variables measuring leadership in this context include the leaders' personal commitment, that is their feeling of being personally responsible for the execution and the outcome of change efforts. Furthermore, it is crucial to look at the leaders' vision regarding technological change and the leaders' perception of how effectively they can sell this vision throughout the organization and to external stakeholders.

Organizational Structure

This construct describes the established systems, processes and exchange relationships within organizations. Size (number of employees), organizational form (hierarchical versus network, number of organizational layers), roles and authorities (broadly defined versus narrow job descriptions), communication structures (long or short, formal or informal) and decision-making channels (top-down or participative), determine the flexibility of an organization and, therefore, its ability to change. Organizational structure can be characterized by how rigid or flexible and how adaptive or non-adaptive an organization is. Rossetti and DeZoort (1989) mention the shape, composition, and degree of decentralization as an important structural factor that influences an organization's capacity to change. The old command-and-control model of organizational structure will not be suitable for the environment organizations are going to face in the 21st century. Informational strategies like knowledge management are a direct threat to the hierarchical nature of most organizations (Steck, 1993). Top-down management reinforces fear, distrust and internal competition and reduces collaboration and cooperation. It leads to compliance, but a high capacity to change requires commitment (Drucker et al., 1997). Rapid change per se is not a problem. The real issue is the organizations' inability to deal with change. This inability stems from the belief that change can be managed using a traditional, bureaucratic management approach. Bureaucracy, however, has been designed to resist change (Waterman, 1990). It is necessary for establishing consistency and stability in an organization, but hierarchies make the free exchange of knowledge more difficult and, thus, limit the organizational capacity to change. Flat organizations, on the other hand, have a built-in flexibility. They have a less rigid division of work, a constant search for innovative solutions, participation in decision-making, a free flow of communication in all directions, very general job descriptions, a delegation of authority, and a greater sensitivity to environmental changes (Zeira and Avedisian, 1989). Organizational structure also refers to the communication infrastructure. The more comprehensive and flexible the corporate communication network is, the more likely employees know where the organization wants to go. This is an important factor for reducing employee resistance and for initiating and sustaining change because change tends to ignore the proper channels and established bureaucratic lines (Waterman, 1990).

Change Management

Change management can be divided into two sub-concepts: 1) Change Management Approach, and 2) Management of Resistance to Change. Change management approach refers to the change management procedures established within organizations. The questions to be addressed in this context deal with whether there are formal change strategies or not, if bureaucratic barriers have to be overcome, who usually initiates and sponsors changes (top-down or bottom-up changes), and if change is typically managed internally or if external help in the form of consultants is obtained (internal versus external change agents). In addition, organizations may differ in their change management approaches as regards how actively and continuously they seek change. A pro-active approach reduces the time gap between the occurrence of an event and the company's respective reaction, which leads to a higher capacity to change. On the other hand, a remedial, discontinuous change approach decreases the organization's flexibility and, therefore, makes a fast adoption of technological innovations a lot harder. Employee resistance is still the biggest barrier to successful change. Successfully addressing resistance means ensuring the existence of incentives for employees to learn and change and the establishment of well-structured plans that embrace employee participation throughout all stages of a change process. The ultimate goal of change management is to incorporate organizational learning into the corporate culture in order to increase an organization's capacity for continuous change. Having a capacity for continuous change means seeing change as a stimulus rather than a threat (Breuer, 1989). Openness to change and anticipating change are vital characteristics of an innovative organization. Since change is taking place with increased speed, new change management techniques are required to achieve such a proactive change approach. Unfortunately, most organizations still change only as little as they must rather than as much as they could and/or should. Research shows that a good change management concept can substantially increase the likelihood of successful IT adoption (Markus and Benjamin, 1997; Baker et al., 1999).

Corporate Culture

DeLisi (1990) identifies culture as the primary driver of strategic organizational change. Being aware of an organization's culture is already a big step towards a higher capacity to change (Hassard and Sharifi, 1989). An organization's culture should be adaptive, yet consistent in pursuing its long-term goals, and responsive to individuals, but within the context of a strong, shared mission. Organizational cultures have enormous inertia and change very slowly, and the larger an organization is, the greater is this inertia (Denison, 1990). Corporate culture determines how organizations process information (Linder, 1985). Knowledge cannot be shared without trust, honesty, and openness. Maintaining this culture of trust is essential for achieving high levels of change readiness because people change for emotional reason far more than for rational reasons (Waterman, 1990). Another very important aspect of corporate culture is an organization's attitude toward risk. This attitude has a direct influence on capacity to change and on technology management. A culture that tolerates high risks and the possible failures that are connected with it, makes it easier for organizations to pursue a proactive change approach and, thus, get less frustrated by volatile environments (Watkins, 1998). To develop a culture that thrives on continuous change is extremely important. Without it, single change projects may succeed, but will make the next change harder (Lewis, 1998). Success has an almost vaccinating effect against change and makes an organization resistant to future changes (Mackiewicz, 1994).

The proposed Internet Readiness model incorporates the concept of "capacity to change" in order to reflect the ability of organizations to successfully alter their structures, systems, values, beliefs, goals, and strategies. More specifically, it assesses the overall flexibility/adaptability of organizations, the organizational ability to react to changing market conditions, the longevity/depth of change efforts, and the extent of change an organization has experienced in the past. It is argued that an organization's capacity to change and its stage of effective technology use co-evolve as organizations progress to higher levels of Internet Readiness. Although certain stages of technology use may be reached with moderate levels of organizational capacity to change, it is posited that a high capacity to change is crucial for sustaining achieved "readiness" in the long run. Internet Readiness, therefore, can be measured as a combination of stages of effective technology use and capacity to change and can be conceptualized as a 3 X 3 matrix (see Fig. 4) with Cells 1, 5, and 9 representing the normative stages of Internet Readiness. This normative model would hypothesize

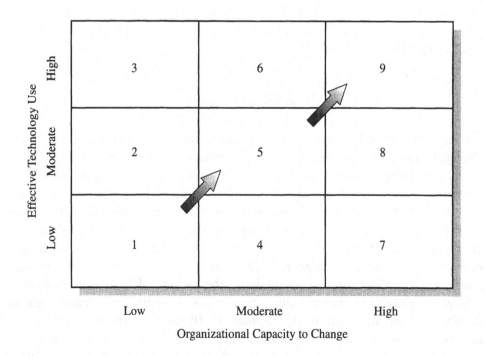

Fig. 4. Internet readiness

that a tourism organization would progress along a path from low capacity/low effectiveness through moderate capacity/moderate effectiveness until they reach high levels of capacity and high effectiveness in their technology use. Alternative paths are possible, however, belonging to other cells can postpone reaching Cell 9, the state where organizations realize the greatest impacts, most effective technology use and best technology/organization fits. Tourism organizations located in Cell 6, for example, appear to have reached high levels of effective technology use but have not made the organizational changes necessary to fully realize the benefits of these investments. Perhaps more important, organizational changes are more difficult and time-consuming than technological changes and co-evolution processes are restricted if the technologies have been set in place to support old practices.

5. Case Study of Internet Readiness Among American Convention and Visitors Bureaus

A study was conducted among American convention and visitors bureaus (CVBs) as a first attempt to empirically test the Internet Readiness model. The survey was based on the measurement models for the stages of effective technology use and the full model of capacity to change, including items to measure Environment, Leadership, Corporate Culture, Organizational Structure and Change Management. Choosing the rather homogeneous sample of American CVBs limits the generalizability of study findings but helped considerably in reducing the complexity of the model.

The primary data collection instrument was a self-administered, Web-based questionnaire. Ease of use was a major concern when designing the Web-based survey. The questionnaire incorporated a total of 38 questions that could be answered, on average, within 10 minutes. Pictures and graphics were avoided to keep downloading time short. Most items were measured using a 5-point Likert-type scale. The response rate was expected to be rather low due to the nature of the questions, the length of the questionnaire, and the electronic administration of the survey. Further, the contact information about potential survey participants was obtained through the Internet and email addresses may become outdated very quickly. The sample size was, therefore, to be held as high as possible. In total 565 addresses with contact names and 308 email addresses without specific contact names were included in the sample, leading to a total sample size of 873 tourism related bureaus/organizations.

A pretest was administered in order to test the layout of the questionnaire and to get some feedback regarding the format of the questions. The pretest sample consisted of 20 convention and visitors bureaus in Illinois and Indiana. A series of analyses were conducted to examine item response, stability and order response bias. The pretest results indicated that no substantial changes to the survey instrument were necessary. Minor changes were incorporated into the survey design such as the possibility to preview the second survey Web page without causing an entry to the database. The initial mailing for the main study was conducted July 26, 2000. A total 74 of the 873 initial email surveys were returned undeliverable; the email addresses were corrected and resent July 27, 2000. Of these, 37 email addresses could not be corrected, reducing the overall sample size to 836. The survey subjects were asked to complete and submit the questionnaire by July 31, 2000. Hard copies of the survey questionnaire were faxed to individual organizations upon request. In an effort to achieve a higher response rate a reminder was sent to non-respondents on August 2, 2000. By August 3, 2000, the database consisted of 241 usable entries. Four respondents provided incorrect ID codes and had to be excluded from the sample. In total, 237 valid surveys were returned resulting in an effective response rate of 28.4 percent.

Results

Descriptive statistics were used to obtain a general understanding of the extent to which the tourism organizations vary in terms of Environment, Leadership, Change Management, Organizational Structures, Organizational Culture, IT Use, Development of Informational Strategies and Capacity to Change. Chi-Square tests and Discriminant analyses were then used to classify the respondent organizations into different stages of effective technology use and organizational capacity to change. Detailed descriptive results and analyses of the validity and reliability of each construct are provided in Gretzel and Fesenmaier (2000). This paper reports the results of analyses focusing attention on the examination of Internet Readiness of the American CVBs and the factors related to the ability of these destination marketing organizations to use Internet technology to compete effectively in the new world economy.

Stages of Effective Technology Use

As discussed earlier, it is argued that technology adoption typically occurs in three stages: Substitution, Enlargement, Reconfiguration. The way organizations use technology and their approach towards knowledge management and organizational learning were used to classify the organizations in the sample into the three stages of effective technology use (see Fig. 5 for a description of the scales used). More specifically, a summated scale was constructed based upon IT use and each CVB was allocated into one of three groups relative to their mean score (i.e., ±1 standard deviation); this approa ch was repeated for the knowledge management construct. A 3 × 3 matrix was then constructed based upon these scales and the destination marketing organizations were assigned into one of nine cells. Last, the respective organizations were compared using Multiple Discriminant Analysis with the nine

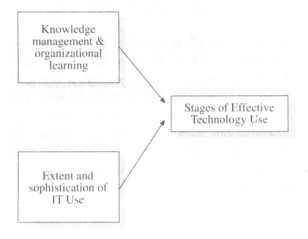

Fig. 5. Measurement model for stages of effective technology use

cells as the grouping variable and the independent variables were the individual items used in scale construction. As expected, this approach yielded highly significant results, indicating a high discriminating power of the items included. The results also indicated that those organizations that *did not* follow the normative model (i.e., not on the diagonal of the 3 × 3 matrix) could be re-assigned to one of three normative stages without substantial loss in an overall goodness-of-fit (e.g. the probabilities of membership ranged between 88–98%). Figure 6 shows the resulting

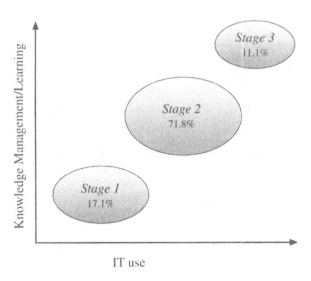

Fig. 6. Stages of effective technology use

three stages and the percentage of organizations in the respective groups. Stage 1 (i.e., those with low level of IT use and with little knowledge infrastructure) is comprised of 37 (17.1%) American CVBs, Stage 2 (i.e., moderate develop of IT and knowledge management strategies) of 155 (71.8%), and Stage 3 (i.e., high levels of IT use and sophistication and knowledge management strategies) comprises 24 (11.1%) tourism organizations. Although group sizes depend strongly on the way the stages were defined, it is interesting to see that most American Convention and Visitor Bureaus have already reached Stage 2. Stage 2 organizations appear to have the potential to reach Stage 3 if they reconfigure certain aspects of their structures, cultures and processes.

Stages of Capacity to Change

American CVBs were assigned to stages of low, moderate, and high capacity to change following a methodology similar to the one discussed above using the following items: 1) the overall flexibility of the organization, 2) the extent to which an organization has changed within the last five years, and 3) the extent to which an organization changes actively rather than reactively (see Fig. 7). The results indicate that most organizations (117 or about 53%) have moderate capacities to change, about 18 percent (40 organizations) achieve only low levels of capacity, and a surprisingly high number of organizations (64 or 29%) have reached the highest level of capacity to change (see Table 3).

Fig. 7. Measurement model for organizational capacity to change

Table 3. Frequencies for stages of capacity to change among American CVBs

Stage	Percent
1. Low	18.1
2. Moderate	52.9
3. High	29.0

Assessing Internet Readiness

The Internet Readiness matrix provides a framework for identifying the extent to which tourism organizations are capable of using Internet technology to effectively compete in the new tourism economy. As discussed earlier, it is expected that tourism organizations should lie on the diagonal cells (Cell 1: low-low, Cell 5: moderate-moderate, or Cell 9: high-high) but combinations outside the normative stages are possible. Few organizations, however, are expected to be assigned to the extreme positions (i.e., Cell 3 and Cell 7). The study among American CVBs confirms this assumption (see Fig. 8). Only one organization has reached the Reconfiguration stage (Cell 3) with low levels of capacity to change and four

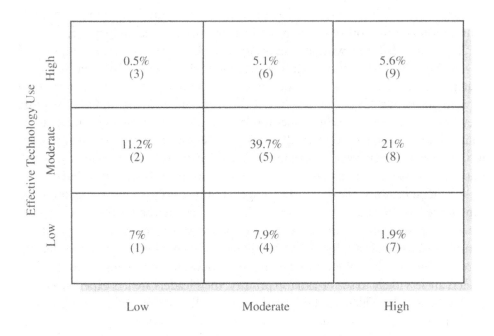

Fig. 8. Internet readiness of American convention and visitors bureaus

organizations have a high capacity to change but realize only low levels of effectiveness in their technology use (Cell 7). Since these numbers are not sufficient to draw
conclusions regarding the characteristics of organizations in these cells, they will be
excluded from further analyses.

A series of analyses were conducted to understand better the nature of those
tourism organizations assigned to the various cells of the Internet Readiness matrix.
The results show that, in general, organizations in the Enlargement phase (Cells 2,
5 and 8) have started to use technology earlier than organizations in the Substitution
phase (Cells 1, 4 and 7). Also, they see a greater impact of technology on their
organizational activities and are more likely to evaluate competitors' Internet
strategies. IT is a greater priority for leaders of organizations in the Enlargement
stage. Organizations in the Reconfiguration stage (Cells 3, 6 and 9) tend to
experience an even greater impact of Internet technologies. Reconfiguration organizations do not only use IT more extensively and in more sophisticated ways, they
also tend to have more full-time staff and larger budgets. Organizations in the low
capacity to change range do not achieve higher scores because they lack leadership/
leader participation in change efforts, teamwork, and a corporate climate of trust,
openness, and honesty. Comparisons of organizations with moderate and high
capacity to change indicate that high levels of capacity (Cells 7, 8 and 9) are
associated with more organizational success, more partnerships, even more leader
participation and more successful leaders in terms of translating the corporate vision
into action, more group decision-making, more management of resistance to
change, broader job descriptions, less hierarchical structures, more informal communication and the cost of training is a smaller barrier to technology use.

A more detailed, pair-wise analysis of American CVBs (i.e., organizations located
in adjacent cells) reveals further differences among the Stages of Internet Readiness
that go beyond variations based on effective technology use and organizational
capacity to change. Organizations in Cell 1 appear to be "stuck" in Cell 1 because
they have started to use technologies too late and do not see enough impact to be
counted as Cell 2 organizations. Cell 1 organizations differ from Cell 4 organizations
in terms of their perceived constraints to technology use and the extent to which
leaders participate in change efforts. Cell 1 organizations are distinctly different from
Cell 5 organizations along a wide range of dimensions: Cell 1 organizations
experience less impact, perceive more constraints, see themselves more as laggards,
are less successful, have a smaller amount of partnerships, are less likely to evaluate
competitors' Internet strategies, tend to have less team-work, trust and leadership
participation, are less likely to take employee opinions into consideration, their
leaders are less likely to see IT as a top priority, their leaders are less experienced and
tend to be female, which can be related to the smaller size of Cell 1 organizations.

What keeps Cell 2 organizations from scoring higher on the capacity to change
continuum is lack of leadership, lack of group decision-making, lack of teamwork,
lack of broader job descriptions, and lack of trust. The difference between Cell 2 and
Cell 6 organizations in terms of effectiveness of technology use is mainly a function

of staff, budget and IT spending. Organizations in Cell 4 have smaller budgets, experience less impact, lag behind in terms of the time they typically start using new technologies, have more problems in justifying IT investments, perceive lack of in-house expertise as a greater constraint, are less successful, have less trust, and their leaders are less likely to see IT as a top priority and are less likely to be successful in translating the corporate vision into action than organizations in Cell 5. Cell 5 organizations lag behind Cell 8 organizations in terms of the constraints they perceive, their management of resistance to change, their communication structure, and the amount of teamwork, trust and leader participation. Cell 5 and Cell 6 organizations differ in terms of staff and budget. Also, Cell 6 organizations are more likely to see themselves as innovators and IT is a greater priority for their leaders.

Tourism organizations located in Cell 9 have achieved high levels of capacity to change and high levels of effectiveness in the way they use technology. They are clearly in the Reconfiguration phase. Cell 8 organizations are in the same capacity to change level, but Cell 9 organizations are larger, have bigger budgets, experience a greater impact of Internet technologies, are more likely to serve international markets and have less hierarchical structures. Also, Cell 8 organizations are more likely to perceive lack of time as a constraint to technology use, which is a characteristic problem of the Enlargement phase. Limitations in terms of staff and budget appear to keep Cell 8 organizations from becoming more effective in their technology use. Cell 6 organizations are extensive and sophisticated IT users, however, they lack informal communication, broader job descriptions, flat structures and leader participation. Cell 6 and Cell 9 organizations all tend to be rather large, but, Cell 9 organizations are definitely more flexible. This does make a difference, which can be clearly seen by looking at the impact of technology experienced in both groups: only 27.3 percent of Cell 6 organizations see a very strong impact compared to 66.7 percent in Cell 9. Thus, although extensive and sophisticated technology use can be achieved by investing enough in the development and implementation of IT strategies, the realization of impacts requires capacity to change.

6. Conclusions

The speed of technological change and the organizational challenges brought about through different models of communication, collaboration, and interactivity lead to immense uncertainties for organizations trying to create competitive advantages in the new e-economy. Thus, tourism organizations are increasingly in search of guidelines or best practices that allow them to evaluate and, if necessary, adapt their Internet strategies. Finding measures to assess Internet Readiness and establishing industry benchmarks will greatly support organizations in their endeavor to cope with the new economic realities. The proposed Internet Readiness framework will help tourism organizations understand the necessity for organizational changes if they want to achieve effectiveness in the adoption and use of innovative information technologies. Since traditional business models and organizational approaches have become increasingly outdated, reconfiguration will be the prerequisite for establishing competitive advantages in the new e-economy.

The results of this study indicate that relatively few (5.6%) American convention and visitors bureaus are currently structured to fully realize the potential impact of Internet technology. These destination marketing organizations are typically large but flat and represent some of the leading tourism destinations in the United States. Another 21 percent of American CVBs have developed much of the organizational capacity to effectively utilize Internet technology but have not invested fully in technology because of limited budgets or lack of time/limited staff. The remaining American CVBs appear to face major challenges in order to fully realize the benefits of Internet technology and, therefore, to compete effectively in the new tourism economy. These challenges include increasing budgets capable of supporting IT infrastructure, building/supporting organizational capacity to change, forming partnerships, recognizing the value of knowledge and investing in systems for updating the skills of their staff.

These challenges appear to be formidable and will substantially limit the ability for the American tourism industry to effectively compete within the international tourism industry. Indeed, recent technology developments and investments worldwide appear to place the American tourism industry at a distinct disadvantage. In particular, destination marketing systems such as TIScover (Austria) and Gulliver (Ireland) currently being used throughout Europe and industry knowledge-based community systems such as the Canadian Tourism Exchange (Canada) and Tour-MIS (Austria) provide substantial capacity for tourism organizations to more effectively develop and market their services (Werthner and Klein, 1999; Wöber and Gretzel, 2000; Fesenmaier et al., 1999). Such systems provide a framework for collaboration, learning and more extensive research and offer tools that support organizations in extending their technology use. Thus, active participation in virtual tourism communities can greatly enhance an organization's effectiveness in technology use and its capacity to change. Also, such platforms represent a very effective way of pooling forces and overcoming limitations due to organizational size. In addition, the ability to compete relies on the recognition that the basic models of organizational structure have and will continue to change, offering new and exciting ways to develop the capacity of tourism marketing organizations to expand and/or service their respective markets. Last, American tourism destination marketing organizations appear unable to effectively utilize the emerging Internet communication strategies (e.g. permission marketing, personalized advertising and virtual community) which could enable them to more effectively and efficiently develop one-to-one relationships with their current and prospective customers. The implications of these findings are substantial, suggesting that the American tourism industry should focus efforts in at least the following areas: 1) Embracing new Internet technologies and creating organizational cultures/structures that are able to empower tourism organizations to more effectively build integrated marketing and management strategies that focus on the changing individual needs of travelers (e.g., customer profiling systems, adaptive/interactive interfaces, etc), 2) Developing education programs with which to train staff on the nature and use of eCommerce and Internet marketing and to prepare them for the new technologies; and, 3) Creating partnerships and platforms for sharing knowledge. With the continued investments of many foreign governmental organizations worldwide, it appears that a substantial proportion of American CVBs will fall further behind in competing for tourists. Thus, it is critical that tourism organizations throughout the U. S. recognize the challenges brought about by the new tourism economy and focus on integrating capacity to change into their organizations, supporting new models which embrace networking strategies and developing new intelligent and integrative ways of using technology.

References

Adams, C., Adams, B. (1995) The birth of transformation. Executive Excellence 12 (12): 15

Arthur Andersen Consulting (2000) Survey of small and mid-sized businesses. Trends for 2000. http://www.arthurandersen.com/resource2.nsf/AssetsByDescription/SSMB_2000 EnterpriseGroup/$file/SSMB_2000.pdf

Baker, M., Sussmann, S., Welch, S. (1999) Information Technology management. In: Brotherton B. (ed.) The Handbook of Contemporary Hospitality Management Research. John Wiley & Sons, New York, pp. 397–413

Breuer, J. E. (1989) Orchestrating Culture Shock: What Happens When Companies Must Change. Inform 3 (4): 11, 46

Bruce, B. C., Rubin, A. (1993) Electronic Quills: A Situated Evaluation of Using Computers for Writing in Classrooms. http://www.lis.uiuc.edu/~chip/pubs/Equills/intro.shtml

Brynjolfsson, E. (1993) The Productivity Paradox of Information Technology. Communications of the ACM 36 (12): 67–77

Burt, R. S. (1998) The Network Structure of Social Capital. University of Chicago (unpublished)

Contractor, N. S., Wasserman, S., Faust, K. (1999) Testing multi-level, multi-theoretical hypotheses about networks in 21st century organizational forms: An analytic framework and empirical example. http://www.spcomm.uiuc.edu:1000/contractor/pstarpaper.html

Contractor, N. S., Stohl, C., Monge, P., Flanagin, A., Fulk, J. (2000) Communication in the Global Workplace: Advanced E-Quad Collaboration Tools to Support Multi-University Cooperative Learning and Teaching. Working paper, University of Illinois

Davis, S., Meyer, C. (1998) It's all a blur. Executive Excellence 15 (9): 11–12

Day, G. S. (1998) Organizing for Interactivity. J Interactive Marketing 12 (1): 47–53

DeLisi, P. S. (1990) Lessons from the Steel Axe: Culture, Technology, and Organizational Change. Sloan Management Review 32 (1): 83–93

Denison, D. R. (1990) Corporate Culture and Organizational Effectiveness. John Wiley & Sons, New York

Dun & Bradstreet (2000) D&B study shows seven out of 10 U.S. small businesses now have Internet access. http://www.dnb.com/newsview/0500news8.htm

Drucker, P. F., Dyson, E., Handy, C., Saffo, P., Senge, P. M. (1997) Looking Ahead: Implications of the Present. Harvard Business Review 75 (5): 18–32

Evans, P., Wurster, T. S. (1999) Blown to Bits. Harvard Business School Press, Boston, MA

Fesenmaier, D. R., Leppers, A. W., O'Leary, J. T. (1999) Developing a knowledge-based tourism marketing information system. Information Technology in Tourism 2 (1): 31–44

Finerty, T. (1997) Evolutionary thinking about business change. People Management 3 (20): 60

Forrester (2000) The eBusiness Voyage. http://www.forrester.com

Garvin, D. A. (1998) Building a Learning Organization. Harvard Business Review on Knowledge Management. Harvard Business School Press, Boston, MA

Greengard, S. (1998) Will your culture support KM? Workforce 77 (10): 93–94

Gretzel, U., Fesenmaier, D. R. (2000) Assessing the Capacity of American Convention and Visitors Bureaus to Effectively Use Internet Technologies – A Pilot Study. National Laboratory for Tourism and eCommerce. University of Illinois, Urbana-Champaign

Gretzel, U., Yuan, Y., Fesenmaier, D. R. (2000) Preparing for the new economy: Advertising and change in destination marketing organizations. J Travel Research 39 (2): 146–156

Hackman, M. Z., Johnson, C. E. (1996) Leadership – A communication perspective, 2nd edn. Waveland Press, Prospect Heights, IL

Hanson, W. (2000) Principles of Internet Marketing. South-Western College Publishing, Cincinnati, Ohio

Hartman, A., Sifonis, J. (2000) Net ready. Strategies for success in the E-conomy. McGraw-Hill, New York

Hassard, J., Sharifi, S. (1989) Corporate Culture and Strategic Change. J General Management 15 (2): 4–19

Huffington, C., Cole, C. F., Brunning, H. (1997) A manual of organizational development: The psychology of change. Psychological Press/International Universities Press, Madison, CT

Kanter, R. M. (1998) Change-adept organizations. Executive Excellence 15 (8): 4

Lewis, B. (1998) Managing change is not enough: You must create a culture that embraces it. InfoWorld 20 (45): 105

Linder, J. C. (1985) Computers, Corporate Culture and Change. Personnel J 64 (9): 49–55

Mackiewicz, A. (1994) The successful corporation of the year 2000. The Economist Intelligence Unit, New York

Madnick, S. E. (1987) Perspectives on the Effective Use, Planning, and Impact of Information Technology. In: Madnick, S. E. (ed.) The Strategic Use of Information Technology. Oxford University Press, New York, pp. 3–14

Mariotti, J. L. (1997) Continuous change. Executive Excellence 14 (10): 8

Markus, M. L., Benjamin, R. I. (1997) Are you gambling on a magic bullet? Computerworld 32 (42): C1-C11

Modahl, M. (2000) Now or Never – How companies must change today to win the battle for Internet consumers. Harper Business, New York

Orlikowski W. J., Yates, J., Okamura, K., Fujimoto, M. (1999) Shaping Electronic Communication: The Metastructuring of Technology in the Context of Use. In: DeSanctis, G., Fulk, J. (eds.) Shaping Organization Form: Communication, Connection, and Community. Sage Publications, Thousand Oaks, CA, pp. 133–171

Poon, A. (1993) Tourism, Technology and Competitive Strategies. CAB International, Oxon, UK

Prokesch, S. E. (1997) Unleashing the Power of Learning. Harvard Business Review 75 (5): 147–168

Rossetti, D. K., DeZoort, F. A. (1989) Organizational Adaptation to Technology Innovation. Advanced Management J 54 (4): 29–33

Senge, P., Kleiner A., Roberts, C., Ross, R., Roth, G., Smith, B. (1999) The Dance of Change. Doubleday, New York

Scott Morton, M. S. (1991) The corporation of the 1990s: information technology and organizational transformation. Oxford University Press, New York

Sheldon, P. J. (1997) Tourism Information Technology. CAB International, New York

Shukla, M. (1997) Competing through knowledge: Building a learning organization. Response Books, New Delhi, India

Steck, R. N. (1993) Don't Automate – Informate. D&B Reports 42 (4): 42–43 (19)

Thorp, J. (1998) The Information Paradox. McGraw-Hill, Toronto

Timmers, P. (2000) Electronic Commerce and the e-conomy. Lecture Series "E-commerce". Vienna University for Economics and Business Administration. http://wwwi.wu-wien.ac.at/Studium/Abschnitt_2/LVA_ss00/LectureSeries.html

Van de Ven, A. H. (1991) Managing the process of organizational innovation. Changing and Redesigning Organizations. Oxford University Press, New York

Vandenbosch, B., Ginzberg, M. J. (1997) Lotus Notes and collaboration: Plus ça Change. J Management Information Systems 13 (3): 65–81

Venkatesh, V., Davis, F. D. (2000) A Theoretical Extension of the Technology Acceptance Model: Four Longitudinal Field Studies. Management Science 46: 186–204

Waterman, R. H. (1990) Adhocracy: The Power to Change. Whittle Direct Books, Knoxville, Tenn

Watkins, W. M. (1998) Technology and Business Strategy: Getting the Most Out of Technological Assets. Greenwood Publishing Group, Westport, Connecticut

Werthner, H., Klein, S. (1999) Information Technology and Tourism – A Challenging Relationship. Springer, Wien New York

Wöber, K., Gretzel, U. (2000) Tourism Managers' Adoption of Marketing Decision Support Systems. J Travel Research 39 (2): 172–181

Yuan, Y. Y., Fesenmaier, D. R., Xia, L., Gratzer, M. (1999) The Use of Internet and Intranet In American Convention and Visitors Bureaus. In: Buhalis, D., Schertler, W. (eds.) Information and Communication Technologies in Tourism 1999. Springer, Wien New York, pp. 365–375

Yuan, Y. Y., Gretzel, U., Fesenmaier, D. R. (2000) Managing Innovation: The Use of Internet Technology by American Convention and Visitors Bureaus and Factors Affecting Its Implementation. University of Illinois, Working Paper

Zeira, Y., Avedisian, J. (1989) Organizational Planned Change: Assessing the Chances for Success. Organizational Dynamics 17 (4): 31–45

Ulrike Gretzel

Ph. D. student in the Institute of Communications Research at the University of Illinois and a research assistant at the National Laboratory for Tourism and E-Commerce. Her research interests lie in the field of marketing information systems in tourism with a special focus on organizational issues in knowledge management, collaboration, corporate culture and change management.

Daniel R. Fesenmaier

Professor in the Department of Leisure Studies and Director of the National Laboratory for Tourism and E-Commerce, University of Illinois. His main research and teaching interests focus on the use of information in travel decisions, the use of information technology for tourism marketing and the development of knowledge-based systems for tourism marketing organizations.

Aggregation and Disaggregation of Information Goods: Implications for Bundling, Site Licensing, and Micropayment Systems*

Y. Bakos[1] and E. Brynjolfsson[2]

[1]Stern School of Management, New York University, and
[2]Massachusetts Institute of Technology, U.S.A.

bakos@stern.nyu.edu
erikb@mit.edu

Abstract
We analyze pricing strategies for digital information goods that are based on aggregation or disaggregation. Bundling, site licensing, and subscription pricing can be analyzed as strategies that aggregate consumer utility across different goods, different consumers, or different time periods, respectively. Using micropayments for rental of software "applets," or other discrete units of information, can be thought of as disaggregation. We show that reductions in marginal costs made possible by low-cost digital processing and storage of information will favor aggregation of information goods, while reductions in transaction and distribution costs made possible by ubiquitous networking tend to make disaggregation more profitable.

Furthermore, offering the goods simultaneously in the aggregated package and as separate components may dominate strategies of both pure aggregation and pure disaggregation. Our model demonstrates how the increasing availability of information goods over the Internet will lead to increased use of both disaggregation-based pricing strategies, taking advantage of micropayment technologies, and aggregation strategies, whereby information goods will be offered in bundles, site licenses, and subscriptions.

---

* In: *Internet Publishing and Beyond: The Economics of Digital Information and Intellectual Property.* Kahin, B., Varian, H. (eds.) (2000) MIT Press. Copyright© 1997–99 by Y. Bakos and E. Brynjolfsson

1. Introduction

The emergence of the Internet as a way to distribute digital information, such as software, news stories, stock quotes, music, photographs, video clips, and research reports, has created new opportunities for the pricing of information goods. Providers of digital information goods are not sure how to price them and are struggling with a variety of revenue models. Because perfect copies of these goods can be created and distributed almost costlessly, some of the old rules, such as "price should equal marginal cost," are not applicable (Varian, 1995).

As noted by Varian (1995), Bakos and Brynjolfsson (1996, 1999a), Odlyzko (1996), Chuang and Sirbu (1997), and others, the Internet has also created new opportunities for repackaging content through bundling, site licensing, subscriptions, rentals, differential pricing, per-use fees, and various other mechanisms; others may yet be invented. All these schemes can be thought of as either aggregating or disaggregating information goods along some dimension. For instance, aggregation can be done across products, as in the case of bundling digital goods for sale in an applications software "suite" or providing access to an online service for a fixed fee. Aggregation can also be done across consumers, as with the provision of a site license to multiple users for a fixed fee, or over time, as with subscriptions (Odlyzko, 1996; Varian, 1995, 1996). Fishburn et al. (1997) argue that the choice between aggregation and disaggregation cannot be made based on utility maximization, and ultimately rely on noneconomic arguments to predict that aggregation will dominate when marginal production and distribution costs become negligible.

In this chapter, we generalize the model of bundling introduced in Bakos and Brynjolfsson (1996, 1999a) by including a parameter that indexes the cost of distributing goods over a network. This, in addition to the parameter for the marginal cost of production introduced in our earlier work, allows us to compare pricing strategies based on aggregation and disaggregation. We find that lower transaction and distribution costs tend to make unbundling (disaggregation) more attractive for sellers, while lower marginal costs of production tend to make bundling (aggregation) more attractive. We then demonstrate how some of our earlier results on bundling can be generalized to other types of aggregation, such as site licensing and subscriptions. We find that, as with bundling, aggregating information goods across consumers or across time is often an effective strategy that maximizes societal welfare and the sellers' profits; however, aggregation is less attractive when marginal costs are high or when consumers are very heterogeneous.

In section 2, we present the basic argument for the impact of aggregation on profits and efficiency and provide a graphical intuition. In section 3, we present a simple mathematical model demonstrating how changes in production and transaction costs affect the profitability of bundling and unbundling goods. In section 4, we show how the formal results can be applied to questions of site licensing, subscriptions, and micropayments. Section 5 discusses some implications for practice and suggests questions for further research.

2. Aggregation Changes Demand

Most goods can be thought of as aggregations, or bundles of smaller goods (Lancaster, 1966). For instance, a spreadsheet program is a bundle of components – the ability to calculate sums, to produce charts, to print in various fonts, and so on (Brynjolfsson and Kemerer, 1996). Similarly, the purchase of a durable good is equivalent to a series of rental contracts (Christensen and Jorgenson, 1966), and sharing of books or videocassettes can be seen as multiple separate transactions (Varian and Roehl, 1996).

Why Aggregate?

There are two main reasons that sellers may wish to use aggregation when selling information goods. First, aggregation can directly increase the value available from a set of goods, because of technological complementarities in production, distribution, or consumption. For instance, it is more cost-effective to deliver a few hundred pages of news articles in the form of a Sunday newspaper than to separately deliver each of the individual components only to the people who read it, even if most of the Sunday bundle ends up in the recycle bin without ever being read. Likewise, having a consumer purchase a movie on videocassette may be cheaper than repeatedly renting it, or for the seller to attempt charging members of the household separately for viewing it. These cost savings increase the surplus available to be divided between the buyer and the seller, although they may also affect the way the surplus is divided.

Second, aggregation can make it easier for the seller to extract value from a given set of goods by enabling a form of price discrimination. This effect of aggregation is subtler and, in the case of bundling, has been studied in a number of articles in the economics literature (Adams and Yellen, 1976; McAfee et al., 1989; Schmalensee, 1984). While the benefits of aggregation due to cost savings are relatively easy to see, the price discrimination effect does not seem to be as widely recognized, although it can dramatically affect both efficiency and profits (Bakos and Brynjolfsson, 1996, 1999a).

The Effects of the Internet and Digitization

Ubiquitous low-cost networking, low-cost digital processing, and low-cost storage of information will profoundly affect the incentives for sellers to aggregate goods that can be delivered in digital form, whether to take advantage of cost savings or to price-discriminate. For example, the Internet is making it feasible to disaggregate news stories that were formerly aggregated in a newspaper simply to economize on transaction and distribution costs. The Internet has also made detailed monitoring and micropayment systems feasible, making it more attractive to sell small units of information, perhaps for use within a limited period of time, by a limited number of people or in a limited set of situations. As a result, many observers have predicted that software and other types of content will increasingly be disaggregated and metered, for instance as on-demand software "applets" or as individual news stories and stock quotes. For instance, Bob Metcalfe writes, "When the Internet finally gets micromoney systems, we'll rent tiny bits of software for seconds at a time. Imagine renting a French spelling checker for one document once" (Metcalfe, 1997).

On the other hand, the near-zero marginal costs of reproduction for digital goods make many types of aggregation more attractive. While it is uneconomical to provide goods to users who value them at less than the marginal cost of production, when the marginal cost is zero and users can freely dispose of goods they do not like, then *no* users will value the goods at less than their marginal cost. As a result, economic efficiency and, often, profitability are maximized by providing the maximum number of such goods to the maximum number of people for the maximum amount of time. In this paper, we show that selling goods in large aggregates will often achieve this goal.

Thus, goods that were previously aggregated to save on transaction or distribution costs may be disaggregated, but new aggregations of goods will emerge to exploit the potential for price discrimination, creating new efficiencies and profit opportunities. We show that strategies involving bundling, site licensing, and subscriptions can each be understood as a response to the radical declines in production, distribution, and transaction costs for digital information goods, while micropayments can be seen as both a consequence and a cause of radically lower transaction and distribution costs.

Graphical Intuition: The Case of Bundling

The possibility of extracting more value from consumers by aggregating information goods can be illustrated by graphically analyzing the effect of bundling on the demand for information goods. Consider a simple linear demand curve for all goods, and assume that the initial fixed costs of producing a good are significant, but that after the first unit, marginal production costs, denoted by c, are close to zero. At price p, the number of units purchased will be q, resulting in profits of pq. However, as long as $p > c$, some consumers who value the good at more than its production costs will not be willing to pay as much as p. As a result, these consumers do not get access to the good, creating a deadweight loss, denoted by the shaded region in Fig. 1. In addition, there are consumers who would have been willing to pay more than p for access to the good, but who have to pay only p to receive it. These consumers enjoy a consumers' surplus, as indicated in Fig. 1.

If the seller is able to price-discriminate, charging a different price to every consumer based on his or her willingness to pay, it will be able to increase its profits. Perfect price discrimination will maximize the seller's profits and will eliminate both

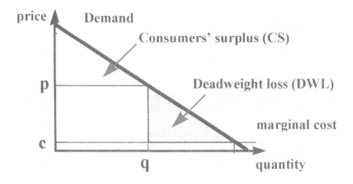

Fig. 1. Deadweight loss from sales of a zero-marginal-cost information good

the consumers' surplus and the deadweight loss (Varian, 1995). If the seller cannot price-discriminate, however, the only single price that would eliminate the inefficiency from the deadweight loss would be a price equal to the marginal cost, which is close to zero. Such a low price would not generate sufficient revenues to cover the fixed cost of production and is unlikely to be the profit-maximizing price. Yet any significant positive price will inefficiently exclude some consumers.

Aggregation can sometimes overcome this dilemma. Consider two information goods, say a journal article and a music video, and suppose that each is valued between zero and one dollar by some consumers, generating linear demand curves such as the one in Fig. 1. Suppose further that a consumer's valuation of one good is not correlated with his or her valuation of the other, and that access to one good does not make the other more or less attractive.

What happens if the seller aggregates the two goods and sells them as a bundle? Some consumers – those who valued both goods at one dollar – will be willing to pay two dollars for the bundle, while others – those who valued both goods at almost zero – will not be willing– to pay even a penny. The total area under the demand curve for the bundle, and hence the total potential surplus, is exactly equal to the sum of the areas under the separate demand curves. However, most interestingly, bundling changes the shape of the demand curve, making it flatter (more elastic) in the neighborhood of one dollar and steeper (less elastic) near either extreme, as shown in Fig. 2.[1]

As more goods are added, this effect becomes more pronounced. For instance, the demand for a bundle of 20 goods, each of which has an independent, linear demand ranging from zero to one dollar, is shown in Fig. 3.

A profit-maximizing firm selling a bundle of 20 goods will set the price slightly below the $10 mean value of the bundle $10, and almost all consumers will find it worthwhile to purchase the bundle. In contrast, only half the consumers would have

---

[1]   See Salinger (1995) for a detailed graphical analysis of the two-goods scenario

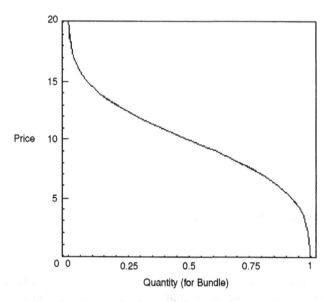

Fig. 2. Demand curve for a bundle of two information goods with independently distributed uniform valuations

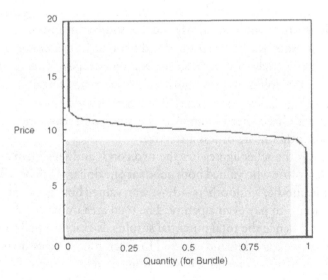

Fig. 3. Demand curve for a bundle of 20 information goods with independently distributed uniform valuations

purchased the goods if they had been individually sold at the profit-maximizing price of 50 cents, so selling the goods as a bundle leads to a smaller deadweight loss and greater economic efficiency. Furthermore, the seller will earn higher profits by selling a single bundle of 20 goods than by selling each of the 20 goods separately. Thus, the shape of the bundle's demand curve is far more favorable both for the seller and for overall economic efficiency.

Why Does the Shape of the Demand Curve Change as Goods Are Added to a Bundle?

The law of large numbers implies that the average valuation for a bundle of goods with valuations drawn from the same distribution will be increasingly concentrated near the mean valuation as more goods are added to the bundle. For example, Fig. 4 shows the uniformly distributed probability of a consumer's valuation for a good with the linear demand shown in Fig. 1.

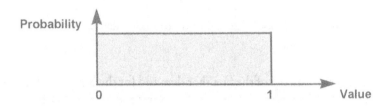

Fig. 4. Uniform probability density function for a good's valuation

If a second good is bundled with the first, the probability density function for the consumer's valuation for the bundle of two goods is the convolution of the two uniform distributions, which will be shaped like an inverted V (Fig. 5).

As more and more goods are added to the bundle, the sum of valuations becomes more concentrated around the mean, reflecting the law of large numbers (Fig. 6). That is, the high and low values for individual goods tend to "average out" so that consumers' valuations for the bundle include proportionately more moderate valuations. For example, some people subscribe to America Online for the news, some for stock quotes, and some for horoscopes. It is unlikely that a single person has a very high value for every single good offered; instead, most consumers will have high values for some goods and low values for others, leading to moderate values overall.

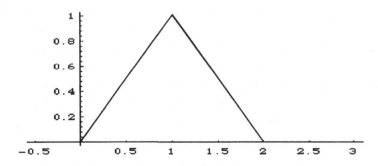

Fig. 5. Convolution of two uniform probability density functions

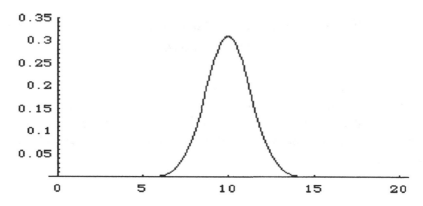

Fig. 6. Convolution of 20 uniform probability density functions

Sellers can take advantage of the fact that demand for the bundle (adjusted for the number of goods) will be more concentrated around the mean valuation than in the case of individual goods. The distribution of valuations for the bundle of 20 goods shown in Fig. 6 corresponds to the demand curve shown in Fig. 3.

Thus, bundling can be thought of as a type of price discrimination, except that instead of increasing the menu of prices to better match the heterogeneous distribution of consumers, bundling reduces the effective heterogeneity of the consumers so that a single price can effectively and efficiently allocate goods to them. Like the Procrustean bed, bundling changes consumers' demands so that a single price fits them all.

If consumers' demands remain heterogeneous even after bundling, then a mixed bundling strategy, which offers a menu of different bundles at different prices, will dominate pure bundling (which is simply a special case of mixed bundling). However, when consumers' valuations for the goods in the bundle are not correlated, the profit advantage of mixed bundling over pure bundling diminishes as the number of goods in the bundle increases.

Similar effects result in other types of aggregation, such as aggregation across consumers, as in the case of selling a single site license for use by multiple consumers. This analogy is explored more fully in section 4. The law of large numbers, which underlies these aggregation effects, is remarkably general. For instance, it holds for almost any initial distribution, not just the linear one shown graphically above.[2] Furthermore, the law does not require that the valuations be independent of each other or even that the valuations be drawn from the same distribution.

The desirability of bundling as a device for price discrimination can break down when consumers' valuations are correlated with one or more common variables. Similarly, applying the same type of analysis to study the impact of marginal costs,

---

[2]   There are several versions of the law of large numbers, but in general the random variables being combined must have only finite variance

we find that when marginal costs are high, unbundling may be more profitable than bundling.

3. A Model for Aggregation and Disaggregation

The above insights can be modeled more formally. In particular, the aggregation of information goods into bundles entails several types of costs:

— *Production cost:* the cost of producing additional units for inclusion in the bundle. For instance, storage, processing, or communications costs incurred in the process.
— *Distribution cost:* the cost of distributing a bundle of information goods.
— *Transaction cost:* the cost of administering transactions, such as arranging for payment.
— *Binding cost:* the cost of binding the component goods together for distribution as a bundle. For example, formatting changes necessary to include a good in the bundle.
— *Menu cost:* the cost of administering multiple prices for a bundle. If a mixed bundling strategy for n goods is pursued, as many as 2^n prices (one for each separate sub-bundle of one or more goods) may be required.

We now focus on the impact of production costs and distribution/transaction costs, which seem to be most important for determining the desirability of aggregation; similar reasoning can be applied to the binding and price administration costs.

Consider a setting with a single seller providing n information goods.[3] Let p_n^*, q_n^*, and π_n^* denote the profit-maximizing price per good for a bundle of n goods, the corresponding sales as a fraction of the population, and the seller's resulting profits per good. Assume that

A1: The marginal cost of producing copies of all information goods and the marginal distribution and transaction cost for all information goods are zero.
A2: Each buyer can consume either 0 or 1 unit of each information good and resale is not permitted.
A3: For all n, buyer valuations are independent, identically distributed (i.i.d.) with continuous density functions, nonnegative support, finite mean μ, and finite variance σ^2.

By applying the law of large numbers to the above setting, we derived the following proposition and the corresponding corollary in Bakos and Brynjolfsson (1996, 1999a):

---

[3]   This setting, the assumptions, and the main result for bundling information goods are derived from Bakos and Brynjolfsson (1996)

Proposition 1 (minimum profits from bundling zero-marginal-cost i.i.d. goods)

Given assumptions A1, A2, and A3, bundling n goods allows the seller to capture as

profits at least a fraction $\left[1-2\left(\frac{(\sigma/\mu)^2}{n}\right)^{\frac{1}{3}}+\left(\frac{(\sigma/\mu)^2}{n}\right)^{\frac{2}{3}}\right]$ of the area under the demand

curve.

Corollary 1 (bundling with symmetric distribution of valuations)

Given assumptions A1, A2, and A3, if the distribution of valuations is symmetric around the mean, a fraction of the area under the demand curve of at least

$\left[1-\frac{3}{2}\left(\frac{(\sigma/\mu)^2}{n}\right)^{\frac{1}{3}}+\frac{1}{2}\left(\frac{(\sigma/\mu)^2}{n}\right)^{\frac{2}{3}}\right]$ can be captured by bundling n goods.[4]

We now extend the original model by substituting Assumption A4 for Assumption A1:

A4: The marginal cost for producing each information good is c, and the sum of distribution and transaction costs for any individual good or bundle is d.

Assumption A4 implies that the total incremental cost of supplying a bundle of n information goods is $nc + d$.

Corollary 2 (bundling with production, distribution, and transaction costs)

Given assumptions A2, A3, and A4, bundling n goods results in profits of π_B^* for the

seller, where $\pi_B^* \geq \left(\mu-c-\frac{d}{n}\right)\left[1-2\left(\frac{(\sigma/\mu)^2}{n}\right)^{\frac{1}{3}}+\left(\frac{(\sigma/\mu)^2}{n}\right)^{\frac{2}{3}}\right]$.

Selling the goods individually, the seller faces a downward-sloping demand curve $q_i(p_i) = \int_p^\infty f(x)dx$ for each individual good, and will select the optimal price p_i^* and corresponding quantity q_i^* that will maximize profits, $\pi_i(p_i) = (p_i-c-d) \cdot q_i(p_i)$ resulting in profits of π_i^*.

---

4   For example, if consumer valuations are i.i.d. with a distribution symmetric around the
    mean and a coefficient of variation $\mu/\sigma = 1/\sqrt{3}$ (e.g., uniformly distributed in $[0,2\mu]$), the
    seller can realize profits of at least 80% of the total area under the demand curve with a
    bundle of 100 goods. For most common distributions of independent valuations, this
    corollary provides a conservative lower bound; for instance, with valuations uniformly
    distributed in $[0,2\mu]$, this level of profits can actually be achieved by bundling eight goods

When the number of goods is large, bundling will be superior to unbundled sales in the limit as long as $\pi_B^* \approx \mu - c > \pi_i^*$. Furthermore, if there is no consumer with a valuation greater than v_{max}, unbundled sales will be profitable only as long as $c + d \leq v_{max}$.

Figure 7 depicts the impact of c and d on the desirability of bundling large numbers of goods. In Area I, unbundled sales dominate bundling. In Area II, bundling is more profitable than unbundled sales. Finally, in Area III, the marginal production, distribution, and transaction costs are high enough to make both bundled and unbundled sales unprofitable.[5]

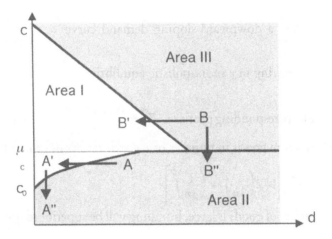

Fig. 7. Phase diagram for bundling and unbundling strategies as a function of marginal cost and transaction/distribution cost

A reduction in distribution or transaction costs can make unbundling more attractive than bundling (a move from A to A'). For example, it is often argued that as micropayment technologies and electronic distribution reduce d, there will be a move toward "atomic" pricing, that is, price per use (Metcalfe, 1996, 1997). However, as soon as the marginal cost falls below a certain threshold c_0, bundling becomes more profitable than unbundling, even if distribution and transaction costs are zero, as demonstrated by the move from A' to A". While bundling is optimal in the neighborhood of A mainly as a way to economize on distribution and transaction costs, the benefits of bundling in the neighborhood of A" derive from its ability to enable the seller to extract more profits from consumers. Therefore, the types of bundles observed in a world of high production, distribution, and transaction costs

---

[5] A similar diagram can be drawn to show when bundling or unbundling is economically efficient from a social-welfare standpoint. Unfortunately, the regions in which bundling and unbundling are socially efficient are not identical to the regions in which each is profitable. In particular, bundling is socially inefficient in a substantial portion of Area II near the frontier with Area I

(near A) may differ substantially from the types of bundles observed in a world with very low production, distribution, and transaction costs.

A reduction in c, d, or both can move a good from Area III (no trade) to either Area I (unbundled sales, if the primary reduction is in the distribution and transaction costs) or Area II (bundled sales, if the primary reduction is in the marginal cost of production).

The threshold level c_0 below which bundling becomes unambiguously more profitable than unbundling depends on the distribution of the underlying valuations. For example, consider consumer valuations that are uniformly distributed in $[0, v_{max}]$, which corresponds to a linear demand function. Selling the goods individually, the seller faces a downward-sloping demand curve $q_i = \dfrac{v_{max} - p_i}{v_{max}}$ for each individual good, resulting in a monopolistic equilibrium price of $p_i^* = \dfrac{v_{max} + c + d}{2}$ for each good, and corresponding profit of $\pi_i^* = \dfrac{(v_{max} + c + d)^2}{4 v_{max}}$ as long as $c + d \leq v_{max}$. Selling the information goods in bundles of n goods results in profits $\pi_B^*(n)$, where

$$\pi_B^*(n) \geq \left(\frac{v_{max}}{2} - c - \frac{d}{n} \right)\left[1 - 2\left(\frac{1}{3n} \right)^{\frac{1}{3}} + \left(\frac{1}{3n} \right)^{\frac{2}{3}} \right].$$

When the number of goods is large, bundling will be superior to unbundled sales in the limit as long as $\dfrac{v_{max}}{2} - c > \dfrac{(v_{max} - c - d)^2}{4 v_{max}}$, $c \leq \dfrac{v_{max}}{2}$ and $c + d \leq v_{max}$. If $c + d > v_{max}$, unbundled sales will be unprofitable, while bundled sales will be unprofitable if $c > \dfrac{v_{max}}{2}$. In this case, c_0 is approximately $0.41\, v_{max}$. Figure 8 shows a "phase diagram" of the corresponding profitability areas.

It can be argued that linear demand functions and the corresponding uniform distribution of valuations are not appropriate for information goods. For example, most consumers may have exactly zero valuation for 90% of the news stories provided by a news service, and a linear demand for the remaining 10%. The resulting piecewise linear demand curve would be similar to the one used by Chuang and Sirbu (1997) and to several numerical examples presented in Odlyzko (1996).

When many consumers have zero valuations for any given good, the effects of any marginal costs will be amplified and the region in which bundling is profitable will be reduced. This is because any bundle will likely include numerous goods with no value to any given consumer; if these goods are costly to provide, they will tend to reduce the value created by providing the bundle to that consumer. For instance, when consumers have nonzero valuations for only 10% of the goods, the threshold value, c_0, at which bundling becomes unprofitable relative to bundled sales declines by a factor of 10 to $0.041\, v_{max}$ (see Fig. 9).

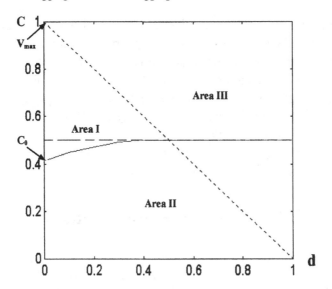

Fig. 8. Phase diagram for bundling and unbundling strategies as a function of marginal production cost and distribution/transaction cost when valuations are uniformly distributed

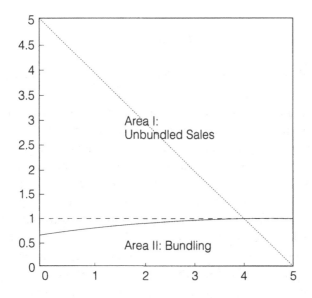

Fig. 9. Phase diagram for bundling and unbundling strategies as a function of marginal production cost and distribution/transaction cost when valuations are exponentially distributed

As another example, when valuations are distributed exponentially – so that only a small number of people have high valuations and a long tail of people have low valuations but no one quite has a zero valuation – and marginal costs are near zero, bundling can allow sellers to profitably provide the goods to the long tail of people who have relatively low valuations for the good. Because the number of such people may be very large, the efficiency and profit effects can be substantial: One could grow quite rich by selling a joke per day to 10 million people, even if most of them valued the joke at only a penny or less. However, as soon as marginal costs begin to approach the average consumer's valuation, bundling becomes unprofitable. In contrast, because the exponential distribution assumes there is always a positive probability that someone will have a valuation equal to or greater than any finite number, unbundled sales are never completely unprofitable; they simply require a price greater than the sum of production, distribution, and transaction costs. Figure 9 shows the "phase diagram" with the corresponding two areas of profitability.

4. Site Licensing and Subscriptions

The preceding section focused on the benefits of aggregation in the context of bundling. As has been noted in two examples by Odlyzko (1996) and several analytical models by Bakos and Brynjolfsson (1999c) and Bakos et al. (1999), parallel arguments can be made for aggregation in other dimensions, such as site licensing (aggregation across users) and subscriptions (aggregation over time).

Site Licensing

As with bundling, there are many reasons that a firm may choose to sell its products through a site license instead of selling them to individual users. For instance, site licensing can reduce administrative costs and transaction costs; reduce or eliminate the need to check for piracy at a given customer's site; facilitate interoperability and foster positive network externalities; and reduce maintenance costs through standardization of software configurations. Many of these costs can be modeled as creating a fixed transaction cost, t, per sale, analogous to the distribution/transaction cost parameter, d, in section 3. When this cost is sufficiently high, aggregation (site licensing) will be more profitable than disaggregation (individual sales).[6]

As shown by Bakos and Brynjolfsson (1999c), an analysis similar to that for bundling shows that site licensing can also be seen as a mechanism for aggregation that increases seller profits and reduces the inefficiency of withholding a good from consumers who value it at more than its marginal cost. Where bundling aggregates a single consumer's valuations for many products, site licensing aggregates many consumers' valuations for a single product. As with bundling, the law of large numbers will lead to a distribution of valuations for the site license that, after adjusting for the number of users, is less dispersed and more predictable than the distribution of individuals' valuations for the same good.

---

[6]   Varian (1997) develops a model for sharing information goods that can be applied to site licensing; however, his analysis is driven by transaction cost considerations rather than the aggregation effects

For instance, some researchers at a university may have high valuations for Mathematica and be willing to pay $500 for access to it; other users might value it only at $50; and still others might be willing to pay $5 or $10 to have easy access to the program in case it is needed in the future. Wolfram Research, the manufacturer of Mathematica, could set a high price and exclude potential users with low valuations, or set a low price that fails to extract most of the surplus from the high-valuation users.[7] Alternatively, Wolfram could offer a site license to the university that gives all potential users access to Mathematica. The value of such a site license to the university is equal to the sum of all potential users' individual valuations. This amount is larger than the profits that can be obtained through individual sales. Thus, both profits and efficiency may be increased if the seller pursues a site license.

If the seller does not offer the goods for sale to individual users, then in principle it could offer the site license for a price just slightly less than the expected sum of individual valuations (i.e., at a price $p \approx m^*\mu$, where m is the number of individuals at the site and μ is the average valuation for the good in this population). Almost all sites would find this price acceptable, and thus almost all users would get access to the good.[8] As with bundling, in the limit, aggregation virtually eliminates inefficiency and maximizes profits, at the expense of consumers' surplus.

One important difference between site licensing and bundling is that the site-licensing strategy requires an agent who has authority to purchase information goods on behalf of their ultimate consumers. An agent may not have perfect information about the preferences of end users, and his or her incentives may not be perfectly aligned with those of the end users; this may reduce the benefits of a site-licensing strategy.

Subscriptions

Our model of aggregation can also be applied to dimensions such as time and space. For example, when the good can be costlessly provided over time, it may be more profitable to sell it as a long-term subscription than to sell individual uses in short periods of time. Since a given user may sometimes have high valuations for the good and sometimes low valuations, per-use (or short-term) pricing might inefficiently exclude use during low-valuation periods, even when the cost of provision is zero.

---

[7] If Wolfram Research can identify the users who have high and low values, it can also price-discriminate by charging different prices to different users. However, because users can often disguise their true valuations, price discrimination typically leaves some rents in the hands of high-value users and excludes some low-value users from access to the good

[8] When individual copies are also available at a price that would leave some surplus in the hands of some consumers, the seller cannot extract the full value of the product through a site-licensing strategy. If the seller attempted to do so, the buyers would be collectively better off by individually buying or not buying the product

Greater efficiency and profits can result from charging a single subscription fee and giving the user long-term access to the good, by an argument corresponding to those for bundling and site licensing.[9]

Similarly, allowing the user to access the good from multiple locations may also provide some of the benefits of aggregation; a requirement that the good be used only on a specific machine or in a specific location would undermine these benefits. Without aggregation, some users might forgo access to the good in places where their valuations were low; when the costs of providing additional access are even lower (or zero), this would create an inefficiency.

There are many other ways to "disaggregate" goods. Technologies such as micropayment systems, cryptolopes, autonomous agents, and object technology are enabling sellers to charge different prices when information goods are disaggregated in various ways. For instance, a seller of software, in principle, could charge users a price for each time a function of its product is invoked on a particular machine. Although such "atomic" pricing may become feasible, it would reduce or eliminate the benefits of aggregation and thus it might reduce efficiency and profits.

When to Use Micropayments: "Mixed Aggregation" Can Dominate Pure Aggregation

Our model indicates that complete disaggregation or "mixed aggregation" (which involves simultaneously selling both an aggregate and disaggregated components) can be more profitable than aggregation strategies in three specific circumstances.

First, if marginal costs are nontrivial, disaggregation can economize on these costs by allowing users to "opt out" of components with a marginal cost greater than their marginal benefit. For example, if the marginal cost of providing an additional component or servicing an additional user is c, a seller that charges a fixed price p plus an additional price of c per component or user will avoid the inefficiency of including too many components in the sale or servicing too many users. If c is very low, micropayment technology may be required to enable the seller to profitably pursue such a strategy.

Second, if some consumers are willing to pay more for all goods, mixed aggregation may be beneficial if it can help sort consumers. For instance, if consumers with high valuations tend to prefer to use more goods or use the goods more often, a mixed-aggregation strategy can induce them to self-select and pay higher prices for larger aggregations.

---

9   A subscription may provide the user with different goods over time; in such cases, the logic of bundling applies directly. However, even when a subscription provides the *same* good in different time periods, the aggregation effects may still be important, since consumer valuations for the good may vary with time. If these valuations are serially correlated, however, the benefits of aggregation will tend to be lower (Bakos and Brynjolfsson, 1996)

Third, even when marginal costs are negligible and consumers are homogeneous, large aggregations of goods (or users) may be required to fully extract profits and to maximize efficiency. Therefore, if the seller can aggregate over only a small number of goods, consumers, or time periods, it may be optimal to also offer some goods outside the bundle, site license, or subscription.

Aggregation and Disaggregation on Multiple Dimensions

Aggregation can also be practiced on multiple dimensions simultaneously. For instance, bundles of goods can be offered on a site-license basis to multiple users for an extended period of time. This strategy may enable the seller to get closer to full efficiency and earn higher profits, since aggregation along one dimension will not generally exhaust the benefits of aggregation in other dimensions. Indeed, when the valuations of the goods are independently distributed and these goods have zero marginal cost, the optimal strategy will be to offer the largest possible bundle of goods through the largest possible site license for the broadest possible set of conditions, and to charge a price low enough to get almost all users to participate. This strategy captures as profits nearly the entire possible surplus from the goods.

In practice, it might make sense to aggregate in some dimensions while disaggregating in other dimensions. For instance, if marginal costs are not negligible, it may be appropriate to offer only subsets of the goods in each of several bundles so that users can choose the sets of goods they find most valuable and avoid the production cost for the ones they do not. Similarly, the seller could choose to disaggregate (or avoid aggregating) in those dimensions that are most effective in getting users to reveal their valuations while aggregating in other dimensions.

5. Conclusions

The Internet is precipitating a dramatic reduction in the marginal costs of production and distribution for digital information goods, while micropayment technologies are reducing the transaction costs for their commercial exchange. These developments are creating the potential to use pricing strategies for information goods based on aggregation and disaggregation. Because of the ability to cost-effectively aggregate very large numbers of information goods, or, at the other end of the spectrum, offer small components for individual sale, these strategies have implications for information goods that are not common in the world of physical goods.

In particular, aggregation can be a powerful strategy for providers of information goods. It can result in higher profits for sellers as well as a socially desirable wider distribution of the goods, but it is less effective when the marginal production costs are high or when consumers are heterogeneous. Aggregation strategies can take a variety of forms, including bundling (aggregation across different goods), site licensing (aggregation across different users), and subscriptions (aggregation over time). These strategies can reduce buyer heterogeneity by aggregating a large number of goods, users, or time periods, and can also reduce distribution and transaction costs. Therefore, a decision to aggregate information goods should be based on the trade-off between the benefits of aggregation and the marginal costs of production and distribution. Low distribution costs make aggregation less attractive, while low marginal production costs make aggregation more attractive.

On the other hand, the low distribution and transaction costs offered by ubiquitous networking and micropayment technologies enable the use of disaggregation strategies such as per-use fees, rentals, and sale of small components. Disaggregation strategies enable sellers to maximize their profits by price discriminating when consumers are heterogeneous. For example, the number of goods desired by individual consumers may be correlated with their valuations for these goods, as when a professional stock trader demands more financial news stories and has higher valuation for these stories than an individual investor. The seller can take advantage of this correlation by incorporating the signal that reveals the consumer's valuation, that is, the number of news stories purchased, in the pricing of the goods, resulting in some type of pay-per-use pricing. In general, the pricing scheme used should incorporate all signals that may reveal a consumer's willingness to pay, and micropayment technologies can enable the implementation of such schemes.

The optimal pricing strategy will often involve mixed aggregation, that is, the simultaneous availability of information goods in aggregates of different sizes and compositions as well as individually. Mixed aggregation will be more desirable in three cases: first, when consumers are very heterogeneous, as it provides a device for price discrimination; second, when the marginal production costs are significant, as this increases the cost of offering goods to consumers who do not value them; and finally, when the number of goods for sale is relatively small, as the aggregation benefits of the law of large numbers will not be as powerful and the menu costs of administering the prices for all bundles offered will not be as high.

Our analysis of aggregation provides a framework in which to understand the pricing strategies of online content providers such as America Online and the Microsoft Network, the widespread use of site licensing of software and data access by companies such as Wolfram Research and Reuters, and subscription pricing in the sale of information goods by companies such as Netscape and *The Wall Street Journal.* It can also explain how the dramatic reduction in marginal production, distribution, and transaction costs precipitated by the Internet is leading to pricing strategies based on both aggregation and disaggregation. Because the reasons for aggregating information goods when production and distribution costs are very low differ substantially from the reasons for aggregating goods when these costs are high, the content and nature of the aggregations (e.g., bundles) may differ substantially in these two situations.

In the models presented in this paper, we have focused on the demand-reshaping effects of aggregation and disaggregation, and have ignored their strategic aspects. In a related paper (Bakos and Brynjolfsson, 1999b), we find that the profit-enhancing potential of bundling will often be increased when competitors are forced to respond.[10] The analysis in this chapter suggests that there may be similar competitive benefits in site licensing and subscription strategies.

Finally, aggregation also has significant effects on social welfare. Specifically, aggregation strategies can substantially reduce the deadweight loss from monopoly, but they can also lower the surplus left to consumers.

References

Adams, W. J., Yellen, J. L. (1976) Commodity bundling and the burden of monopoly. Quart J Econ 90 (August): 475–498

Armstrong, M. (1996) Multiproduct nonlinear pricing. Econometrica 64, 1 (January): 51–75

Bakos, Y., Brynjolfsson, E. (1996) Bundling information goods: Pricing, profits and efficiency. Working Paper, MIT Sloan School

Bakos, Y., Brynjolfsson, E. (1999a) Bundling information goods: Pricing, profits and efficiency. Management Science 45, 12 (December) Available at http://www.stern.nyu.edu/~bakos

Bakos, Y., Brynjolfsson, E. (1999b) Bundling and competition on the Internet. Management Science, 2000. In press. Available at http://www.stern.nyu.edu/~bakos

Bakos, Y., Brynjolfsson, E. (1999c) Site licensing. Working Paper

Bakos, Y., Brynjolfsson, E., Lichtman, D. G. (1999) Shared information goods. J Law Econ 42 (April): 117–155

Brynjolfsson, E., Kemerer, C. F. (1996) Network externalities in microcomputer software: An econometric analysis of the spreadsheet market. Management Science 42, 12 (December): 1627–1647. Available at http://ccs.mit.edu/erik

Chuang, J. C.-I., Sirbu, M. A. (1997) Network delivery of information goods: Optimal pricing of articles and subscriptions. In: Hurley, D., Kahin, B., Varian, H. (eds.) Internet Publishing and Beyond: The Economics of Digital Information and Intellectual Property. MIT Press. In press. Available at http://www.epp.emu.edu/~chuang

Christensen, L. R., Jorgenson, D. W. (1969) The measurement of U.S. real capital input, 1929–1967. Review of Income and Wealth 15 (4): 293–320

Fishburn, P. C., Odlyzko, A. M., Siders, R. C. (1997) Fixed fee versus unit pricing for information goods: Competition, equilibria, and price wars. In: Hurley, D., Kahin, B., Varian, H. (eds.) Internet Publishing and Beyond: The Economics of Digital Information and Intellectual Property. MIT Press. In press

Hanson, W., Martin, K. (1990) Optimal bundle pricing. Management Science 36, 2 (February): 155–174

Lancaster, K. J. (1966) A new approach to consumer theory. J Political Economy 74, 2 (April): 132–157

McAfee, R. P., McMillan, J., Whinston, M. D. (1989) Multiproduct monopoly, commodity bundling, and correlation of values. Quart J Econ 114 (May): 371–384

Metcalfe, R. (1996) It's all in the scrip – Millicent makes possible subpenny 'net commerce'. Infoworld, January 29, 1996

---

[10] Specifically, in the presence of fixed production costs (and low or zero marginal costs), aggregation can drive competitors out of the market, even when their products are qualitatively superior. Such a response will often increase the profitability of aggregation

Metcalfe, R. (1997)Pollinate lets you rent the software you need for just the right amount of time. Infoworld, June 9, 1997

Odlyzko, A. M. (1996) The bumpy road of electronic commerce. In: Maurer, H. (ed.) WebNet 96 – World Conf. Web Soc. Proc., AACE, 1996, 378–389

Odlyzko, A. M. (1996) On the road to electronic publishing. Euromath Bulletin 2 (1): 49–60

Salinger, M. A. (1995) A graphical analysis of bundling. J Business 68 (1): 85–98

Schmalensee, R. L. (1984) Gaussian demand and commodity bundling. J Business 57 (1): S211–S230

Stigler, G. J. (1963) United States v. Loew's, Inc.: A note on block booking. Supreme Court Review, pp. 152–157 [Reprinted in Stigler, G. J. (1968) The Organization of Industry. Richard D. Irwin, Homewood, IL.]

Varian, H. R. (1995) Pricing information goods. Proceedings of Scholarship in the New Information Environment Symposium, Harvard Law School, May 1995

Varian, H. R. (1997) Buying, sharing and renting information goods. Working Paper, School of Information Management and Systems, University of California at Berkeley, May 1997. Available at http://www.sims.berkeley.edu/~hal

Varian, H. R., Roehl, R. (1996) Circulating libraries and video rental stores. Available at http://www.sims.berkeley.edu/~hal

Yannis Bakos
Associate Professor of Management at the Stern School of Business at New York University. His research focuses on the impact of information technology on markets, and in particular on how internet-based electronic marketplaces affect pricing and competition. He is also studying pricing strategies for information goods. Professor Bakos is the co-founder of the Workshop on Information Systems and Economics (WISE), which has become the leading forum for research at the intersection of the Information Technology and Economics disciplines. He received his MBA and Ph.D. from the Sloan School of Management at MIT, and holds Bachelors and Masters degrees in Electrical Engineering and Computer Science from MIT.

Erik Brynjolfsson
Associate Professor at the MIT Sloan School of Management and Co-director of the Center for eBusiness@MIT (http://ebusiness.mit.edu). His research analyzes how businesses can effectively use the Internet and other information technologies. Prof. Brynjolfsson is an award-winning researcher, and a Director or Advisor for numerous ecommerce firms. He lectures and consults worldwide on topics related to Internet strategy, pricing models and intangible assets. Prof. Brynjolfsson is an associate member of MIT's Lab for Computer Science and the co-editor of Understanding the Digital Economy (MIT Press). He holds Bachelors and Masters degrees from Harvard University and a Ph.D. from MIT.

Auctions – the Big Winner Among Trading Mechanisms for the Internet Economy

R. Müller

International Institute of Infonomics & Department of Quantitative
Economics, Universiteit Maastricht, The Netherlands

r.muller@ke.unimaas.nl

Abstract

Auctions are probably the most important mechanism for dynamic pricing in electronic commerce. Although they constitute a very old mechanism as well, the new popularity has raised a lot of questions on the appropriate design of an auction mechanism for a particular situation. This chapter describes reasons for auction popularity by setting them into the context of trends in electronic commerce. We then illustrate the main issues in auction design. Our analysis starts with simple single-item auctions, as we can see them in many B2C markets. We then look at the more complex auction designs, which are necessary for B2B markets. For the latter design has to take into account that buyers want to purchase collections of items and services, and that the valuation for winning collections is not simply equal to the sum of valuations of single items. We show how multi-item auction mechanisms can benefit from a synthesis of microeconomic and mathematical optimization models.

1. Introduction

An auction is a mechanism to re-allocate a set of goods to a set of market participants on the basis of bids and asks. In its classical form one seller, the auctioneer, wants to find a buyer for a single, indivisible item among a group of bidders. The best known auction design for this case is the increasing bid auction, or *English auction*. In this auction the auctioneer receives bids until she decides to terminate the auction, at which point the bidder with the highest bid receives the item, unless this bid is below the auctioneer's reservation price. The price that the bidder has to pay is equal to her last bid. An auction design is specified through three elements:

1. the *bidding rules* define what bidders may bid for and when;
2. the *market clearing rules* define when and how the allocation of items to bidders is decided and what bidders have to pay;
3. the *information disclosure rules* define when and which information is disclosed to whom.

The English auction has the simple bidding rule that every bidder can make a bid at every time, the market clearing rule that the highest bid wins and has to pay this bid, and the information disclosure rule that the highest bid is known. If the auction takes place in a room where all bidders are present, then bids are known to all bidders. In English auctions done on the Internet, only the price of the current high bid may be announced.

Auctions may not only be used to sell items or services but also to purchase them. We call them in this case a *reverse auction*. For purchasing *first price, sealed bid auctions* are the common format. Here bidders submit sealed bids. The bidding rules define who is allowed to participate. The market clearing rule assigns the bid to the bidder with the lowest price for the item. The price that is paid by the auctioneer is equal to this bid price. This format is typical for contracting complex services in the construction industry. The advantage of a reverse auction is that the buyer can specify in detail the service, and due to sealed bids is not required to take the cheapest offer, but to apply other criteria than price in the market clearing phase.

As another example for a classical auction we mention the *Dutch auction*. It uses a price clock that starts at a high price, which steadily decreases until a bidder decides to buy at the current price. By shouting or other means she stops the bidding process and receives the item at the current price. The Dutch auction is typically used for selling agricultural products. It is fast since it ends with the first bid from a bidder, and thus in particular appropriate for markets that have to negotiate a high volume of transactions in a short period of time.

Finally, there are so-called *double auctions* in which buyers make bids and sellers make asks, where a participant may be buyer and seller at the same time. Bids and asks are displayed in an order book. As soon as a bid for an item is higher than the current ask, the item is traded for a price in between of the two values. Double auctions are used at stock exchanges, and now frequently at spot markets for commodities in B2B marketplaces.

The Internet has become an important platform for trading, which is illustrated through all chapters of this book. Auctions got within Internet trading a much more prominent role than they had in offline trading. Reasons for that are discussed in section 2. Section 3 is dedicated to the fundamental choices one has in auction design. We illustrate them along single item auctions. In Section 4 we introduce the more complex setting, where several indivisible items are auctioned at the same time.

Such auctions are of particular relevance in B2B e-commerce. Section 5 illustrates possible designs for such multi-item auctions, as well as the challenges in implementing such design. We summarize in Section 6.

The goal of this article about auctions and the Internet is to provide an introduction to the topic. We summarize those features of auctions that have to be understood for users and providers of Internet auctions. We try to omit mathematical details where possible, but do nevertheless try to explain the mathematical problems that have to be solved in auction design. We hope to stimulate the reader to start from this article for a more detailed tour through the recent auction literature. Last but not least we try to combine quite different aspects of auction theory in an interdisciplinary approach. A reader who would like to learn at this point more about the history of auctions, or read about the different formats in more detail, should have a look at (Agorics Inc., 1996). For diving deeper into the topic we recommend (Klemperer, 1999).

2. Auctions on the Internet

Why are auctions such a popular trading mechanism on the Internet? Broadly spoken, the reason for this popularity is that Internet enables a wide range of organizations and people to use auctions for a wide range of items and services at rather convenient transaction costs. Let us elaborate on this in some more detail, without repeating however the many possible explanations that can be found in (Herschlag and Zwick, 2000).

Before the Internet could be used as communication platform for auctions, the range of potential participants in auctions, either as a bidder or an auctioneer, was rather limited. Now with the Internet, and with auction platforms accessible via the Internet, everybody can participate and even create an auction. At first place this is a phenomenon of tremendously decreased transaction costs. Physical presence at the auction is not necessary anymore, when product information as well as bids and asks can be communicated electronically. Many companies have seen this opportunity in an early stage of E-commerce penetration on the Web and set-up *private-to-private* auction platforms. Trading of collectibles has soon been complemented by using auctions as trading mechanism in retailing. Auction sites functioned as an "electronic catalogue with dynamic pricing", selling new products in *business-to-private* auctions. Finally, the business-to-business applications entered the stage. Meanwhile the Internet hosts a huge collection of auctions. The best way of getting an overview is probably to consult listings like http://www.internetauctionlist.com/ or http://www. auctionguide.com/.

The popularity of Internet auctions goes hand in hand with other business trends observed for the Internet. Three of these should be mentioned here.

Firstly, we see *changing roles of intermediaries* and *new forms of intermediation* (Sarkar et al., 1998; Scott, 2000). Already in October 1998, the Keenan report stated

"The power of instant communication destroys the power of middleman to hide the real price from buyers and sellers, creating new intermediaries who will control the distribution of basic goods. Distribution channels that are inherently inefficient, such as wholesale-retail chains, may be re-intermediated by a new middleman equipped with Internet Exchange technology" (Kennanvision.com, 1998).

Auctions on the large scale are only feasible due to the Internet. They are thus examples of *cybermediaries*. To some extend they constitute dis-intermediation as they are likely to replace a significant part of the business of brick-and-mortar auction houses. Whether the Internet auctions will be sustainable is likely to depend on whether or not they can provide a reliable service to their customers at a reasonable price. The first generation Internet auctions seem to require just a software platform to create a successful auction business. This rather simple business model for consumer-to-consumer auctions, which lets the participants take care of all other phases of the transaction, seemed to be sufficient for success. This is best explained by enormous *first mover advantages*, as an auction is a perfect example for strong network externalities. Sellers like to use sites that have many visitors, since a large number of bidders increases the expected revenue. Bidders again prefer these sites because they can chose from a large number of different offers. They might hope that the segmentation of the market has the effect of less competitors in a specific auction, ignoring to some extent that they are looking for precisely that product and value it therefore higher.

With more and more auction sites entering the stage, and with the trend that portals or companies that started with traditional retailing use now auctions as one of many versions of trading, the very simple model of trading platform can however risk to become a commodity. The trading itself is only a small part of the total change of ownership that, at the end has to include financial and physical settlement. Herschlag and Zwick (2000) give the example of Teletrade as an auction site that adds services for settlement for buyers and sellers, while ebay likes to classify itself as a "person-to-person" trading community. Whether the latter is a sustainable business model depends very much on the experiences that consumers make with their private trading partners. It could well be that online auction sites develop their own netiquete, maybe established through ratings of the auctioneers and bidders. But it could also be that on the long term auction sites which take care of logistics and settlement have an advantage against the platform only solutions. When more customer service is required, the traditional auction houses may even become the strongest competitors as they can rely on an established brand name as well as on their experiences in all phases of the settlement. However this brand name has to be protected and thus these sites will have to provide an above average service. It seems likely that we will see a range of service versions, where higher quality of service might have to be paid for by participation fees. Such fees could also serve partly to provide customers an insurance against bad fulfilment of the contract.

The second business trend is *customising*, hand-in-hand with *personal pricing*. The principal idea of an auction is to find among a set of potential buyers those with the highest willingness to pay, where the second highest valuation is about what can be expected as revenue (due to a fundamental theorem on auctions this is true for all major single-item auctions with private, independently distributed valuations of bidders, see the next section). Auctions make therefore sense in cases where the valuations are diverse, and where identification of the customer with highest valuation is difficult. However this concept seems to be in contrast to the expectation that consumers of an online auction have. Typically, they would like to make a bargain. Auctions would certainly become unpopular if they were used by the high-end customers, driving prices to the same level or above prices in the store or catalogue. Therefore online auctions which sell new products have to put much attention on proper product selection. There has to be a kind of scarcity and the product has to address a consumer group that observes a discount through the auction. Typical products are thus completely new products which are not available yet, or products that are replaced by a new version. In both cases the auction implements a two-fold segmentation. It selects through the type of products consumers who, in the first case, do not want to wait for until the next generation is in the store, and, in the second case, do not care for the most recent technology. Among those it applies personal pricing by finding the consumer with highest willingness to pay.

Real customizing in such a market is rather limited. There has to be more than one bidder interested in the same copy, since otherwise the second price would be zero. A typical customisation dimension is time. If for example bandwidth in a telecommunication network is required for a certain time-interval at a certain capacity, or if a traveller needs a ticket for a very specific time, an auction can have the strength that searching and negotiating an alternative trade is not feasible, as it would exceed the time limit. On the other hand, auctioning last minute tickets identifies those travellers who are not bound to a certain time.

Auctions are not the only trading mechanism that can realise personalised pricing. There are for example one-to-one price negotiation sides on the Web, in which a customer negotiates individually with a merchant on the price. From the list of frequently asked questions at haggelzone.com one can read (as of 11. 12. 2000) "Hagglezone.com is the anti-auction. At www.hagglezone.com, prices go down, not up. The buyer is in control of negotiating the price down against the chosen Haggler, instead of bidding prices up against hordes of other consumers". A "haggler" means a salesperson the customer tries to negotiate with a price. Note that the underlying mechanism is similar to a Dutch auction, rather than an "anti-auction". Namely, in case the merchant is negotiating at the same time with several customers (which is not observable by the buyer), he can lower the price steadily until the first customer is willing to buy. If there are several items to sell, she can however continue decreasing prices for the other customers. Only if there is exactly one customer interested in the item it differs from a Dutch auction. In this case an auction would not be recommendable to the merchant, so the advantage is on the merchant's side. One-to-one price negotiation is actually most appropriate, if more terms than the price are part of the negotiation, in which case there is likely exactly one customer for a given mix of terms. Furthermore, the price serves as a trade-off between matched and un-matched customer expectations. An example is given by www.tradeaccess. com. Finally, there are sites like www.priceline.com realising B2C reverse auctions, and sites like www.letsbuyit. com that realises a flexible price through bundling of demand.

The third business trend is *customer involvement*. At an auction site it is the customer who determines the price, not the auctioneer. With many items on sale at the same time, the customer gets a huge selection of items. In particular for moderated auctions, as they can be found on various sites (for example at www.ricardo.de) the customer contributes to the entertainment to non-active visitors of the auction site by taking part in an open, observable competition. Finally, customers of private-to-private auctions contribute to the success by setting up own auctions. Customers can even become almost professional traders by the help of the online auction infrastructure. Auctions like www.ricardo.de observe that items in their private-to-private auctions have previously been purchased in the business-to-consumer area. The Keenan report cites www.eBay.com with the information that in 1999, 10.000 customers made most of their personal income from trading goods with eBay (Keenanvision, 2000).

3. Auction Design

There are three major categories of auctions

1. The classical auction in which an auctioneer sells to a group of bidders. The introduction presented already the main versions: *English auction, first price sealed bid auction,* and *Dutch auction.* A fourth member of this category is the *second-price sealed bid auction,* also called the *Vickrey auction,* in which the winner has to pay only the second highest bid price.
2. The reverse auction in which the auctioneer wants to purchase items from a set of bidders. One may use all of the four formats here, although the first-price sealed-bid auction seems the most used one.
3. The double auction in which a group of buyers and sellers meet each other. The classical model is an *exchange.* Here sellers post asks and buyers post bids.

Inside each of these categories, many parameters have to be chosen to fine-tune the auction procedure. These include features like activity rules, minimum increments, or decrements, as well as information disclosure policy in multi-round auctions. A mix of general format and features can be used to address specifically the goals of an auction, given a certain market situation. Of increasing interest are hereby *multi-item auctions*, where the seller has a set of items to sell, and buyers are interested in purchasing certain subsets of this set. In this section we look at the role of information in auction design for single items, and then see in the next section why multi-item auctions require a special treatment.

Why is it such an important factor in the design of an auction, which information bidders and the auctioneer have about the value of the items on sale, and the information that they have about the other agents' value estimates? We will describe in the following two extremes, in order to give an answer to this question. Again, when compared with the rich literature on auctions, see e.g. (Klemperer, 1999), our treatment has to be rather introductory. Furthermore, information distribution in practice is usually in between the two extremes.

The first extreme is that where every bidder has *private value* of the item. The mathematical formalization is a value v_i of bidder i. To capture the degree of information that other bidders have about i's valuation we assume that they observe it as *random variable X_i*. In case of a discrete random variable they know thus the probability that the valuation of i takes a certain value. The private value model assumes that these random variables X_i are *independent random variables*. It is save to assume that the random variables are all identical, if bidders have no information about differences in the competitors' values for the item. An example for an auction with a private value model is that of auctioning a collectible, e.g. some painting from an *unknown* painter from the 19th century, where the value for every bidder is a function of personal taste. We assume an unknown painter, because we want to exclude that the purchase is meant as an investment for later sale, in which case we would loose some of the independence of valuations.

The second extreme is that of a *common value*. In this case the value of the item is independent of the bidder, or in other words common to every bidder. Mathematically this situation is modelled by a single random variable. The exact distribution of the random variable is unknown to the bidders, and possibly as well to the auctioneer. However all parties may have a certain degree of information about this random variable, by having done a priori some research. An example is shares on the stock market. Their value in the future, i.e. the price at which the stock market will trade them, is completely independent of bidders' personal taste. The value is a random variable, of which well-informed bidders have a better estimate than less informed bidders.

Auctions in practice are situated in between these two extremes. Buying a painting might well be seen as an investment, in which case the future demand for the painting, in other words the possible price that it might achieve in an auction, plays a significant role for its value. The decision which shares to buy at which price can also be influenced by preferences for a brand name, or from hedging considerations for the own portfolio, which adds a private value component.

Let us see now how the two cases influence the choice for the auction design. Notice that the bidding process may reveal information, in other words it signals other bidders. The auctioneer might want to support these signals, if it reduces the risks of bidders and thus increases the willingness to pay. She might want to mind these signals, if bidders can collude this way and decrease the outcome of the auction.

Consider the ascending price English auction. If bidders have private valuations v_i, and if they behave rationally, they should participate in the auction until the bid reaches v_i. Indeed at that point a bidder's *utility* u_i which is defined by $u_i = v_i - p$, p being the price that the winner has to pay, is becoming 0, so she becomes indifferent between win or not to win. Observing the bid prices of other bidders is not of relevance for her. The only impact that they have to her strategy is that they determine at which price she is able to win the item. If she has the highest valuation and all bidders participate actively, she will purchase the item at a price slightly higher than the second highest bid from her competitors. If competitors follow the same rationale, this bid is equal to the second highest valuation of bidders. In this case the English auction realizes a so-called *second price auction*.

Three factors play an important role here. Firstly, it is the *activity* of bidders. If activity is not stimulated, then the bidder with the highest valuation risks to make an initial bid that is already strictly higher than the second highest valuation. In this case all others drop out and she doesn't realize the maximum possible utility. It's thus wise for all bidders to start with a careful low bid. It's also advisable for the auctioneer to let the auction start with a low initial bid, even if her reservation price is higher. The *reservation price* is the lowest price at which the auctioneer is willing to sell. In Ebay.com private-to-private auctioneers can for example set a start price *and* a reservation price. The latter is not visible to the bidders.

Secondly, the *termination rule* of the auction plays a role. In the traditional offline auction setting, the auctioneer uses the *going, going, gone* mechanism to finalise the bidding. This enables the auctioneer to evaluate carefully, whether the current highest bidder is also the one with the highest valuation. If, like in many online auctions, the end is a fixed point in time, the auction looses its flavour of a second price auction. Now a bidder with a low non-competitive valuation may succeed to win by making the highest bid just before the auction finishes. Bidders can protect themselves against such competition only if they make a high bid early enough. But this makes it likely that a winning bidder has to pay a price that is very close to her own valuation, which turns the auction mechanism into a *first price auction*. Online auctions are therefore considered typically as a hybrid of a first and second price auction (Ockenfels and Roth, 2000). Some auction sites, e.g. www.amazon.com, avoid this by extending the auction automatically for a couple of minutes after the last bid was made. Quite astonishingly, the bidders can in principle avoid to pay more than the second highest valuation in a first price auction by using their information and doing some calculus. Indeed if they know how the random variables determining other bidders' valuations are distributed they can calculate a strategy that gives them an expected utility that is equal to that in the English auction. Basically, they have to calculate the *expected value of the second highest bid*. For the interested reader we recommend an auction survey by Wolfstetter (1996), or the original paper by Myerson (1981), to learn more about the precise conditions under which the *revenue equivalence theorem* applies.

Thirdly, *minimal bid increments* are of relevance. A minimal bid increment is the amount by which the next bid has to be higher than the current highest bid. Minimum bid increments can have the effect that not necessarily the bidder with highest valuation wins the auction. Say, for example, that the highest valuation among all bidders is 98, the minimal increment is 5 and the auction is at price of 95. If the current highest bid has not been by the bidder with highest valuation, the latter has to drop out, since winning with 100 would have a negative utility.

Fixed end times and minimal increments may thus both lead to the effect that the auction is not *efficient*. Efficiency is defined as the property that the bidder with highest valuation will win the auction. Efficiency is desirable from a welfare perspective, and also from an auctioneer's perspective. If the bidder with highest valuation wins, and if there is a strong competition, meaning that the second highest valuation is close to the highest, an efficient second price auction is close to optimal for the auctioneer. In economic literature an auction design is said to be *optimal* if the expected revenue for the auctioneer is maximized. We will use the attribute optimal in a different way throughout this paper, namely with respect to a specific instance of bidder valuations. We say that the auction is optimal for this instance if the revenue is equal to the maximum valuation.

Let us now turn back to the role of information, and consider the case of a common value, where the final value of the item will be the same for every bidder, but the bidders have different estimates about this value. We look first at the English auction. We observe easily that the bidders should become careful with every bidder who drops from the bidding, since this indicates that her estimate tells that the (common) value of the item will be less than or equal to the current highest bid. The more bidders drop out, the more reliable becomes this signal from the auction process. An ascending price auction thus reveals information. Necessary is however activity by the bidders. We saw above that with a fixed termination date early bidding is discouraged, and thus information revelation is abandoned. The auction becomes a first price auction, with a significant risk of a *winner's curse*. The winner's curse is the effect that a winner in a common value auction pays more than the (later) value of the item. The winner's curse is actually not tied to first price auctions, and can also occur in second price auctions with common value, though it will be less severe of course.

The possibility to exchange information during the auction process makes up for the main difference between open outcry auctions and *sealed bid* auctions, in which the auctioneer collects bids in sealed envelopes and decides who wins the auction. Certainly, sealed bid auctions have the advantage of further lowering transaction costs, but the stronger the common value component is in the valuation of the item, the higher the risk of a winner's curse. Furthermore, sealed bid auctions require trust in the auctioneer that she does not manipulate the bids. The sealed bid auction knows two versions: the first price sealed bid auction, and the Vickrey auction in which the price is that of the second highest bid. The revenue equivalence theorem (Myerson, 1981) tells us that the expected revenue for the auctioneer is the same for both models in the case of private values, since in the first price auction the bidder should adjust his bid to the expected second highest bid. Under common value situations this is not necessarily the case.

The online auction www.ricardo.de experimented in May 2000 with a second price Vickrey auction. They called it an *undercover auction*. Results have been reported on their site at http://www.undercover.ricardo.de/undercover/mid.htm (11.12.2000). Comments to an announcement of that auction at www.zdnet.com showed that bidders have a hard time understanding the principle of the second price. A concern was that a bidder might be tempted to bid very high, because this increases the chance to win the auction, while only the second price has to be payed. However this strategy would lead to a large loss if more than one bidder applies it. Rather than excluding by this argument the strategy, comments at www.zdnet.com brandmarked the auction mechanism as extremely unfair! Online auctions can well offer Vickrey auctions in a less explicit way. So does www.qxl.com, which offers to set a maximum bid upto which a bidding agent will increase the bid on behalf of the bidder whenever her bid is not the highest: "When you bid, we ask you to put in the maximum bid amount you are willing to pay for the item. Remember that bid amount reflect the amount you are willing to pay per item. So, if you bid £10, and you select to buy a quantity of 10, that means your total bill could be £100 for this auction. Once you set your Max. Bid, we place a bid on your behalf to enter you in the auction, and every time you're outbid, to make sure you stay the high bidder, up to the bid you specify."

The ricardo case indicates that smart auction design should take the user into account, in the sense that it might be too complex for her to behave optimally. If we follow this argumentation in a more formal way, we see that different auction designs have quite different *computational complexity* for the bidders and the auctioneer. The reader should take computational complexity as a measure of mathematical tasks that have to be solved in order to optimize the own strategy. In an English auction this is quite simple: the bidder observes and decides at every point whether she is willing to increase the bid or not. In the common value case the decision has to take the bidding of competitors into account, in the other case not. Two recent papers that take the cognitive costs of bidders into account are (Parkes et al., 1999), and (Nisan and Ronen, 2000).

Let us finally consider the Dutch auction. In the case of private valuations the bidder should use the same strategy as in the sealed bid first price auction or in the auction with a fixed termination date: forecast the second highest valuation of all bidders, and stop the descending auction clock at this value, in case that the own valuation is higher. Notice once more the computational problem of calculating this termination point! Without computational effort, maximum expected utility is not realized, because the bidder either fails to win, or she wins at a price strictly higher than the second highest valuation among the bidders. In case of a common value auction, the Dutch auction has the disadvantage that it does not reveal any information about other bidders' estimates. Bidders can simply not observe other bidders' decision to leave the auction. This delivers again a high risk for a winner's curse.

What we learn from this discussion is that auction theory is a very complex field of mathematical research. Although there are strong theorems that can be used to reduce the number of cases to be considered, like the revenue equivalence theorem or the revelation principle (Myerson, 1979), these theorems have to make assumptions that are not necessarily applicable in practice. Firstly, they assume *rational decision making*, secondly they assume unbounded computational and mathematical capabilities of decision makers, and thirdly they seem not to reflect that the process of an auction can have a strong psychological influence on the decision behaviour, which is in any case not necessarily completely rational. Every specific auction design requires not only a detailed theoretical foundation, but also empirical and experimental analysis, in order to be able to predict its outcome for bidders and auctioneer. The many auctions on the Internet do not only challenge auction research for that, but also turn out to become a means to improve the understanding of auctions. With millions of auctions going on all the time, auction research gets the empirical data required to fine-tune designs. As an outstanding example of such online research we refer here to (Ockenfels and Roth, 2000).

To summarise, we can say that research on single-item auctions has to look in detail on bidders information about the item, on the spread of this information among bidders, the computational complexity of evaluating this information, and the diffusion of information during the auction process.

4. Complements and Substitutes

So far we considered the case that exactly one item is sold in an auction, and that the bidders valuation of that item is completely independent from other events. This assumption is hardly feasible in practice. Bidders might at the same time be active in many auctions, and the value of an item that they can win might well depend on other items they can purchase. For example, they might succeed to buy a *complement* for an item, giving the union of the two items a higher value than the sum of individual values. They might also face the situation in which they have purchased items that *substitute* each other. We consider in this section auctions in which one auctioneer tries to sell a *set of items* to a group of bidders. Such auctions are called *multi-item* auctions. The items may be different or identical. In the pure case of identical items we talk about *multi-unit* auctions. We assume furthermore that items are not divisible, such that it is not possible, say, that two bidders win both half of an item.

Multi-item auctions have numerous applications, like selling airport time slots (Rassenti et al., 1982), railroad segements (Brewer, 1999), and shipping contracts (Caplice, 1996). They are of interest as coordination mechanism in multi-agent systems (Nisan and Ronen, 2000), and have recently been investigated largely from a computer science and operations research perspective (e.g., Fujishima et al., 1998; Leyton-Brown et al., 2000a, b; Rothkopf et al., 1998; Sandholm, 1999; Sandholm and Suri, 2000; Tennenholtz, 2000; Vohra and de Vries, 2000; Wellman et al., 1998).

In terms of the broad range of auction features that we discussed in the previous section we have to restrict ourselves. We assume in the following private value. The value is now not anymore related to one single item, but is a function that maps every subset of items to a real, non-negative number. Such a function determines the *type* of a bidder. A type is thus a mapping $v: 2^S \to \mathfrak{R}$. The outcome of the auction is an allocation of subsets of items to bidders. We denote by I the set of items and by B the set of bidders. Let J be a numbering of the union of all possible bids from all bidders. The set J gives a unique identifier to every subset for every bidder. We use it in the following to simplify our notation.

As in every auction mechanism it has to be decided which are the winning bids. Based on our notation we can use an 0–1 vector x to model this decision, with the interpretation that $x_j = 1$ if and only if bid j is assigned. By w_j we denote the bid price. Efficiency of the auction can now be expressed as follows. The final allocation x should maximise the expression $\sum_{j \in J} v_j x_j$. If p_j denotes the price which has to be paid for winning bid j, then optimality is achieved if $\sum_{j \in J} p_j x_j$ equals this maximum value.

Already the number of possible allocations of items, it is $(|B| + 1)^{|S|}$, indicates that multi-item auctions can be expected to be far more complex than single-item auctions. They are almost the most general market mechanism for markets with indivisible goods, and have in particular been studied in the literature on resource allocation in multi-agent systems. What they don't capture are preferences of a bidder on allocations among the other bidders. They are also a special case of multi-attribute auctions. To see this observe that we can represent a subset by an attribute vector, with one component for every item in I, and an attribute having value 1, if the corresponding item is contained in the subset, 0, otherwise. This way every bid, becomes a bid on a *product*, which satisfies certain attributes. The fact, that only a limited number of copies are available of each item translates into the fact that the auctioneer in the multi-attribute auction can only fulfil a certain mix of contracts.

Multi-item auctions started to gain scientific popularity in terms of the huge frequency auctions organised by state authorities since about 1994. Some failures of the first designs of such auctions in New Zealand, and Australia, caused the FCC in the US to invite auction experts to help in creating an appropriate multi-item auction (McMillan, 1994). The result was a multi-round, parallel single-item auction, with rules for minimum increments and participation. Let us try to illustrate why, aside from the sheer number of possible allocations, multi-item auctions are such a complex issue.

A major challenge in multi-item auction design is to solve the *exposure problem*. Suppose that items Q and R are strong complements to each other for a bidder A, thus she would be willing to pay \$ 100 if she can purchase both of them, while she values Q and R alone only at \$ 20 each. Suppose that competitors B and C have only interest in Q and R, respectively, with a valuation of \$ 30. If Q and R are auctioned independently in single-item auctions, then A may have to bid on both, Q and R, higher than 30, due to the competition by B and C. At this time she might well win Q at, say, 30, but fail to win R, leaving her with a negative utility of -10. If bidder A can announce her high valuation for $\{Q, R\}$ to the auctioneer, B and C might on the other hand be discouraged by the *threshold problem*. Individually they are not able to compete against the high bid of A. Together their value might however add to more than the $\$100$ by A. If the auction design is not capable to reveal this, A might win despite the higher revenue obtainable for the auctioneer if she assigns to B and C. However revealing this information in an ascending price auction might also be tricky for B and C. If for example B makes a high bid for Q, then a relative low bid from C for R is enough to beat A. C enjoys in this case *free riding* on the high bid from B.

A way out of this dilemma is to use a *utilitarian revelation mechanism*, in which bidders tell the auctioneer their type and the auctioneer computes an allocation based on this information. A problem with this approach is that bidders might be better off if they do not tell the truth, but report a wrong type w instead. This problem will be discussed below. A second problem of the revelation mechanism relates to the fact that an open, ascending price auction may function to inform other bidders in common value auctions. This issue is not addressed here, as we said to restrict ourselves to private value auctions. One might however argue that a utilitarian revelation mechanism may be repeated in several rounds, allowing bidders to adjust their type by withdrawing or reducing a bid made in a previous round. This kind of mechanism has to our knowledge not been studied in the literature, although several authors did propose ascending price combinatorial auctions in order to overcome the complexity of winner allocation in an revelation mechanism. This will be the topic of the next section.

5. Sealed Bid Combinatorial Auctions

In a sealed bid combinatorial auction bidders make bids for subsets of items. We assume for a moment that this gives a bid vector w. The auctioneer computes on this basis an allocation x. If the bids reveal the true valuations of bidders, i.e. $w = v$, then finding an optimal solution of the following integer linear program yields an efficient allocation:

max wx
s.t. $Ax \leq 1$
         $x\ integer$

In this formulation A is a matrix of zeroes and ones with a row for every item i, and a 1 at position j of row i, if and only if item i is contained in bid j. The right-hand side 1 stands for a vector with as many components as A has rows, with a 1 in each component. Two issues have to be considered at this point. The first is whether this is a reasonable way of representing the allocation problem. The second is how bidders can be given incentives to bid $w = v$. This is necessary to make the approach efficient, and due to a result of Monderer and Tennenholtz (1998) it is a basis to design an optimal auction, i.e., an auction with maximum possible revenue for the auctioneer.

6. Coding and Computational Complexity of Sealed-bid Combinatorial Auctions

Let us look at the integer linear programming model above and discuss how well it is suited to find an allocation of subsets to bidders in a sealed bid combinatorial auction.

Firstly, we observe that several bids from the same bidder may win at the same time, as long as they are disjoint. This happens however only in the case of substitutes, since only in this case the sum of the values of two disjoint bids may be higher than the bid for the union of the two sets. To protect the bidder against winning several bids at the same time we have to add additional constraints to the linear programming model. If the bidder wants to win at most one bid from all her bids, one additional row per bidder suffices. It has a 1 in every column of the matrix that represents a bid by this bidder, and a 1 as right-hand-side, all other coefficients are equal to 0. If a single bidder wants to express that there are several subsets of bids, where she wants to win one from each subset, but possibly several bids in total, we have to add such a constraint for each of these subsets. Such a bid is called an OR of XOR bids (Nisan, 2000). Notably, other logic constraints, like *if winning this bid I want also to win another bid*, can be expressed by adding linear constraints to the model. Nisan describes in a recent paper how different representations of combinatorial auctions can be converted into each other (Nisan, 2000).

Secondly, the simple encoding of bidders' types by listing *all* subsets for *every* bidder is not feasible for even small numbers of bidders and items. For 20 items and 100 bidders the matrix has already 20 rows and more than 20 million columns. It's not only the storage that causes a problem here, but also the fact that every bidder would have to communicate more than a million values. A sealed bid combinatorial auction has thus to restrict itself to a small number of bids from each bidder. Subsets for which a bidder does not make a bid are assumed to have a default value. For example, one might assume that such subsets have a value equal to zero. Many authors make also the free *disposal assumption* saying that getting additional items does not decrease the value. If the model does not exclude that the same bidder wins several subsets, the value of every subset that can be composed as disjoint union of subsets for which a bid has been made is assumed to be equal to the sum of the values of the subsets.

The restriction to a reasonable number of bids is less serious when a combinatorial auction is done in several rounds, versus in one round of sealed bids. In this case a bidder has a chance to submit in a later round bids which she did not consider in the beginning, and thus even learn her true valuation during the bidding process (Parkes and Ungar, 2000). This can be seen as adding in every round columns to the integer linear programming problem, which relates nicely to a *column-generation algorithm* in combinatorial optimisation. In such an algorithm we start with a small number of columns and find the optimal solution (in our terms this means a small number of initial bids). We then "generate" new columns which, once added to the linear program, can improve the optimal solution. Note that every new column extends the number of possible solutions of the optimisation problem (all previous solutions plus solutions that use that column), thus with a column added the optimal solution is at least as good as before. In a multi-round combinatorial auction, column generation means that bidders can submit bids in every round which improve the revenue for the auctioneer. In a one-round sealed bid auction one can use a similar approach by letting bidders submit a *pricing procedure*. This is a software agent that is able to calculate for every subset the price that a bidder is willing to pay for that subset. An approach like that can be found in various online auctions for single items. It is called a *bidding agent*. A bidder parameterises this agent by her maximal price, and the agent will generate minimal incremented bids in an ascending price auction, until this price reached.

Thirdly, and most important the above integer linear programming problem is NP-hard. This means that there will be no algorithm that can solve this problem in a number of operations that is polynomial in the encoding length of the problem, as far as $P \neq NP$, which, although never formally proven, is generally assumed to be true. This is already true if every bid contains not more than 3 items, and all bid prices are *1* or if every bidder makes exactly one bid with bid price 1 (Rothkopf et al., 1998; van Hoesel and Müller, 2000). On the other hand the problem is polynomial solvable if there exists a sorting of items such that every bid contains a set of neighboured items (Rothkopf et al., 1998). This latter result holds only in the case of complements. If bids substitute each other, and therefore additional constraints are required telling that every bidder is allocated at most one bid, it becomes NP-complete. This follows from a result about the complexity of certain scheduling problems (Keil, 1992).

Complexity results for the winner determination problem have to be taken with some care. Note that we want to have an algorithm that is polynomial in the length of the encoding of a problem. Now, if every bidder would submit a bid for every subset, the encoding would already take a huge amount of space. Indeed, it can be shown that with this huge input the winner determination problem can be solved in polynomial time (Müller and Schulz, 2000). But with a large number of items, an exponential number of bids would not be realistic from a bidders point of view, therefore it is reasonable that in many applications we are not in this extreme case of an exponential number of bids.

The fact that the winner determination problem is NP-hard is the most serious obstacle towards the application of sealed bid combinatorial auctions, and will form the core of the discussion of the remaining part of this chapter. We will first explain the classical Vickrey-Clarke-Groves pricing mechanism for sealed bid combinatorial auctions. We give a very simple proof that it is truth revealing. If it is used in combination with a heuristic or an approximation algorithm it requires a warranty on the allocation algorithm that leads at the same time to some abnormal effects. These are recent results by Nisan and Ronen (2000), which we summarise without giving proofs. We will then illustrate that the complexity of computing a good allocation in a combinatorial auction has to do with the complexity of defining market clearing prices in a market with indivisible items. We finally give a framework to solve the allocation problem with a primal-dual algorithm. This framework computes such prices, however with the disadvantage of being not optimal. If it is combined with a carefully adjusted pricing mechanism, it gives a truth revealing combinatorial auction mechanism, however only for special cases.

7. The Vickrey-Clarke Groves Mechanism

A combinatorial auction is one of many mechanisms that could be thought of as a clearing mechanism for a market with indivisible items. A general analysis of such markets is far beyond the scope of this paper, so we will have to make some assumptions in this section.

Our first assumption is that the auctioneer has the goal to maximize own revenue. The best result that can be achieved, given certain types of bidders, and assuming that bidders do not bid more than their valuation, is the solution of the above integer linear optimisation problem with $w = v$. A bidder may however be better off in bidding less than her valuation. In order to achieve nevertheless an allocation that is close to this optimum the auctioneer has to set incentives to bidders to report their *true* valuation in their bids.

Take for example the case of a sealed-bid auction for a single item. Bidders submit sealed bids with a price w_j. If the auctioneer chooses the highest bid as winning bid, bid 1, say, and sets $p_1 = w_1$, then the corresponding bidder would have been better off if he had submitted a bid that is just above the second highest bid. Thus the auction mechanism sets incentives for strategic behaviour. However, a classical mechanism is available to avoid strategic behaviour. We have seen it already in the introduction. It is based on an appropriate modification of the payment scheme: winning bid 1 has only to pay the second highest bid, i.e., $p_1 = w_2$, say. Under this design, which is called the Vickrey auction, the best strategy for bidders is to reveal their true valuation (Vickrey, 1961). We observe that in a highly competitive market the auctioneer makes still almost optimal revenue, as the second highest valuation is likely to be almost equal to the highest valuation.

To put these ideas into formulas for the general case we need the following definitions. A set J_c of bids of a bidder c is said to constitute a *weakly dominant* strategy, if for every set of bids by other bidders any other set J'_c of bids from c would not improve her revenue. In other words, independent of what other bidders bid, the set J_c is always the best response. An auction mechanism is called *truth revealing* if for every bidder, bidding her true valuation is a weakly dominant set of bids.

Remember that we call an auction mechanism *efficient* if the total valuation of the allocation is maximal with respect to all feasible allocations, i.e. it maximises total welfare. Suppose we have a truth revealing mechanism and all bidders use their weakly dominant strategies. We will then have an efficient mechanism if the allocation x is an optimal solution for the above integer linear optimisation problem. Thus a truth revealing mechanism does provide the auctioneer with the right data to achieve efficiency.

For multi-item auctions the *Vickrey-Clarke-Groves mechanism* (Clarke, 1971; Groves, 1973), which is frequently also called the *Generalized Vickrey Auction*, is an auction design that satisfies truth revealing. It works as follows. Suppose w are the bid prices reported by bidders, and A is the matrix of bids, as described above. Let x' be the optimal allocation with respect to these bids, i.e. the optimal solution of the integer linear program given by A and w. The vector x' defines the winning bids. Next the auctioneer computes the prices for the winning bids. Let c be some winning bidder, and let x'_c be the part of x' related to bids from bidder c, and x'_{-c} the other components of x', and the same convention apply to other vectors and matrices involved. The auctioneer now deletes for a moment all bids from bidder c, and solves the integer optimization problem given by the objective $w_{-c}\,x_{-c}$ and the constraint $A_{-c}\,x_{-c} \le 1$. Let z_{-c} be the optimal solution, in other words the best allocation of winning bids if bidder c would not have particiapted in the auction. The price $p(c)$ to be paid by c is $p(c) = w_c x'_c - (w x' - w_{-c} z_{-c})$. The term in brackets that is subtracted from the bidder's bid price can be viewed as the marginal contribution of bidder c to the auction. This price is computed for every bidder who wins a bid under the allocation x'.

To give an illustration, consider our example from the previous section. We have seven bids, 3 from bidder A, and two from bidders B and C, respectively. The optimisation problem to solve is:

$$
\begin{array}{llllllllll}
\text{Max} & 100\,x_1 & + & 20\,x_2 & + & 20\,x_3 & + & 30\,x_4 & + & 30\,x_5 & + & 30\,x_6 & + & 30\,x_7 \\
\text{s.th.} & x_1 & + & x_2 & + & & & x_4 & + & & & x_6 & & & \le 1 \\
 & x_1 & + & & & x_3 & + & & & x_5 & + & & & x_7 & \le 1 \\
 & x_1 & + & x_2 & + & x_3 & & & & & & & & & \le 1 \\
 & & & & & & & x_4 & + & x_5 & & & & & \le 1 \\
 & & & & & & & & & & & x_6 & + & x_7 & \le 1 \\
\end{array}
$$

$$x_1, x_2, x_3, x_4, x_5, x_6, x_7 \in \{0,1\}$$

The optimal solution is $x_1 = 1$, and all other $x_i = 0$. The price to be payed by bidder A is 100 minus her marginal contribution. The latter is equal to (100–60), as excluding every bid from A leaves us with the integer linear programming problem:

Max $30\ x_4 + 30\ x_5 + 30\ x_6 + 30\ x_7$

s.th. $x_4 +$ x_6 ≤ 1

                    $x_5 +$ $x_7 \leq 1$

                $x_4 +$ x_5 ≤ 1

                          $x_6 +$ $x_7 \leq 1$

          $x_4,\ x_5,\ x_6,\ x_7 \in \{0,1\}$

which has an optimal value of 60. Therefore A wins the set $\{Q,\ R\}$ for a price of 60.

We shall briefly give the proof for truth revelation. For that we have to compare a bidder's revenue for arbitrary bid prices w with the revenue when she changes to her valuation. With similar conventions as above, and an easy calculation, the first value is $v_c x'_c + w_{-c} x'_{-c} - w_{-c} z_{-c}$, and the second value is given, as $v_c x'_c + w_{-c} x'_{-c} - w_{-c} z_{-c}$, using x' for the optimal allocation under the true valuation. The last term is identical in both formulas. The sum of the first two terms is in the first case equal to the objective value of the feasible allocation x' with respect to the objective composed from v_c and w_{-c}. In the second case the sum of the two terms is the objective value of the *optimal* feasible allocation under this objective. Therefore the value of the second formula is larger than the value of the first.

As VCG is truth revealing it is also efficient. And again it is likely to get very close to the optimum value for the auctioneer, when for example for every winning set there is a loosing bid on that set (or on a subset) that makes almost the same price offer. Truth revealing requires however to reveal the complete type, which might be information that is exponential in the number of items, as we discussed above. Another disadvantage of VCG is that it requires solving the winner determination problem once in phase 1 and again for each winner of a bid in phase 2. Although the later would be polynomial in the size of the input if all bids are reported, the overall mechanism of reporting bids and computing an allocation and prices needs an exponential number of operations.

One might argue that a good heuristic algorithm could replace the exact computation of the winner determination. Based on this idea, Nisan and Ronen defined *VCG-based mechanisms* (Nisan and Ronen, 2000). Such a mechanism uses the same second price formula as the VCG mechanism. However the vectors x and z are replaced by the solutions computed by the heuristic. Truth revealing VCG-based mechanisms can be characterized as follows (Nisan and Ronen, 2000). Let the *range* of an allocation mechanism be defined as the set of all different allocations that can be proposed by a mechanism. For example, a very simple mechanism might assign the whole set of items always to one bid and chose for that the bidder with highest bid for the set (or a subset, if we assume free disposal). In this case the range of the algorithm consists of as many different allocations as there are bidders, namely assigning everything to bidder 1, or to bidder 2, or to bidder 3, etc. A sufficient condition for a truth revealing VCG-based mechanism is that it is *maximal in its range*. This means that the allocation algorithm chooses always an allocation that is at least as good with respect to the current bids as any other allocation in its range.

If one looks at the proof above one observes that this property guarantees indeed truth revealing as it leaves no benefit for strategic behaviour. Furthermore, Nisan and Ronen showed that being maximal in the range is also *necessary* for a VCG based mechanism in order to be truth revealing.

From this result they make some astonishing observations. If the range does contain every allocation, then it is clear that the allocation algorithm has actually to find the optimal allocation. But this problem is NP-hard. If the range is however a subset of all allocations, then the algorithm must have some very counter intuitive behaviour. To see this, let x be an allocation that assigns some set S_1 to bidder 1, a set S_2 to bidder 2 and so forth, but that is *not* in the range of the algorithm. Whatever bidders will bid, the algorithm will not suggest this allocation. Then look at the following valuation: bidder 1 values all items in S_1 by 1, bidder 2 values all items in S_2 by 1, etc., while every bidder values all the other items by 0. The allocation algorithm would in this case not do the obvious allocation x, namely giving S_1 to 1, S_2 to 2, etc.

8. Supported Allocations

It is important to mention that the direct equivalence of the winner allocation problem in sealed bid combinatorial auctions and the set packing problem from combinatorial optimisation gives us as well a huge family of polynomial solvable cases. For example, we may associate every bid with a node in a graph, give it the weight w_j, and connect two nodes by an edge if the bids compete on a common item. This leaves us with the problem to calculate a *maximum weighted stable set* in a graph. Combinatorial optimisation research has identified many classes of graphs for which the stable set problem is polynomial solvable (see, e.g., Skiena, 1998). In particular in cases where the bids have a geometric or geographic interpretation the graph is often a so-called *intersection graph*. In many such cases the geometric representation can be used to design polynomial algorithms (see, e.g., Felsner et al., 1997).

Important, and this not only from the algorithmic perspective, are those cases for which winner determination is polynomial due to the fact that the linear program that we get when we drop the integer constraints from the above ILP has nevertheless an integer optimal solution. In this case we can use a polynomial algorithm to solve the winner determination problem, or to speak more pragmatically, every commercial linear programming solver can be used to compute the best allocation. Nisan observed that the fact that the LP has integer optimal solution is actually directly related to an economic property underlying the combinatorial auction (Nisan, 2000). This property is the topic of this section.

An allocation x in a combinatorial auction is *supported by single-item prices y_i,* if for all bids j, $x_j = 1$ implies $\sum_{i \in j} p_i \le w_j$, and $x_j = 0$ implies $\sum_{i \in j} p_i \ge w_j$. It is *exactly supported* if $x_j = 1$ implies $\sum_{i \in j} p_i = w_j$. An allocation x is called *full* if every item is contained in some winning bid. From an application point of view a supported allocation has the advantage of publishable prices that explain to the bidders why they lost or won a bid. From a computational point of view it is of importance because of its relation to the solvability of the allocation ILP. It is an immediate consequence of linear programming duality that a combinatorial auction instance admits an optimal allocation x that is exactly supported by single item prices if the linear relaxation of the allocation ILP has an integral optimal solution. Indeed, the single item prices are equal to the dual variables, one for every item, and the dual feasibility together with the complementary slackness condition $x_j(\sum_{i \in j} y_i - w_j) = 0$ prove that the solution is exactly supported. The dual of the linear relaxation of the allocation ILP is

$$
\begin{aligned}
\min \quad & y\,1 \\
\text{s.t.} \quad & y\,A \geq w \\
& y \geq 0
\end{aligned}
$$

Nisan showed almost the opposite direction as well. Namely, if a combinatorial auction instance admits a *full* allocation supported by single-item prices, then this allocation is optimal and the allocation LP has an integral optimal solution. Furthermore, it has a full allocation that is exactly supported (Nisan, 2000). Let us show the very simple proof of that result. Suppose x is a full allocation supported by single item prices y. First we may assume without loss of generality that the allocation is supported exactly, since for a winning bid j with $\sum_{i \in j} y_i < w_j$ we can increase y_i to make the left-hand-side equal to the right hand side (Note that every i is contained in at most one winning bid). After this modification, the prices y_i form a feasible dual solution. Let us now compare the primal and dual objectives of x and y, respectively. We see that $\sum_j w_j x_j = \sum_{j\,:\,x_j = 1} \sum_{i \in j} y_i = \sum_i y_i$. The last equation holds because x is a full allocation, thus this condition is essential in the proof. By this equality we have a primal feasible x, and a dual feasible y, with identical objective value, proving the optimality of both.

There are many cases for which the allocation LP has an integral optimal solution, and is therefore supported (Müller and Schulz, 2000; Vohra and de Vries, 2000). In many cases the solution procedure does not have to rely on a LP solver, but could be done directly by a combinatorial algorithm, which is in most cases the faster approach. There are also classes for which one has a polynomial algorithm, but for which the LP does not necessarily have an integer solution. Here the allocation is in general not supported.

9. Primal-dual Algorithms

Primal-dual algorithms have particularly nice properties when applied to the winner determination problem in combinatorial auctions. Firstly, they compute solutions that are exactly supported. Secondly, for some special cases the payment phase can be adjusted in a way that makes the auction mechanism truth revealing. Thirdly, a primal-dual approach certificates the quality of the current allocation with respect to the criterion revenue maximization for the auctioneer. Indeed, the primal objective is a lower bound and the dual objective gives an upper bound on the revenue that can be achieved with respect to the current bids.

When adapted to our context a primal-dual algorithm works as follows. We are given the binary optimization problem to maximize the function wx subject to the intersection constraint $Ax \leq 1$ and the constraint that primal variables are binary. The dual program we look at is the dual of the linear relaxation of this binary program. It is given by the objective $y1$ and the constraint $yA \geq w$. We try to construct a feasible primal solution x, i.e. an allocation, and a dual feasible solution y, i.e., single-item prices such that x and y together fulfil the primal complementary slack constraint $x_j (\sum_{i \in j} y_i - w_j) = 0$. Together with dual feasibility, this slack condition translates to the condition that the allocation x is strictly supported by prices y.

Remember that a Dutch auction is an auction in which prices are descending. A *Dutch primal-dual algorithm* (Müller and Schulz, 2000) for winner determination mimics the principle of a Dutch auction. Single-item prices (dual variables) are iteratively reduced to levels at which the price of a bundle j, say, with respect to these single-item prices hits the bid price for the bundle. At such a level further reduction of prices of items in bundle j is not possible without becoming dual infeasible. The Dutch primal-dual algorithm decides for j whether it is assigned or not, fixes all prices of items in j and continues to reduce prices of other items. The algorithm terminates when no more dual variables can be reduced, or all bids are decided. The choice of variables, which are going to be reduced in the next iteration, and how much they are reduced, makes different versions of this scheme.

The following example illustrates the algorithm. There is a set of two items, a and b, and there are three bids: 12 for $\{a\}$, 10 for $\{b\}$, and 23 for $\{a, b\}$. Suppose we do a greedy allocation of bids, which means that we assign a bid whenever its dual constraint becomes tight, and all items in the bid are still available. We start with prices for a, and b to be equal to 23. Prices will first go down to 12 for a, and b, the bid for $\{a\}$ is assigned. Now, only the price for $\{b\}$ can be further reduced. At price 11 the dual constraint on the set $\{a, b\}$ becomes tight. This bid cannot be assigned. Now all prices are frozen and the algorithm stops. If we had not assigned $\{a\}$, then $\{a, b\}$ could have been chosen. In both cases the dual objective equals the optimal solution, only in the second case the primal solution is optimal, too.

Lehmann, O'Callaghan and Shoham investigated the special case of combinatorial auctions in which every bidder is interested in at most one subset of items (Lehmann et al., 1999). For this case they prove sufficient conditions for a combinatorial auction mechanism, i.e., a winner determination and payment algorithm, to be truth revealing. Key to their result is to adjust the payment scheme in a way that bidders cannot regret too high bids. The payment scheme is not equal to the VCG scheme. In order to explain their approach we need some definitions.

A combinatorial auction mechanism for single-minded bidders is called *exact*, if it assigns to a bidder either the empty set or exactly the set she is interested in. It is called *monotone* if winning bids would keep winning, if they would be replaced by a higher bid on the same set, or the same bid on a subset of items. In other words if a bid j with $x_j = 1$ is replaced by a bid k with $I_k \subseteq I_j$, and $w_k \geq w_j$, then $x_k = 1$. Lehmann et al. prove that in a mechanism that satisfies exactness and monotonicity, given a bid j together with a fixed set of other bids, there exists a *critical value* c_j such that for $w_j < c_j$ the mechanism will set $x_j = 0$ and for $w_j > c_j$ the mechanism will set $x_j = 1$. This motivates the following definition. An exact and monotone mechanism is called *critical* if $x_j = 1$ implies $p_j = c_j$. As a final condition in order to make a winner determination algorithm truth revealing they need *participation*. A mechanism fulfils *participation* if $x_j = 0$ implies $p_j = 0$. The result is then that a mechanism for single-minded bidders, which fulfils exactness, monotonicity, critical and participation is truth revealing.

The Dutch primal-dual allocation algorithm fulfils exactness. Furthermore it fulfils monotonicity. First, assume a bidder replaces a bid j by a bid k that bids a higher price on the same set. Then tightness of the dual constraint for k is not later achieved than it has been achieved for j. Second, suppose a replacement of a bid j by a bid k on a subset of its items.

Then the dual constraint becomes tight at higher individual prices for each item in the bid, which again moves the decision about this bid to an earlier stage of the algorithm. But at earlier stages of the algorithm no bid l with $I_k \cap I_l \neq \emptyset$ can exist. From monotonicity it follows that there exists a critical price p_j for every bid. Using this in the payment phase of the mechanism guarantees participation and by that we get a truth-revealing mechanism.

The primal-dual view has recently proven to be rather helpful in understanding combinatorial auctions. In particular one can interpret ascending price auctions with combinatorial bids as primal-dual algorithms (Parkes and Ungar, 2000). Furthermore, the modeling of markets for indivisible items by integer linear programming models, their relaxations, and the dual programs of the later can lead to valuable insights in market design (Bikchandani and Ostroy, 2000).

10. Conclusions

This chapter has given an introduction on auction mechanisms as means of dynamic pricing on the Internet. We have explained how the popularity of auctions can be explained by general trends in the digital economy, like new forms of intermediation, customization, and customer involvement. We then outlined several design issues of an auction. Starting at simple single-unit, single-item auctions, we showed how in particular business-to-business applications require more complex auction formats. Such auction formats have to address the needs coming from complementarity or substitutability of items in a multi-item setting. Designing such auctions requires an integrated treatment of the computational aspects of auction design, i.e. how much information has to be communicated and how does the auctioneer process this information, and the economical aspects of the design, i.e., what are the strategies of bidders, what revenue can the auctioneer make, and is the allocation of items efficient with respect to the bidders preferences.

We could certainly not cover all aspects that should be covered if this chapter would claim to be a survey paper. However this has not been the intention. We rather want to encourage the reader to use the references of this chapter and dive into the theory. Touching this theory at least to some extent, rather than leaving it aside, had the intention to convince the reader that auction design is a far more complex engineering task than one might expect at first glance. The author maintains a Web portal listing resources on the subject at www.etrade.infonomics.nl.

Acknowledgements

I would like to thank A. Schulz for many fruitful discussions on the subject when I visited MIT in summer and autum 2000, and V. Feltkamp and S. Onderstal for their valuable suggestions.

References

Agorics Inc. (1996) Auctions – going, going, gone. A survey of auction types. Agorics Inc., Los Altos, CA. Available at http://www.agorics.com/new.html (11.12.2000)

Barun Sarkar, M., Butler, B., Steinfield, C. (1998) Intermediaries and Cybermediaries: A Continuing Role for Mediating Players in the Electronic Marketplace. JCMC 1(3). Available at http://www.ascusc.org/jcmc/vol1/issue3/sarkar.html (11.12.2000)

Bikchandani S., Ostroy, J. M. (2000) The package assignment model. Working paper. An earlier version is available at http://www.cramton.umd.edu/conference/auction-conference.html (11.12.2000)

Brewer, P. J. (1999) Decentralized computation procurement and computational robustness in a smart market. Economic Theory 13: 41–92

Caplice, C. G. (1996) An Optimisation Based Bidding Process: A New Framework for Shipper-Carrier Relationships. Thesis, Department of Civil and Environmental Engineering, School of Engineering, MIT

Clarke, E. H. (1971) Multipart pricing of public goods. Public Choice 11: 17–33

Felsner, F., Müller, R., Wernisch, L. (1997) Trapezoid Graphs and Generalizations, Geomety and Algorithms. Discrete Applied Mathematics 74: 13–32

Fujishima, Y., Leyton-Brown, K., Shoham, Y. (1999) Taming the computational complexity of combinatorial auctions: Optimal and approximate approaches. In: Proceedings of IJCAI'99, Stockholm, Schweden. Morgan Kaufmann. Available at http://robotics.stanford.edu/~kevinlb/ (11.12.2000)

Groves, T. (1973) Incentives in teams. Econometrica 41: 617–631

Herschlag, M., Zwick R. (2000) Internet Auctions – a popular and professional literature review. Quarterly J Electronic Commerce 1 (2): 161–186. Available at http://home.ust.hk/~mkzwick/download.html (11.12.2000)

Hoesel, S. van, Müller, R (2001) Optimization in Electronic Markets: Examples in Combinatorial Auctions. Netnomics 3: 23–33

Keil, J. M. (1992) On the complexity of scheduling tasks with discrete starting times. Operations Research Letters 12: 293–295

Kennanvision.com (1998) Exchange in the Internet Economy. The Keenan Report No. 1. Available at http://www.keenanvision.com (11.12.2000)

Klemperer, P. (1999) Auction Theory – A Guide to the Literature. J Economic Surveys 13 (3): 227–286. Available at http://hicks.nuff.ox.ac.uk/economics/people/klemperer.htm (11. 12.2000)

Lehmann, D., O'Callaghan, L. I., Y. Shoham, Y. (1999) Truth Revelation in Rapid, Approximately, Efficient Combinatorial Auctions. Working Paper, 1999

Leyton-Brown, K., Pearson, M., Shoham, Y. (2000a) Towards a Universal Test Suite for Combinatorial Auctions. Proceedings of the 2000 ACM Conference on Electronic Commerce (EC'00). Available at http://robotics.stanford.edu/~kevinlb/ (11.12.2000)

Leyton-Brown, K., Shoham, Y., Tennenholtz, M. (2000b) An algorithm for multi-unit combinatorial auctions. Proceedings of National Conference on Artificial Intelligence (AAAI), Austin, TX, July 31–August 2. Available at http://robotics.stanford.edu/~kevinlb/ (11.12.2000)

McMillan, J. (1994) Selling Spectrum rights. J Economic Perspectives 8 (3): 145–162

Monderer, D., Tennenholtz, M. (1998) Optimal Auctions Revisited. In: Proceedings of AAAI-98

Müller, R., Schulz, A. (2000) Combinatorial Auctions from a computational perspective. Working paper, available from the authors

Myerson, R. B. (1979) Incentive Compatibility and the Bargaining Problem. Econometrica 47: 61–73

Myerson, R. B. (1981) Optimal Auction Design. Mathematics of Operations Research 6 (1): 58–73

Nisan, N. (2000) Bidding and Allocation in Combinatorial Auctions. In: Proceedings of the ACM Conference on Electronic Commerce (EC-00). Available at http://www.cs.huji.ac.il/~noam/ (11.12.2000)

Nisan, N., Ronen, A. (2000) Computationally Feasible VCG Mechanisms, in Proceedings of the ACM Conference on Electronic Commerce (EC-00). Available at http://www.cs.huji.ac.il/~noam/ (11.12.2000)

Ockenfels, A., Roth, A. (2000) Late Minute Bidding and the Rules for Ending Second-Price Auctions: Theory and Evidence from a Natural Experiment on the Internet. Working Paper, Harvard University. Available at http://www.uni-magdeburg.de/vwl3/axel.html (11.12.2000)

Parkes, D. C., Ungar, L. H. (2000) Iterative Combinatorial Auctions: Theory and Practice. In: Proceedings of AAAI-00.

Parkes, D. C., Ungar, L. H., Foster, D. P. (1999) Accounting for Cognitive Costs in On-line Auction Design. In: Noriega, P., Sierra, C. (eds.) Agent Mediated Electronic Commerce (LNAI 1571). Springer, LNAI 1571, pp. 25–40

Rassenti S. J., Smith V. L., Bulfin R. L. (1982) A combinatorial auction mechanism for airport time slot allocation. Bell J Economis 13 (2): 402–417

Rothkopf, M. H., Pekec, A., Harstad, R. M. (1998) Computationally manageable combinatorial auctions. Management Science 44 (8): 1131–1147

Sandholm, T. (2000) Approaches to Winner Determination in Combinatorial Auctions. Decision Support Systems 28(1–2): 165–176

Sandholm, T., Suri, S. (2000) Improved Algorithms for Optimal Winner Determination in Combinatorial Auctions and Generalizations. Proceedings of National Conference on Artificial Intelligence (AAAI), Austin, TX, July 31–August 2, pp. 90–97

Scott, J. (2000) Emerging Patterns from the Dynamic Capabilities of Internet Intermediaries, JCMC 5 (3). Available at http://www.ascusc.org/jcmc/vol5/issue3/scott.html (11. 12. 2000)

Skiena, S. S. (1998) The Algorithm Design Manual. Springer, The Electronic Library of Science Series

Tennenholtz, M. (2000) Some tractable combinatorial auctions. Proceedings of National Conference on Artificial Intelligence (AAAI), Austin, TX, July 31–August 2

Vickrey, W. S. (1961) Counterspeculation, auctions and competitive sealed tenders. J Finance 16: 8–37

Vohra R., Vries, S. de, Combinatorial auctions – a survey. Working paper, 2000. Available at http://www.kellogg.nwu.edu/faculty/vohra/htm/res.htm (11.12.2000)

Wellman, M., Walsh, W., Wurman, P., MacKie-Mason J. (1998) Auction protocols for decentralized scheduling. Proceedings of the 18th International Conference on Distributed Computing Systems.

Wolfstetter, E. (1996) Auctions: An introduction. J Economic Surveys 10: 367–421

Rudolf Müller
Associate Professor for Operations Research at Maastricht University. He is program leader of the e-organisation research unit of the International Institute of Infonomics. He completed his PhD in Mathematics in 1993 at Technical University Berlin, and has been Assistant Professor for IS at Humboldt-University in Berlin. His research interests include electronic markets, Internet information services, and combinatorial optimisation.

Security in E-Commerce

G. Müller

Telematics, University Freiburg, Federal Republic of Germany

mueller@telematik.iig.uni-freiburg.de

Abstract

Future networks will be open, heterogeneous and complex systems consisting of many independent nets. Classical services like e-mail and file-transfer will only be components of these information networks, which resemble more social rather than technical infrastructures. While the technical development is predictable, the social and economic direction is less clear. Security is a key factor (Schoder et al., 1998). It is, however, no longer limited to the protection from physical dangers, but rather the ability to protect virtual assets and privacy. As in any human communication, it should be seen as an element of technical communication and is a matter to be negotiated between partners. This paper describes multilateral security (Rannenberg et al., 1996) as the requirement to act self-determinedly in a global network and relates the social term "trust" and the technical term "security". While the functions of technology are all related to cryptography, infrastructures enable communication and institutions have the task of assuring trust in functions and promises of infrastructures. Even though governments may have to change their policy towards regulation, a realm of regulations in providing future infrastructures may remain. This paper elaborates on concepts and ideas of the Kolleg "Sicherheit in der Kommunkationstechnik" (Müller et al., 1997, 1998), supported by the Gottlieb Daimler- und Karl Benz-Stiftung, Ladenburg-Berlin.

1. Introduction

Future networks will be open, heterogeneous and complex systems consisting of many independent nets. The initial purpose of Internet was the exchange of information with classical services like e-mail and file-transfer. Future applications will be much more complex and will generate social "spaces" where, for example, economic transactions take place. Internet develops along the extension of its range and the power of its components (Fig. 1). Global infrastructures of the future are decentralized, lacking centralized control institutions. The development of trust becomes an issue between participating parties. This will be elaborated using the efforts to generate electronic commerce:

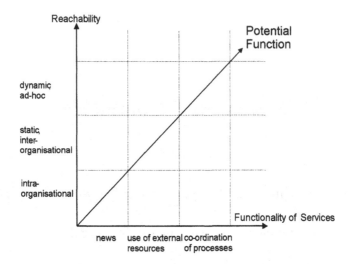

Fig. 1. Potential function of telematics

Electronic commerce is the favored vision for technical justifications (Spar et al., 1996). As at a marketplace, the main purpose of e-commerce is to bring buyers and sellers together at any time, in any place (Müller et al., 1997)

1. Sellers offer their goods and buyers order these goods.
2. Sellers and buyers might need a certificate to assure each other of a special quality, e.g. correctness of the signature.
3. Sellers deliver goods and buyers make payments.
4. Instead of goods, the buyers might receive a certificate to allow them the use of specific services, e.g. subscription of journals.
5. Dissatisfaction is part of any market system. These are handled by exception handlers. Mostly, socially accepted institutions are needed.
6. Some services require third parties to participate, e.g. notary or financial services.
7. Some sellers might wish to attract their customers by registering them and giving special certificates or directory services.

All this requires negotiation processes with a coherent set of rules, transparency of security mechanisms, their potentials, workings and also their drawbacks. Trust is a consequence of the quality of the technical security mechanism. Security is a quality of the whole system and can be accomplished as a result of three phases of system development:

1. *Functionality defines the services offered by an individual system.*
2. *Infrastructure offers services trusted and used by all participants.*
3. *Institutions guarantee the properties of the actual communication system.*

In the past, these requirements were assured by any government with more or less liberal attitudes. In the future, this is impossible since cyberspace and Internet are borderless and no single institution can impose its concept of regulation upon this infrastructure. The concept of "multilateral security" (Müller et al., 1997, 1998) is a possible guideline or architecture with a wealth of ideas on preserving privacy for the individual and protecting the assets of businesses in cyberspace communication.

2. Functionality of Multilateral Security

Internet, as a model of emerging communication infrastructures, has an open architecture giving independence to applications and autonomy to users and service providers at the first glance. The common address-space and common protocols allow anyone to become an operator of a transmission node or even a whole network. Anyone can become a user by declaring – sometimes unilaterally – to an operator that he wants to be a customer. Centralized security systems are counterproductive. The challenge is to develop decentralized control systems and functionality to allow the user to move freely in the electronic world. Multilateral security defines these functions.

All participants in an open network like Internet have to be trusted and distrusted at the same time. All are potential attackers. In the following, a categorization of criteria is proposed that helps the participants in an open network to express their individually perceived security level (Rannenberg et al., 1996):

A: Confidentiality
1. Contents of messages should be able to be protected from all channels, except the communication partner.
2. Sender and receiver should, if they agree, remain anonymous and should not be observed.
3. Sender and receiver should be able to be protected from concatenating communication acts by third parties, their location and identity (pseudonyms) should remain unidentified and they should be able to rely on the fact that unauthorized use of systems is prevented (secure hardware).

B: Integrity
1. Falsifications of contents should be recognized.
2. The scope of accountability systems has to be limited to one transaction.

C: Availability
1. Everybody should be allowed to use the system according to defined rules.
2. Access to request services cannot be denied, if specified in advance.

D: Accountability
1. For a third party, the receiver is able to use the message as proof.
2. The sender should be able to prove the fact of having sent a message and contents.
3. Payment for services are a defining part of communication systems.

This list of functions for multilateral security is not free of conflicting requirements. While the user may prefer anonymity, the service provider must insist on payments. Communicating partners have different roles. Users would probably not like the operator of a network to store, archive or even sell data describing how long or how often the users communicate with each other or the subject they talk about. The recording of data of this kind leads to profiles of users. Profiles are files to record the behavior of specific users over a certain period of time to make better forecasts about the behavior. Profiles receive, from a user's point of view, a very ambiguous evaluation. While loss of privacy is not in the interest of the user, low service quality may also not be in his best interest. Cryptography is the technical means to provide the individual participant with the means to define a personally perceived, and with the communication partner agreed upon, level of security for exactly one transaction.

3. Cryptographic Options

The decentralized nature of modern global communication networks is too complex to ensure trust by its users without additional efforts. On the one hand it allows freedom, on the other hand it removes the accountability. Cryptography, combined with the power of modern computer systems, will even increase this conflict.

In the following, a classification of cryptographic (Schneier, 1995) and steganographic /watermarking (Westfeld, 1997) systems is introduced. While in the first case it is known that a message is encrypted, in the second case the message is hidden. Watermarking is a specific version of cryptography with an open "hidden" message. In Fig. 2, we distinguish between the purpose of assuring confidentiality and systems

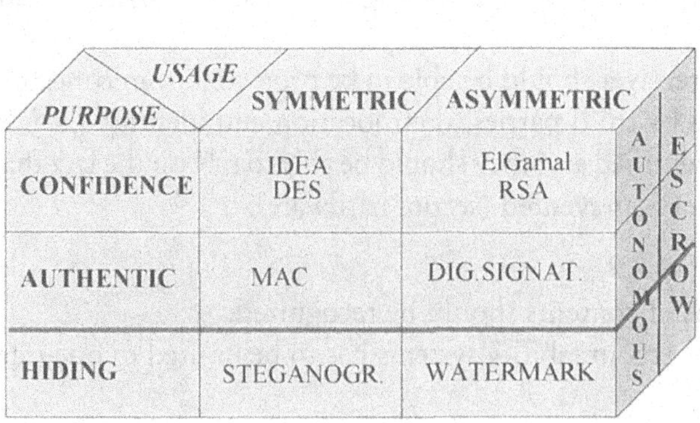

Fig. 2. Classification of cryptographic methods

whose primary purpose is to ensure authentication. Beyond this classification, on a technical level, there is a difference between symmetrical and asymmetrical methods. In the first case, keys are only known to the communicating partners, while public key cryptography divides a key into a secret part, known only to one participant. To be prepared against attacks, one has to distinguish between an area where attacks can be launched (area of attack), and an area where we depend upon trust (area of trust). If, in the "area of trust", the protection fails, cryptographic functions are useless and provide false feelings of security.

Confidentiality Systems

The oldest and most famous systems for concealing information are the symmetrical systems (Fig. 3). The most used representatives are DES and maybe the most interesting, scientifically, is IDEA (Schneier, 1995).

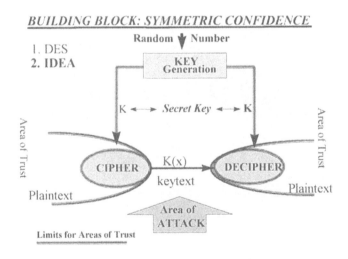

Fig. 3. Symmetric confidentiality system (SCS)

Whenever users want to communicate they need a common key, e.g. K. They may generate this key themselves and exchange the result or use a central institution. Of course, key generation can always decipher the messages and must be a component of the trusted area.

Asymmetric Confidentiality Systems (ACS) are based upon non-reversible mathematical functions, e.g. while it is easy to compute the product of two prime numbers, it is difficult to tell their factors from the result. Today's ACS need up to 1000times more compute power than symmetric systems and, as a result, they are mostly used in a hybrid fashion, where only the keys are exchanged at the beginning of a session. The session itself is conducted in a symmetric mode. Asymmetric systems require several keys, e.g. in Fig. 4, D and C, where D must be kept secret. The trusted area here is that, with affordable effort, factorization is impossible and D cannot be calculated from either C or the original text.

ACS have one property that makes them a good candidate for establishing decentralized control structures. Every participant with access to a computer system can generate keys. The secret key D is for deciphering, and must be kept private, while the public part of the key may be enlisted in any on-line database of public nature or attached to any message. Given technical reasons alone, a central institution is not needed to generate keys. In case of crime or evil purposes, however, the message cannot be enciphered by a third party.

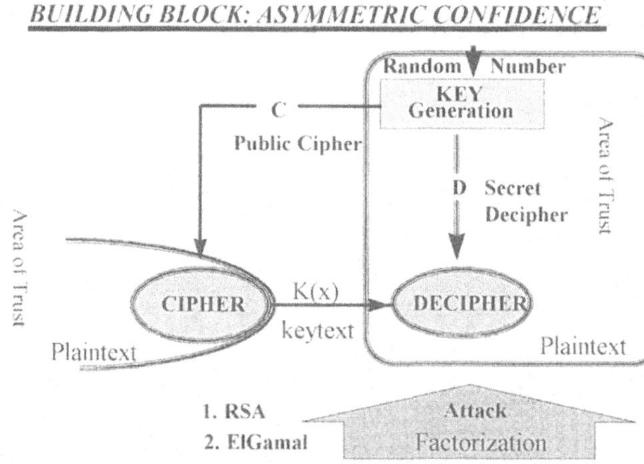

Fig. 4. Asymmetric confidentiality system (ACS)

Authentication Systems

In Fig. 5, a symmetrical authentication system (SAS) is shown. The characteristic is the attachment of a Message Authentication Code (MAC). The receiver can use the key K and the message to compute MAC, and to check whether the message received is the same as the one sent.

Asymmetric authentication systems (AAS) are known as digital signature systems. They offer the possibility of proving that a message was sent from a specific, identifiable sender. For all signature systems, so-called certification authorities or trusted third parties are proposed to build an area of trust. Any decentralized generated key is easy prey for any attacker and may not be accepted as proof in court in case of disagreement and lawsuits.

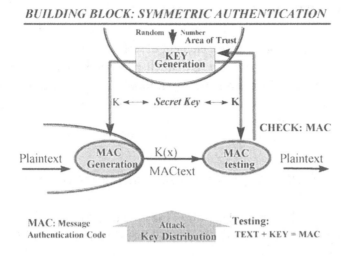

Fig. 5. Symmetric authentication systems (SAS)

Symmetric authentication systems do not have this property. Even if the certification authority verifies the identity of the MAC, there is no guarantee that the MAC has not been generated by a fake party. The flow of information and key distribution is shown in Fig. 6.

For Digital Signature Systems, one cannot rely on just the algorithm and the generated keys. It is important to know who generates and administrates a key to develop trust. Key generation, distribution, and registering of keys, as well as their certification, are the elements for a secure or trustworthy infrastructure.

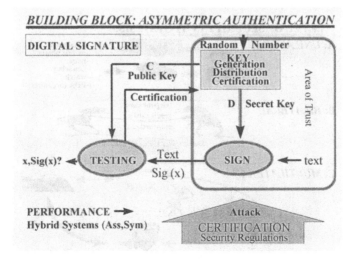

Fig. 6. Asymmetric authentication systems (AAS)

4. Infrastructures and Institutions – Elements to Trust

Cryptographic functions are just one element of security, but while they are needed, they are not sufficient. The main issue is that self-generated and exchanged keys may serve for authentication between partners and may also generate confidence. But there is empty room for any kind of fake behavior, such as pretending to be a specific person or changing contents of information.

Relationships of Communicating Partners

Trust in security of IT-systems determines the level of achievable security between communicating partners. One may distinguish between uni-, bi-, and multilateral security. In the first case, security is at its maximum level and is defined by the technical device one deals with, since no control is given to other people or institutions. If we trust the implementers, it is safe to assume that attacks within this system will not happen. However, the implementation of a system under complete control of a user is unrealistic. Attacks on bilateral relationships and their area of trust are always based upon giving up control of the device, e.g. tampering telephone cards, spying or giving away credit cards, using chip cards and inserting them into unknown and unproved devices, e.g. in a store when payments are to be made. These relationships are depicted in Fig. 7.

For electronic commerce the most common scenario is the multilateral case where new partners of communication, without satisfactory authentication and without the possibility of identifying the other partner beyond any doubt, have to be dealt with. The only realistic assumption for the multilateral case is that the

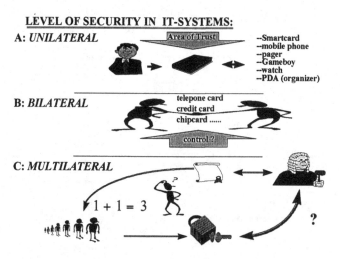

Fig. 7. Levels of security

environment is hostile. Multilateral security cannot be accomplished without a sophisticated and trustworthy infrastructure.

Technology and Infrastructures

The central issue of technology is that it cannot guarantee without any doubt that the partners in any communication are really the ones they claim to be. The technology for authentication is not yet satisfactory. The "trusted" infrastructure is related to the functionality of security, but already requires significant amounts of trust. One has to be aware that security technology changes, while the level of trust has to be maintained. Areas and criteria to judge both technology and infrastructures are the following:

1. *Interfaces and Functionality*: From a user's point of view, the interface must provide the expected functionality.
2. *Extendibility*: Extension encompasses new addition of functions as well as including new hardware and end-devices.
3. *Standards*: Global infrastructures require an agreement upon the execution of the security functions. For this purpose, standards on protection, keys, key distribution, and key generation, as well as the semantic definition of functionality are required.
4. *Certified Blocks*: Cryptographic methods and software or hardware used to realize them are not essentially secure. One can only be sure that they do what they are supposed to be doing, if they are certified by a certifying and trustworthy agency.
5. *Secure Hardware*: Maximum security comes with unilaterally used equipment. Connectivity enhances the functionality and the scope, but also serves as an entrance for attacks.

In the *unilateral case*, a device must act according to the user's wishes, while it is in the user's hands. The chain of trust ranges from the manufacturer, shipment, device personalization, and interaction between user and device. For the use of security modules, this report concentrates on the initialization, usage and maintenance of security modules.

1. Considered applications require personalization of the end-device by a secret key. For this purpose, the device should generate the key after shipment, never divulge it, and should output only the public key which can be certified by request. Key generators need an initial random string from a few to up to several hundred bytes. A protocol is needed to ensure that the string is really random, e.g. by having the user and maybe the certification authority provide one share of the string each. Experiments are being carried out to study collective coin-flipping protocols by implementing XOR. (Boolean that returns true if, and only if, one of its operands is true and the other false.)

2. The next most important feature is the user interface. Devices without interface are vulnerable to fake attacks, as attacks on ATM machines show. It is expected that manufacturers will be forced to standardize these interfaces. Users may be given, together with their key, a trusted document of numbers that allow the user to test the correctness of the interface. The end-device should also contain output slots to fax machines or printers to have a printed proof of the document shown on the interface.

3. If a security module needs maintenance, users should be able to invoke a special mode that allows this without relinquishing the module or exposing functions activated by it in the mobile device.

4. To prevent theft and loss, the mobile devices have either to be very small or the security module should be removable and plugged into any device on demand. The other type of security module is external and requires secure communication channels like radio, infrared, or induction communication to the mobile device.

In the *bilateral case*, the main issue is that a device must remain secure, even if it is stolen or, for the purpose of executing a task, control is temporarily given up, e.g. a smart card is inserted into the slot of a reading or writing device in a supermarket.

1. At present, we use identification techniques, e.g. PIN, pass phrases, and biometrics. This secures the application, but also allows attacks. One possibility of making the known techniques safer is to introduce identification whenever a security critical command is issued, e.g. a signed document is sent or sensitive data are shown on display.

2. Fake devices can be built, they can use internal manipulation to intercept a PIN, change the OK and CANCEL Buttons. The proposed plug-in security modules provide a solution to this. The device number of the security module interacts with the device number of the other device, after identification the PIN may be requested. There is a need to ensure that the module is really plugged in. Distance Bounding Protocols have to be developed.

If the device cannot be used directly, one may try to get to its contents, i.e. they must be *tamper-resistant*.

In general, the balance between the price of security, the options of which seem limitless, and the price of secure end-devices users are willing to pay for must be investigated and are, as yet, unclear.

In the *multilateral case*, the main challenge is to design scenarios and systems that operate in a consistently hostile environment. The difference to bilateral security is that, in the multilateral case, not all applications can be stopped when a security issue is detected. For example, in payment systems checks may be signed individually, if one check is cashed twice, not all other forms of payments should be stopped.

1. The identification of persons has to be replaced by the identification of devices. A person or a process, if atomized, communicates with another device or process or person only through other devices, e.g. a bank communicates to ATM or trusted mobile devices only through its own trusted central computer.

2. The concepts so far require that all parties involved, e.g. bank, user, phone company, employer, etc., rely on one security module for one mobile end-device or one transaction at a time. A security architecture has to be defined to reduce the amount of security modules needed. The user should also not have to change security modules for each transaction. Since it is not expected that parties involved agree on a specific security module, each mobile device should have its own module. For this purpose, the trusted memory of the security module may be too small for all applications. The security module needs an operating system to enable it to store a trusted application, to get a history of conduct or use lesser security measures.

3. If two security modules of two different mobile agents interact, protocols of interaction are needed. Some applications require the permission of both modules, e.g. spending cash by an ATM needs the authorization of the bank's security module and the customer. These protocols can be designed by using digital signatures.

Example: Trust in Digital Signatures

Signatures have five functions:

1. Guarantee: With a signature, a person authorizes the contents of a document.
2. Identification: The characteristics of a signature define the person.
3. Commitment: With a signature, a person defines the borders of a document and the will to stick to the contents.
4. Warning: Before signing, the small time slot makes people aware of their actions.
5. Proof: With the signature, the authentication of any document can be proven in court.

Secure systems mode these functions by employing technology, the cryptographic functions, the environment of the computers and machines used, as well as defining all the rules to generate, exchange and certify the keys.

1. *Generation of keys*: Should a key be generated by the user or by a central agency? The most famous representative for the first approach is PGP (Pretty Good Privacy) product. The latter approach is favored by the PEM (Privacy Enhanced Mail) (Linn, 1993). PGP only relies on the distribution of key and certificates through a "web of friends", while PEM assumes a strictly hierarchically organized structure for certification. Digital signatures allow the exchange or distribution of keys to generate confidence. Technically, anyone with a computer and some software can generate the keys privately.
2. *Trust Centers*: Trust centers are institutions run by third parties to generate, certify, and distribute keys. In order to trace the actions of trust centers in case of conflict, it is recommended to have the whole certification chain added to the signature.

3. *Certification Process*: A participant signs with his private key D his public key C to assure everybody that all signatures with this public key are really from him. The trust center signs with its own secret key D the public key of the issuer to assure the authenticity of the signature.

4. *Test of a Certificate*: All participants can test the correctness of the signature of the trust center by using the public key of the trust center to verify the signature. This is, of course, a recursive process. The correctness of the trust center must be certified by another, probably hierarchically higher trust centers, etc.

Options for Social Institutions

For the first time in history, computers enable end-users to encrypt communication. Until now, this has been a privilege of governments. Despite the decentralized nature of control in modern communication systems, centralized systems have their purpose and require special attention. Governments, especially, claim the need for archiving and monitoring the traffic to avoid crime. The proposed systems for this purpose are known as key-escrow systems. Taking into account the flexibility of technology, i.e. mixture and combined use of steganography and encryption, the complexity of the problem on a technical level is obvious. The root of the controversial political discussion is that instead of giving a confidence generating system the message directly, first a publicly known key is transmitted. The receiver now has two options: he either encodes the message with the key or uses the key to transmit another key, e.g. symmetric ciphering. For future communications, the messages may then be ciphered any number of times. If a key is used that does not allow the restoration of the message, this may be taken as evidence that something is being hidden and maybe illegal. In the decentralized case, the generation of the key, as well as the storage of the key, is uncontrolled by a central institution. While the prime argument of the first case is to protect the majority from crime, the argument of the second case is that exactly this is not possible, e.g. steganographic options, and that only the irrelevant ones will be captured, while organized crime is technically capable enough to use all kinds of masquerading technology.

If, for example, a confidence system has the property that the recovery of messages encoded earlier is not possible, theoretically a public certification authority is not necessary. Private institutions are sufficient. Three results are possible:

1. The Certification Authority (CA) can decipher the message.
2. The CA detects a ciphered message they cannot read.
3. The CA detects the container of a stegomessage and cannot even tell the existence of a message.

The objectives of centralized social infrastructures are only accomplished in the first case. The cases two and three will always be used, when the danger of decryption should be avoided by the individual. This way a false feeling of security will be generated and in the long term trust in the communication system may be lost.

5. Conclusions

The increasing introduction of mobile user devices into the mass market represents a security challenge, and, at first glance, makes security on an individual level a task that cannot be accomplished. However, it is perceivable that these challenges can be met on a technical level together with the introduction of appropriate social infrastructures and the concept of multilateral security. If the devices are truly personal, the level of security may even be enhanced since they are easier to evaluate, certify, and supervise than stationary PC or workstations. They have to have their own interfaces. Smart cards are therefore most likely to be a temporary technology with less usage than hoped for by the proponents.

References

Abelson, H. et al. (1997) The Risks of Key Recovery, Key Escrow, and Third party Encryption. http://theory,ics.mit.edu/

Cheswick, W. R. (1995) Firewalls and Internet Security. Add. Wesley, Reading

Deering, S. et al. (1995) Internet Protocol Version 6, RFC1883, December 1995

Fabre, J. (1996) FRIENDS: A Flexible Architecture for Implementing Fault Tolerant and Secure Distributed Applications. In: 2. Dependable Computing Conference, Italy, 1996

Federrath, H. et al. (1996) MIXES in Mobile Communication Systems, Location management with Privacy, Proc. Workshop on Information Hiding, Cambridge, UK, 1.6.96

Federrath, H. et al. (1997) Bausteine zur Realisierung mehrseitiger Sicherheit. In: Müller, G., Pfitzmann, A. (eds.) Mehrseitige Sicherheit in der Kommunikationstechnik. Add. Wesley, Reading

Grimm, R. (1997) Sicherheit für offene Kommunikationsnetze. In: Müller, G., Pfitzmann, A. (eds.) Mehrseitige Sicherheit in der Kommunikationstechnik. Add. Wesley, Reading

Linn, J. (1993) Privacy Enhancement for Internet Electronic Mail, RFC 1421, February 1993

Müller, G., Kohl, U., Strauß, R. (1996) Zukunftsperspektiven der digitalen Vernetzung. dpunkt, Heidelberg

Müller, G., Kohl, U., Schoder, D. (1997) Unternehmenskommunikation: Telematiksysteme für vernetzte Unternehmen. Add. Wesley, Reading

Müller, G., Pfitzmann, A. (eds.) (1997) Mehrseitige Sicherheit in der Kommunikationstechnik, Verfahren, Komponenten, Integration, Bd 1. Add. Wesley, Reading

Müller, G., Stapf, K. (eds.) (1998) Mehrseitige Sicherheit in der Kommunikationstechnik, Erwartung, Akzeptanz, Nutzung, Bd 2. Add. Wesley, Reading

Müller, G., Rannenberg, K. (eds.) (1999) Multilateral Security – Technology, Infrastructure, Economy, Vol. 3. Add. Wesley, Reading

Rannenberg, K., Pfitzmann, A., Müller, G. (1996) Sicherheit, insbesondere mehrseitige IT-Sicherheit. In: Müller, G., Bunz, H. (Hrsg.) Schwerpunktheft "Sicherheit in der

Kommunikationstechnik" in: Informationstechnik und Technische Informatik (it+ti) 38, Heft 4, August 1996: 7–10

Schoder, D., Strauß, R., Welchering, P. (1998) Electronic Commerce Enquete 1997/98. Empirische Studie zum betriebswirtschaftlichen Nutzen von Electronic Commerce für Unternehmen im deutschsprachigen Raum, Stuttgart 1998

Schneier, B. (1995) Applied Cryptography. John Wiley, New York

Spar, D. et al. (1996) Ruling the Net. Harvard Business review, May-June 1996

Voydock, V. L. (1983) Security Mechanisms in High-Level Network Protocols. In: ACM Computing Surveys 15

Waidner, M. (1996) Development of a Secure Electronic Marketplace for Europe. In: ESORICS, Rome 1996. Springer, Berlin Heidelberg New York Tokyo (http://www.semper.org)

Westfeld, A. (1997) Steganographie am Beispiel einer Videokonferenz. In: Müller, G., Pfitzmann, A. (eds.) Mehrseitige Sicherheit in der Kommunikationstechnik. Add. Wesley, Reading

Wilhelm, U. G. et al. (1997) Sicherheit in Corba und TINA. In: Müller, G., Pfitzmann, A. (eds.) Mehrseitige Sicherheit in der Kommunikationstechnik. Add. Wesley, Reading

Wolf, G. et al. (1997) Sicherheitsarchitekturen. In: Müller, G., Pfitzmann, A. (eds.) Mehrseitige Sicherheit in der Kommunikationstechnik. Add. Wesley, Reading

Günter Müller

Professor of Telematics at the University of Freiburg, was previously a director of IBM Europe. International relationships, especially with Japan and USA, lead 1993 to a consortium on security sponsored by Daimler-Benz. Since1999 he is speaker of the German Research Council (DFG) on the focal point "security". In 1999 he held the Alcatel Professorship at the Technical University in Darmstadt.

XML@work: The Case of a Next-Generation EDI Solution

P. Buxmann

Department of Information Management, Technical University, Freiberg,
Federal Republic of Germany

buxmann@bwl.tu-freiberg.de

Abstract
Only about 5% of the companies which could profit from EDI actually use it. The main reason is that especially small and medium-sized enterprises (SMEs) try to avoid the considerable setup- and operating costs of traditional EDI solutions. We demonstrate how new emerging network technologies, in particular XML, can open communications networks and shape the way businesses can interact with one another. Together with our partner Lufthansa AirPlus we developed a next generation EDI solution that aims at opening EDI networks.

1. Introduction

The usage of EDI (Electronic Data Interchange) enables the inter-organizational exchange of business documents. A typical field of usage is the sending and receiving of sales orders. A carmaker, for example, can send sales orders to his suppliers via EDI, who can then process them immediately in their computer systems. Another example is a company from the telecommunication sector that can use EDI to submit invoices to their customers.

After a short glance into the common literature the first impression could be that the usage of EDI is plainly the "killer-application" which offers the opportunity of millions cost cuts and supports just-in-time-production. Ultimately EDI is levied to a strategic factor of competition (Emmelhainz, 1993). But there also is a down side to the medal: Today the usage of EDI is mainly restricted to large companies. In an empirical study the pressure of large business partners is named as an important reason for the introduction of EDI (Westarp et al., 1999). Only approximately five percent of the companies that could benefit from EDI actually use it (Segev et al., 1997). Often the high costs of implementation and maintenance are named as the reason to refrain from the introduction of EDI especially in small and medium-sized enterprises. Moreover, many of the existing solutions are platform dependent which results in further capital investment for hardware and software to enable the usage of EDI.

The Internet with its wide diffusion, easy access, and worldwide infrastructure could give a new boost to EDI. The analysis of new opportunities based upon open web standards is the subject of this article. A key role for the future of EDI is shown here by the usage of the Extensible Markup Language (XML). This standard serves as a basis for describing EDI documents and supports both easy processing and integration of data into the processes of the involved business partners.

In the second section of this paper we will give an overview about the status quo of EDI. Section 3 is about the opportunities of XML to support modern EDI solutions. In section 4 we will introduce a next generation EDI solution using a case of Lufthansa AirPlus. Finally, we will present five statements about the future of EDI.

2. Electronic Data Interchange – Status quo

An empirical survey we conducted in the summer of 1998 among the 1.000 largest companies in Germany and the US shows that about 52 percent of the responding enterprises in Germany and about 75 percent in the US actually use EDI. On average, German enterprises use EDI with 21 percent of their business partners, while it is 30 percent in the US. With these business partners, 38 percent of the revenue is realized in Germany and 40 percent in the US. This confirms the hypothesis that EDI is primarily applied with important customers. It also seems that EDI plays a more important role in the United States than it does in Germany. Moreover, the current situation in the field of EDI is marked by the usage of a wide variety of heterogeneous and partly incompatible standards. The dominating standard in the US is ANSI X12, while EDIFACT is the European one (Westarp et al., 1999) (see Fig. 1).

Let us take a look at the advantages and disadvantages of using EDI.

First of all, the implementation of EDI causes *one-time costs*. These could be costs for software, training or additional staff as well as possible costs for organizational changes. In particular, costs for restructuring internal processes are difficult to quantify and are often underestimated when anticipating the implementation costs of an EDI system. These costs can vary tremendously depending on the number of

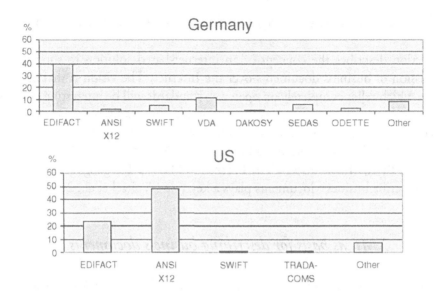

Fig. 1. Status quo of EDI standards

business partners as well the underlying technology. The US Chamber of Commerce estimates that implementation costs average about $50.000 (Waltner, 1997).

Furthermore, the usage of EDI leads to *current costs*. A major role play communication costs that have to be paid to a VAN provider for the usage of his communication infrastructure.

According to our empirical study, the usage of EDI results in a cost reduction of about $208.000 per year. Furthermore, immediate access to data leads to time savings and allows a less capital binding just-in-time-production. Finally, strategic advantages arise through a better customer orientation.

Moreover, the empirical study reveals that time savings are the number one reason to implement EDI – 83% of the people questioned in Germany and 82% of the people in the US named that aspect (Westarp et al., 1999).

So far, we emphasized the advantages of EDI. Thus, what could be the reason for the fact that only 5% of the companies for whom the usage of EDI would be an advantage actually use EDI as we have mentioned in the introduction? If we look at the companies using EDI today we find that mainly large companies apply it. To give an example: A large tire manufacturer receives sales orders via EDI in many cases from only a few selected customers, e.g. carmakers. Other customers like large gas stations or supermarkets have been excluded yet. The reason for that, next to the relatively high cost for the implementation of EDI technology, can be seen in the lack of IT-know-how. While large companies usually have a large IT staff at their disposal, small and medium-sized enterprises cannot rely on similar resources.

3. Concept and Implementation of an Internet-based Solution

This section describes the concept of an internet-based solution to support the transmission of business documents over the Internet. The vision is that an EDI solution which relies completely on open web standards will be interesting even for those users that until now have chosen not to implement traditional EDI solutions. This could be the basis for reducing the investments in information technology in order to support both short-term and long-term inter-organizational relationships (Bakos and Brynjolfsson, 1993). The Extensible Markup Language (XML) that is used to describe business documents plays a key role (Weitzel et al., 2001).

XML as basis for describing business documents

XML is a meta language used to describe data, e.g. business documents, in a way it can be exchanged and further processed between a large number of applications. The following example describes a sales order using XML (see Fig. 2).

In comparison to HTML it becomes clear that the document gets understandable using semantic tag names. Moreover, XML is able to describe the structure of a

```
<?xml version="1.0" ?>
<!DOCTYPE ORDER SYSTEM "ORDER.DTD">
<ORDER>
   <HEAD>
       <NAME>Mustermann</NAME>
       <DATE>02.10.1998</DATE>
       <E-MAIL>customer@anywhere.com</E-MAIL>
   </HEAD>
   <BODY>
       <ITEM>
           <DESCRIPTION>cd rom drive</DESCRIPTION>
           <ARTICLE-NO>123456</ARTICLE-NO>
           <AMOUNT>5</AMOUNT>
       </ITEM>
       <ITEM>
           <DESCRIPTION>monitor</DESCRIPTION>
           <ARTICLE-NO>9876</ARTICLE-NO>
           <AMOUNT>1</AMOUNT>
       </ITEM>
   </BODY>
</ORDER>
```

Fig. 2. Sales order as an XML document

document (Bosak, 1997). As we can see in the figure above, a sales order consists of two parts, the head and the body. The body itself consists of several items which involve description, article-no, as well as the amount. HTML is not able to show this kind of structural information, either.

Another advantage of XML is the availability of additional standards like DOM or SAX (W3C_DOM, 2000; W3C_SAX, 1999). These standards provide new opportunities to process XML documents. Today, powerful parsers are existing. For example, in our work we made good experiences with XML 4 Java (http://xml.apache.org).

Moreover, a so-called Document Type Definition (DTD) can be assigned to an XML document to describe its syntax as it is shown in the second line of the document above. The DTD describes mandatory and optional tags as well as the permitted nesting of the tags (content model). With the help of these DTDs XML documents can, for example, be tested on their validity. The following DTD example describes the general structure of a sales order (see Fig. 3).

Beside DTDs, so-called schemes are available for describing document structures, which provide extensions like inheritance, more data types, etc. (Weitzel et al., 2001).

Due to the following characteristics XML is a suitable basis for the development of a WebEDI solution:

– XML has the potential to become the standard description language for the WWW.
– Complex data structures (like EDI standards) can be described in XML.
– A XML document can be processed through an application as well as displayed in a Webbrowser using style sheets. XSL is a definition language for style sheets by means of XML syntax (W3C_XSL, 2000). It consists of two sections: A language for the transformation of XML documents and a XML vocabulary for the specification of representing semantics.

```
<!ELEMENT ORDER          (HEAD, BODY)>
<!ELEMENT HEAD           (NAME, DATE, E-MAIL)>
<!ELEMENT NAME           (#PCDATA)>
<!ELEMENT DATE           (#PCDATA)>
<!ELEMENT E-MAIL         (#PCDATA)>
<!ELEMENT BODY           (ITEM)+>
<!ELEMENT ITEM           (DESCRIPTION, ARTICLE-NO, AMOUNT)>
<!ELEMENT DESCRIPTION    (#PCDATA)>
<!ELEMENT ARTICLE-NO     (#PCDATA)>
<!ELEMENT AMOUNT         (#PCDATA)>
```

Fig. 3. DTD for a sales order document

Standardization Activities in the field of XML/EDI

In this section we will briefly present two selected standardization initiatives which demonstrate the use of EDI on the basis of XML. For further discussion of standardization activities see (Weitzel et al., 2001).

The XML/EDI Group (www.xmledi.com) including companies such as Sun Microsystems, Microsoft, POET, AT&T, or IBM already published the XML/EDI framework in its year of foundation 1997. This framework describes how traditional EDI can be led in XML considering a 100% backward compatibility. EDI messages in this approach correspond to standard formats such as EDIFACT and ANSI X12. Templates contain the processing rules for exchanged messages and data. Agents interpret templates and are used to carry out predefined functions. They are also able to generate new templates if necessary. Moreover, repositories are part of the framework which enable users or applications to look up the meanings and definitions of EDI items.

The Common Business Library (http://www.commerceone.com/xml/cbl) was originally developed by Veo Systems which was taken over by Commerce One. Today, the library is called xCBL 2.0. Commerce One defines xCBL as a "set of XML building blocks and a document framework". xCBL contains a collection of XML specifications as well as modules for business documents like product descriptions, orders, or invoices. Furthermore, xCBL defines a strict separation between the content of XML documents and their transport or logistic of transaction.

EDI standards served as a basis for the definition of xCBL contents. Starting point were subsets of EDIFACT standards and transaction sets of ANSI X12.

Within the xCBL specification further experiences are included. These experiences were gained by Commerce One being a member in standardization committees such as W3C, IETF, Commerce Net's eCo Working Group, OBI, IOTP, RosettaNet, BizTalk, ebXML and OASIS. Section 4 will return to xCBL.

More open standards

As shown in the last two sections, XML is able to describe multiple data structures such as different EDI standards. However, using XML is not enough to set up an internet-based EDI solution. As mentioned in the beginning of this section, our vision was to develop a solution which is completely based upon open standards. Therefore, the following technologies have been used:

- The exchange of XML-documents is supported by the HTTP-protocol.
- In order to ensure a secure data transfer the partners identify themselves via smartcards, and the data is encoded and transmitted using SSL (Secure Socket Layer) (Thomas, 2000). Therefore, the data can neither be read nor manipulated by a third party.
- The application is completely written in Java.

```
<?xml version="1.0"?>
<!DOCTYPE Invoice SYSTEM „CBL.dtd">
<Invoice>
   <InvoiceHeader>
   <InvoiceDate>19990517</InvoiceDate>
   .....
   </InvoiceHeader>
   <InvoiceParties>
   <Buyer>
      <NameAddress>
.....
      </NameAddress>
   </Buyer>
   <Supplier>
   .....
   </Supplier>
   </InvoiceParties>
   <ListOfInvoiceDetail>
<InvoiceDetail>
      <BaseItemDetail>
        <LineItemNum>1</LineItemNum>
        <SupplierPartNum>
           <PartNum>
<Agency AgencyID= „AssignedBySupplier"/>
             <PartID>SKU123</PartID>
           </PartNum>
        </SupplierPartNum>
        <Quantity>
           <Qty>10</Qty>
<UnitOfMeasure><UOM>EA</UOM></UnitOfMeasure>
        </Quantity>
      </BaseItemDetail>
<InvoiceUnitPrice> 13.95</InvoiceUnitPrice>
   </InvoiceDetail>
   ...
   </ListOfInvoiceDetail>
   <InvoiceSummary>
   <SubTotal>328.50</SubTotal>
   <Tax>
      <TaxPercent>8.2</TaxPercent>
      <Location>Santa Cruz County</Location>
      <TaxAmount>26.947</TaxAmount>
      <TaxableAmount>328.50</TaxableAmount>
   </Tax>
   <Total>355.437</Total>
   </InvoiceSummary>
</Invoice>
```

Fig. 4. XML-invoice of the xCBL

The concept of the solution is shaped open to ensure that the exchange of any business document is possible. Currently the business processes "receive/send sales order" as well as "send/receive invoices" are supported. In the next section we take a closer look at the exchange of invoices. Our prototype served as a basis for the launch of Seals (www.seals.net).

4. The Exchange of Invoices – The Case of Lufthansa Airplus

This section provides a description of an application of our solution at Lufthansa Airplus. First, invoices in the Lufthansa Airplus specific invoice-format LARS are converted into XML and saved in an Oracle database. For this purpose, a template containing a dictionary with the attributes of the invoice's data types and the tags and structure of the XML-invoice is used to create an XML-file for prospective presentation in a browser. This XML file is based on the invoice standard of the xCBL (see section 3.2). Figure 4 shows an invoice in the xCBL format.

All a Lufthansa AirPlus customer needs is a browser, Internet access and a smartcard which offers access to the Extranet, based upon a public-key infrastructure with Global Sign being the certificate authority (Weitzel et al., 2000).

A customer who wants to participate in the system gets a smartcard containing a personal certificate and a smartcard reader. If customers want to access their invoices, they contact the homepage of AirPlus and identify themselves by using the Smart-card. The Webserver checks the validity of the certificates and customers' access rights via a directory server giving them access to their respective invoices. As already mentioned in section 3.3, communication is secured using 128-bit SSL.

Figure 5 shows secure transfer and exchange of invoice data.

Presenting the invoice in a browser is made possible by using XSL style sheets where the layout of the invoice is defined. Since XML distinguishes between data and presentation format, invoice data can be adapted to different needs using different style sheets without having (see Fig. 6) to change the XML-file in any way. Ideally, the customer uses an XML-capable browser like Internet Explorer 5 or Netscape 6 which can directly process the XML-invoice document. Alternatively, the XML-file can be rendered to HTML on the server-side using the style sheets and the invoice-file enabling browsers that are not XML-capable to present the invoice anyway.

If the customer wishes to import data from the (XML-) invoice into his internal systems, this can be done with the help of a signed Java-applet (Weitzel et al., 2000). It is transmitted together with the invoice. By signing the applet it can individually be granted access to databases outside the Java-sandbox. At mouse-click, the customer can import the defined data from the invoice into a local database. This is possible with all databases for which JDBC or ODBC-drivers are available.

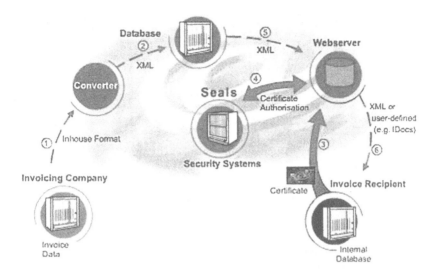

Fig. 5. Secure transfer and exchange of invoice data

Before the first data import is done, it is necessary to carry out a mapping where the customer defines, which data is to be imported into which tables and their fields of the local database. After this mapping is done, any future import will work automatically.

Our mappingtool, which is a Java-applet ready for use on the AirPlus-Server, completely supports a visual mapping. The applet accesses the local database using JDBC to oppose the database structure with the structure of the XML-invoice-format. The dictionary (also an XML-file) that was already used for generating the XML-invoices, contains not only the above mentioned information about the invoice-format but also a description of all invoice elements in explicit and human-readable form, thereby serving as a documentation of the XML invoice format. All the customer has to do is map the database field to the respective invoice element he or she wishes to import. This way, the use of 'full-size EDI' is no longer necessary, when 'custom-size EDI' is to be used. In order to make sure that only meaningful allocations are made, a check of data types and a check of the relations between the tables is performed during this mapping. The result of the mapping is a so-called import-template in XML-format that is stored on the customer's system for later automatic import of invoice data. This template specifies which elements of the (XML-)invoice are imported into which table-fields.

During the import, the applet, which is transmitted together with the invoice, synchronizes the import template and the respective invoice and generates valid SQL-commands for the import by utilizing the relationships between the XML-elements of the invoice. Among other things, XPointers are used during this import, with which single elements of the XML-documents can be selected.

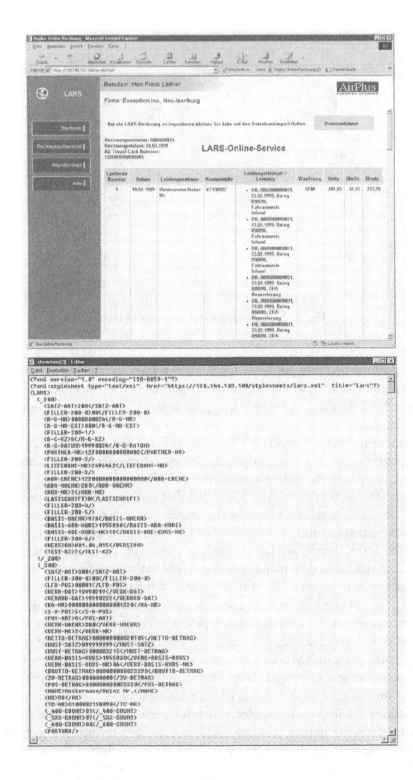

Fig. 6. Invoice presented in a browser and as source code

The open architecture of the solution also enables the support of multiple standards. Each of those standards only requires a separate XML document that synchronizes appropriate information in the data fields of the respective standards with the inhouse system. This way, applications which process documents in foreign formats can understand these documents, even if they only have access to the contents of the communication. Aside from the possibility of supporting different standards, this method enables an easy and flexible alteration of the transaction contents, i.e. the data to be exchanged (see Fig. 7).

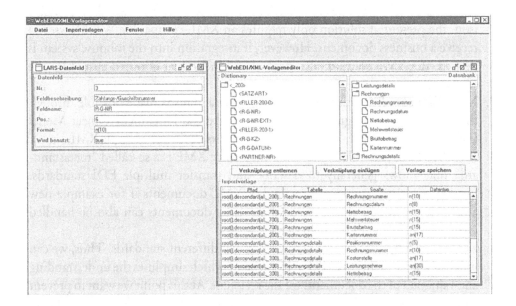

Fig. 7. Mapping to inhouse structures

The number of business documents the solution is capable of supporting is basically unlimited. For example, product catalogs could be distributed over this architecture. All that is needed is a format dictionary to configure the system for different business documents. The data source is not necessarily some particular inhouse format like LARS but can also be any database or a SAP system.

Beside the integration into databases, the solution also provides further integration opportunities, e.g. SAP integration by using BAPI technology or IDOCs (Buxmann and König, 2000) or the download of EDIFACT-files.

5. Conclusions

In the previous chapter we presented a XML-based EDI solution. Through that the question arises if and how far XML/EDI will replace traditional EDI. Do the classical solutions still have a right to exist or will they be replaced step by step or respectively in the context of a big bang?

To answer that question we analyze the advantages of XML/EDI and compare those with traditional EDI. This leads to five statements about the role of XML in future EDI solutions.

1. XML/EDI does its part in the reduction of entrance barriers for the participation in EDI networks. The reason for this can be seen in the high effort and sometimes the lack of know how that is necessary to build up traditional EDI relations. Thus, for the traditional EDI a special converter is needed. In comparison, the presented solution only requires an XML-compatible Webbrowser to receive a business document. However, if integration into the inhouse system is desired, the XML solution also needs some individual effort to customize the solution.

2. XML/EDI simplifies further processing of data. This is made possible through the availability of programming interfaces like the Document Object Model (DOM) (W3C_DOM, 2000) and powerful parsers (in our example XML4Java).

3. XML/EDI can lead to a higher flexibility, since XML is a so-called "metastandard" that allows generally to describe and transfer multiple EDI standards. Furthermore, it is quite easy to modify XML-documents if for example new attributes are added. The presentation of the documents can also be handled relatively flexible with the help of style sheets.

4. XML/EDI simplifies the conversion between different standards. Thus, we can link XML documents to DTD or to a scheme which simplifies the understanding and valuation of the documents for the recipient. At this point we want to prevent a misunderstanding: Even though XML allows a semantical description of data it does not automatically assure a common understanding. For example, an analysis of the context of data modeling in a chemical industry company, revealed 14 different meanings for the word "revenue". The vision of a troublefree understanding of information as well as an automated conversion will also not be completely fulfilled through XML. A promising approach, however, is the development of XSLT, which provides powerful concepts to conduct translations between different XML standards.

5. XML/EDI leads to low communication costs, since we can use the Internet as infrastructure. Compared to the current costs that have to be paid to the VANs, the costs for Internet usage are nearly zero.

The bottom line is, that XML can do its part to open up EDI networks. This can, on the one hand, enable small and medium-sized enterprises to build up their own EDI networks in a relatively simple manner. On the other hand existing EDI networks can be expanded. This will, with some time, lead to the replacement of traditional EDI networks.

References

Bakos, Y., Brynjolfsson, E. (1993) Information Technology, Incentives, and the Optimal Number of Suppliers. J Management Information Systems 10: 37–53

Bosak, J. (1997) XML, Java and the future of the Web, October, 3rd, http://sunsite.unc.edu/pub/sun-info/standards/xml/why/xmlapps.html

Buxmann, P., König, W. (2000) Inter-organizational Cooperation with SAP Systems, Berlin et al.

Densmore, B. (1998) EDI vs. The new kids. Computerworld, 06. 04. 1998, http://www.computerworld.com/home/Emmerce.nsf/All/980406edi

Emmelhainz, M. (1993) EDI – A Total Management Guide, 2nd edn. Van Nostrand Reinhold, New York

Marcella, A., Chan, S. (1993) EDI Security, Control, and Audit. Norwood

Megginson (2000) SAX 2.0: The Simple API for XML. http://www.megginson.com/SAX/index.html

Segev, A., Porra, J., Roldan, M. (1997) Internet-based EDI Strategy. Working Paper 10–21, Fisher Center of Management and Information Technology, University of California Berkeley, http://haas.berkeley.edu/~citm/wp-1021.pdf

Thomas, S. (2000) SSL & TSL Essentials: Securing the Web. Wiley, New York et al.

Tucker, M. (1997) EDI and the Net: A profitable partnering. Datamation, April 1997. http://www.datamation.com/PlugIn/issues/1997/april/04ecom.html

Turowski, K., Fellner, K. (eds.) (2000) XML in der betrieblichen Praxis – Standards, Möglichkeiten, Praxisbeispiele. dpunkt, Heidelberg

Waltner, C. (1997) EDI Travels The Web – EDI over the Web offers companies cheaper E-commerce and messaging via browsers. Internetweek, Issue 668, 16.06.1997. http://www.techweb.com/se/directlink.cgi?CWK19970616S0066

Weitzel, T., Buxmann, P., Ladner, F. (2000) The Extensible Markup Language – New opportunities in the area of EDI. In: Proceedings of the 8th European Conference on Information Systems (ECIS 2000)

Weitzel, T., Harder, T., Buxmann, P. (2001) E-Business und EDI mit XML. dpunkt, Heidelberg

Westarp, F., Weitzel, T., Buxmann, P., König, W. (1999) The Status Quo and the Future of EDI – Results of an empirical survey. In: Proceedings of the 7th European Conference on Information Systems (ECIS'99), Copenhagen 1999, pp. 719–731

W3C_DOM (2000). Document Object Model (DOM), 14. April 14 2000, http://www.w3.org/DOM/

W3C_SOX (1999) Schema for Object-Oriented XML 2.0, W3C Note 30. July 1999. http://www.w3.org/TR/NOTE-SOX

W3C_XSL (2000) Extensible Style Sheet Language (XSL). http://www.w3.org/Style/XSL

Peter Buxmann

Received a diploma in Business Administration in 1990 from Frankfurt University. At the same university, he received the Ph.D. degree in 1995 and completed his habilitation in 1999. In 1997 he was Visiting Scholar at the Walter A. Haas School of Business, U.C. Berkeley. Since 2000 he is Professor of Information Systems at the Technical University of Freiberg. His research interest is in e-business, XML/EDI, Supply Chain Management, and Economics of Standards.

E-Commerce/E-Business Education: Pedagogy or New Product Development?

P. M. C. Swatman[1] and E. S. K. Chan[2]

[1]Faculty of Informatics, University of Koblenz-Landau,
Federal Republic of Germany
[2]School of Management Information Systems, Deakin University,
Melbourne, Australia

paula.swatman@uni-koblenz.de
elsie.chan@deakin.edu.au

Abstract

E-commerce/e-business has been developing at a tremendous pace over the past few years – indeed, since the creation of the NASDAQ index, e-business has become one of the most widely-discussed and rapidly-growing parts of the business world. New types of businesses are evolving within this New Economy and, with them, new business models (or modified versions of traditional business models) are being created to cater for the new business activities and new transactions which are taking place.

Education, too, is undergoing significant changes. The increasing demand for skilled and experienced IT people with both technical and creative skills has combined with an already serious pre-existing shortage of staff having such qualifications to produce an almost insatiable demand for training at all levels – post-graduate, under-graduate and technical. Universities, many of which are in any case under pressure to bring in industry funding to fill the gap left by lower levels of government support, are responding by developing specialist subjects, degrees and diplomas at under-graduate and, particularly, at graduate level. The rate of development and the reactive nature of many of these offerings, however, suggest that what is occurring is not so much an exercise in pedagogy as a marketing activity.

Over the past two years, the rate at which e-commerce/e-business university programs have been introduced around the world has escalated dramatically. This chapter looks at the underlying issues prompting universities to engage in this flurry of new program/course creation. We make use of some preliminary statistics gathered in the Asia-Pacific region to suggest that what is actually taking place is new product development, rather than new program development; and then consider the implications of this marketing-based approach to degree/ program/course creation.

1. Introduction

The introduction of the word wide web in 1992/3 had a profound impact on the then primarily business-focused electronic commerce market, offering a consistent and usable interface which was readily available to SMEs and even individuals (Poon and Swatman, 1999). Since that time, electronic commerce has evolved rapidly – becoming, in the process, a more universal and complex phenomenon than the EDI pioneers of the 1970's and 1980's could ever have imagined. Towards the end of the 1990's there was a US-based move to rechristen the overall trend of electronically-enabled business activities e-business – and to reserve the previous generic term e-commerce for the actual (and more limited) exchange of value-based goods and services (see, for example, the discussion in Mesenbourg, 1999). In this chapter we use the terms e-commerce and e-business interchangeably, largely because many of the authors we cite are themselves still unsure of which term has become the de facto "standard".

The rise of the Information Economy has had significant effects across most business sectors – both public and private. The University of Texas at Austin's Center for Research in Electronic Commerce notes that *'the Internet Economy supported an additional 650,000 jobs in 1999 as revenues soared to over half a trillion dollars'* (University of Texas, 2000). As more and more businesses turn to the Internet to gain strategic advantage – or even just to keep up with their competitors – the demand for employees skilled in a variety of IT, and creative functions grows. Unfortunately, this demand has come at a time when there was already a shortage of skilled workers, and has therefore exacerbated the existing scarcity in this area (FACTOTUM 1996, AIIA, 1999). As companies vie with one another to attract the most skilled and most entrepreneurial staff, demand is placed on educational institutions to provide graduates who can fill these gaps (Snoke and Underwood, 1998; Young and Keen, 1998; Castleman and Coulthard, 1999; Rao, 1999). The Australian government's National Office of the Information Economy (NOIE) points out that: *'the demand for IT&T skills has risen strongly over the past decade. An adequate supply and appropriate mix of IT&T skills is crucial in ensuring that the skill requirements of industry are met'* (NOIE, 2000).

Educational institutions at all levels – universities, polytechnics and technical colleges – are rushing to offer programs and courses in a variety of e-commerce/ e-business areas. While one obvious area is the technical skills required to design and build web sites, there is substantial demand for experienced people with managerial ability who also have a good understanding of e-business and related fields such as e-marketing, logistics, or the legal implications of the developing New Economy

(Chan and Swatman, 1999, 2000). This rapid growth in e-commerce/e-business education programs can be seen in virtually every part of the world. Numbers of programs have grown dramatically over the past two years. For example, in 1998 only two US universities offered accredited degrees in e-commerce (Nickell, 1999), but by 2000 there were:

- 7 bachelors degrees with a major in electronic commerce (AACSB, 2000a)
- 15 e-business/e-commerce masters programs (AACSB, 2000b) and
- 47 Master's degree with an e-business/e-commerce concentration (AACSB, 2000c).

This dramatic growth is not limited to the United States – although 6 out of 8 universities in Hong Kong are already offering e-business/e-commerce programs the Hong Kong government's Education and Manpower Bureau believes that there will still be a shortage of 56,000 IT professionals in 10 years' time. Consequently, the Hong Kong government has provided funding to the City University of Hong Kong to support 120 places in an Associate Degree in e-business which will start in September 2001 (Australian Chinese Daily, 2000).

Although the creation of tertiary programs in the e-business/e-commerce field is solving some of the immediate problems of skill shortages, this rapid development creates problems of its own. Traditionally, university degrees are offered after a careful analysis of the market's needs, the expertise available within the offering institution and the resources which can be drawn upon for new initiatives. e-commerce/ e-business degree development does not appear to be following that pattern.

This chapter initially looks at the issues for service industries in the New Economy, touching on disintermediation, re-intermediation and the rise of the cybermediary; and then considers the role which marketing and, in particular, new product development techniques can play in assisting the developers of new service products to match their expertise to market requirements. We then discuss the issue of e-commerce/e-business program/course development and, using a preliminary survey of new e-commerce/e-business offerings in the Asia-Pacific region as a case example, argue that it appears that many (if not all) the educational institutions offering new e-commerce programs are actually following a new product development strategy, rather than the traditional pedagogic development process and are themselves becoming cybermediaries – with all the complications such a change in market positioning can bring. Finally, we consider the issues for academics faced with a need for rapid program/course development in a domain where skilled staff are as hard to find as they are in industry; and where expertise in marketing techniques is not widespread.

We appreciate that business-to-consumer (B2C) e-commerce activities (those transactions which occur between a business organisation and its end-customers) make up only a small component of the total e-commerce marketplace – indeed, the investment and consulting company Goldman Sachs suggests that B2C may eventually provide as little as 5% of total e-commerce. Our focus, however, is on

e-commerce education which, while clearly a B2C activity, is nonetheless a significant contributor to the overall economy in almost all developed countries. It seems
likely that the rapid growth of what might be termed 'eEducation' will increase the
proportion of B2C activities well beyond the 5% mark (University of Texas, 2000).
International Data Corporation (IDC) estimates that the number of college students enrolled in distance learning courses will reach 2.2 million by the year 2002,
up from 710,000 students in 1998 and eCollege.com reported US$4.7 million in
revenues for 1999 (a 178% increase on 1998).

2. Disintermediation and Reintermediation in the New Economy

Intermediaries offer a wide range of service and facilities, including agents, traders,
brokers, dealers, wholesalers/distributors and providers of specialised information –
among many others. Some of the facilities available through the service industry can
be replicated by the determined citizen, while others are difficult to replace (the
purchase of large quantities of foreign currency, for example, can only occur legally
through the official foreign exchange market, operated by a bank or reputable
NBFI).

The role of the intermediary has been well understood since at least the days of
the pharaohs, but the commercialisation of the Internet and the development of the
world wide web have changed the role of the intermediary almost beyond recognition. The Web allows each individual to search for his or her own information and
to make purchases of goods or services directly from the provider, without needing
assistance from a broker or dealer. The world wide web offers a perfect medium for
the disintermediation of the middleman. Davenport (1996) summarised the
defining attributes of disintermediating technologies as being broadly available, so
that almost any potential buyer can reach the seller; easy to use; able to truly portray
the product being sold (i.e. being able to display colour, audio and video images);
and able to offer information in whatever way is required (i.e. brief, succinct – or
more detailed, once the would-be buyer's interest is piqued).

Yet there is another side to the intermediation coin. While many companies –
and even industries, such as the travel industry – have suffered badly from direct
consumer access to the Internet, the business-to-business (B2B) market is thriving
(see, for example, Hicks, 1999; Berst, 2000). Those organisations (or individuals)
clever enough to recognise the opportunities provided by the Web are reinventing
themselves as 'cybermediaries' – intermediaries offering value-added services to
consumers and vendors over the Internet. While sellers really only need to be put in
contact with purchasers, buyers have many needs which can be met by cybermediaries, ranging from price/quality information to online interest calculators, specialist
advice on problems, or online alerts to the advent of a particular occurrence, such as
the imminent auction of a work of art (Tillett, 2000).

Nunes and Papas (1998) call this 'modelling the electronic channel system' and identify five roles for cybermediaries (or 'electronic intermediaries' as they name them):

- Seller agents, who make markets more accessible to;
- Buyer agents, who search and evaluate goods and services for purchasers; and provide decision support advice to consumers;
- Context providers, who are essentially portal;
- Payment enablers who manage the financial side of Internet purchases; and
- Fulfillment specialists who move the goods from the manufacturer to the consumer.

The creation of new online service industries is an example of 're-intermediation', which has evolved as the previous generation of service offerings are slowly disappearing. The ever-increasing number of 'hubs', 'portals', 'aggregators', 'clearinghouses' and 'exchanges', to name but a few of the terms currently being used to describe B2B Internet-based e-commerce, show that entirely new ways of doing business are being created (see, for example, Democker, 2000; McKeown and Watson, 1997). The development of business models is tending to follow the creation of the actual business, so great is the speed of uptake and innovation in this area.

One area in which disintermediation and re-intermediation is only just beginning to be understood is the education market. Universities have tended to see themselves as the sole providers of high-quality education for adults – and many are struggling to come to terms with the growth of cybermediaries who offer not merely short courses, but even full degree programs over the Internet in a manner designed to be very attractive to cash-rich/time-poor New Economy citizens (see, for example, OnlineEd 2000, EdSurf 2000, or ApTech 2000, which provide a good picture of the variety of programs and courses available online through commercial vendors). These education cybermediaries, being primarily profit-focused, are very much aware of the marketing issues involved in offering new education 'products' to a hungry audience. Universities which cannot recognise this challenge may well find themselves disintermediated in their own market sector.

3. New Product and New Service Product Issues

A considerable amount of research has been undertaken in the area of new product and service development since the beginning of the 1990's. To cite merely a few, in 1991 Mahajan and Wind conducted a survey of 69 firms to assess the role of 24 new product models. They found that the use of new product models was not widespread but that, despite their infrequent use, developers tended to use these models to improve the success rate of new products, as well as to identify problems with the product and alternative marketing strategies. In the same year, Lovelock (1991) developed a framework for understanding the services market. Urban and Hauser

(1993) suggested a new product design process for customers' needs. Wind and Mahajan (1997) addressed 18 critical issues in new product development (NPD). They believed that current approaches to NPD and marketing research and modelling for NPD were inadequate. Rao (1997) noted a need for advanced books on research methods and models for NPD which would include some of the recent methodological advances in the analysis of customer perceptions, preferences, and choices. Langford and Cosenza (1998) suggested using Service/Good analysis to develop good service strategy.

This plethora of research into the development of new goods and services does not, however, clarify the distinction between physical products and service products. Corkindale et al. (1989) distinguished two basic types of services: service products and product services. Service products are marketed purely as services, e.g. banking, insurance, consultancy and education. Product services, by contrast, are quite frequently an inseparable part of a package, such as computer installation and maintenance, customer training for after-sales, and other similar 'add-ons'. Lovelock et al. (1998) distinguished between physical products and service products as follows: the performance of service products are intangible; customers have greater involvement in the production process in service products; people are a part of a service product; there are greater difficulties in maintaining quality control standards in service products; it is more difficult for customers to evaluate service products; there is an absence of inventory in service products (as service cannot be stored); the time factor is important in service products; and, finally, the structure and nature of the distribution channels are different in the case of service products.

4. Designing a New Service Product

A new service product is composed of the following attributes: level of innovation, distinguishable characteristics, types and scope of services, naming and branding, accompanying goods and supplementary services, added value for customers, duration of ownership, business and customer relationships, delivery channels; and, finally, the price of the product and its method of payment (McCarthy et al., 1997; Hart, 1999).

Innovation

When designing a new service product, it is important to clarify the level of innovation which is involved. Generally speaking, the higher the level the longer the development time and the greater the risk of the new product – although more innovative products are also those which yield the highest potential returns. Gruenwald (1992) stated that being new is important; and that being different is also important. Being both new and different provides a major impetus to new product success.

Distinguishing Characteristics

The distinguishing characteristics of a new service product bring with them the chance of greater success – or of greater lack of success. For example, as Bebko (2000) points out: *'It has been argued that the single most important difference between products and services is the characteristic of intangibility. In fact, it has been said that intangibility is the key to determining whether or not an offering is a service or product (Zeithaml and Bitner, 1996). This characteristic has a profound effect on the marketing of services (Lovelock, 1991; Rushton and Carson, 1989). Levitt (1981) argued that special difficulties arise from this intangibility which lead to quality control problems for the producer and evaluation problems for the consumer. It is this intangibility, or lack of physical attributes, that most likely is the reason for service variability, inseparability and perishability.'* (Bebko, 2000)

Type and Scope

These are among the attributes of a service product which determine its development time and cost. Service products which require significant lead times for development will require significantly greater sales volumes or higher prices for success, while whose scope is wide-ranging and/or which require significant amounts of hands-on support are likely to be expensive to maintain and to require highly skilled support staff.

Naming and Branding

These attributes will influence the acceptance of a new service product by its customers. It is clear that well-established brands have less difficulty in gaining acceptance of new service products than do brands which are relatively unknown to the consumer. Similarly, service products which can take advantage of the names of well-known existing physical products face fewer obstacles in achieving success. Ries and Ries (2000) describe the 'Eleven Laws of Internet Branding' which cover the aspects of: business tool, interactivity, common name, proper name, singularity, adverting, globalism, speed, vanity, divergence and transformation.

Other Attributes

Other relevant attributes may include (i) accompanying goods and supplementary services, (ii) whether the product offers added value for customers, (iii) the duration of ownership (the length of time over which the service is provided), (iv) the relationship between customers and the business (Lovelock et al. 1998) and (v) delivery channels. A further important issue is whether this relationship continues after the service has been provided.

Price and Payment Methods

The final attribute is the *price of the service product and the payment method(s) available*. Here market research and modelling are needed to arrive at the optimum price which can be charged for a new offering. New payment methods in B2C transactions such as e-Cash, e-Check or security credit-card charging should certainly be considered for their appropriateness (Turban et al., 1999), although the little evidence we have to date suggests that customers continue to prefer their familiar credit card when paying for electronic services. Once the new service product is designed, an action plan for marketing should, ideally, be produced by the organisation to implement its new concept.

These attributes, which are clearly applicable to physical goods in a physical consumer marketplace, are equally applicable to education products in an online education market-space.

5. E-Commerce/E-Business Education – Applying a Service Product Logic

We have, for some time, been investigating the explosive development of tertiary e-commerce programs in universities within the Asia-Pacific region. During the early days of this research project we focused on the issues of curriculum development associated with this rapid program development process – but it became apparent over time that these courses and programs were being developed in a manner which was more akin to the concept of 'service products' than to traditional pedagogic curriculum development. Universities were offering programs and courses with great rapidity and, it appeared, little regard to the e-commerce domain expertise available within the institution. Market demand was clearly the driving force behind this phenomenon – how else could we explain such examples as the development and offering of an e-commerce degree at either under-graduate or graduate level (or even both), over a period of two years, by six of Hong Kong's eight universities?

Among the earliest of these offerings were single subject general introductions to e-commerce, usually offered by Business or Information Systems Schools/Departments in universities (see, for example, Hampe, 1998; McCubbrey, 1999; Davis et al., 1999 or Hecht, 2000). Wang and Williams (1997) divided the continuum of e-commerce subjects into eight components: Management Information Systems,

Technical Fundamentals of IT, Accounting Information Systems, Business Law, Organization Theory, Marketing, Policy and General Management – a coverage which shows just how broadly-based the e-commerce phenomenon is, even within a Business faculty. Figure 1 shows that Universities, like private sector corporations, have a value chain which must be kept in mind by the developers of new programs and courses – universities which do not consider the 'purchaser' of their 'product' (in this case, both the student and the ultimate employer of that student) run the risk of creating a valueless product (see Fig. 1).

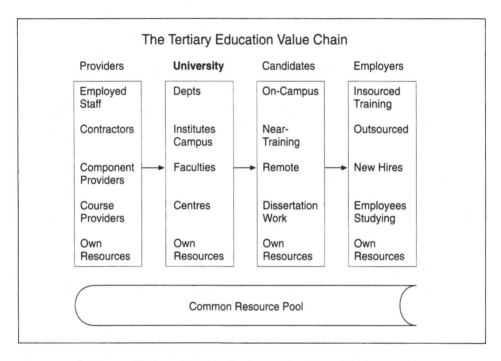

Fig. 1. Higher education also has a value-chain (Clarke, 2000)

If we look once again at the new service product attributes identified from the work of McCarthy et al. (1997) and Hart (1999), listed in the previous section, we can see that the same attributes apply to the development of new and fashionable degree programs:

Innovation

In terms of developing an e-commerce/e-business educational program, where the new program is based on a core of existing subjects with the addition of only a few new e-commerce subjects, less development time is required than for a program in which all subjects are developed *ab initio*. In terms of innovation, the first program is clearly far less innovative, takes less time to develop, is less risky for the offering institution – but offers less market visibility and, potentially, has a lower long-term return. A university which develops an entirely new program, composed of entirely new subjects, has the potential to reap a richer reward.

Distinguishing Characteristics

E-commerce/e-business educational programs are currently in very high demand (particularly at the graduate level). What are the characteristics which distinguish this service product from other, apparently similar service products, such as Information Systems or Information Technology? In some cases there may be little difference apart from the name of the degree or the subjects which comprise that degree. In other cases, however, the new e-commerce offerings are significantly different from IS/IT programs and are composed of tailored and newly developed subjects. Bebko points out that: *'There are five dimensions by which consumers evaluate service quality:*

1. *Tangibles: The appearance of physical facilities, equipment, personnel and communications material.*
2. *Reliability: The ability to perform the promised service dependably and accurately.*
3. *Responsiveness. The willingness to help customers and provide prompt service.*
4. *Assurance: The knowledge and courtesy of employees and their ability to convey trust and confidence.*
5. *Empathy: The caring, individualized attention the firm provides its customers.* (Bebko, 2000)

Clearly, there is considerable room for differentiation within these five criteria – students undertaking new e-commerce/e-business programs will be evaluating their degree on these issues, as well as on the actual content of the subjects offered.

Type and Scope

As the Internet enables global product and service offerings, degree programs are also becoming international commodities, which can be sold cheaply and effectively to students around the world. For example, a number of prestigious European and US universities, supported by a grant from the European Commission, are jointly offering a Master of e-commerce program – the GEM program – which will provide an executive masters degree, based on a mix of online and residential education over a 15-month period (GEM, 2000). E-commerce/e-business programs are finding enthusiastic markets in both their original locations and offshore, both in face-to-face offerings in other countries, and as online offerings. One major disadvantage of this rush to offer programs offshore, however, is the need for high quality, knowledgeable staff who can teach both in the local program and at the offshore locations as well. These degrees are very labour-intensive, requiring constant updating of course content and an excellent understanding of the issues and real-world problems involved. Students paying high prices for imported degrees will not be satisfied with 'ring-ins' having less knowledge and/or commitment than the staff teaching at the home campus.

Naming and Branding

This criterion exists at two levels – the branding of the offering institution, as well as the branding/naming of the degree itself. It is interesting to note that, whereas the earlier degree and program offerings almost universally had the term e-commerce in their title, more recent offerings are tending to use the newer term e-business. One risk for universities moving their e-commerce/e-business offerings online, of course, is that if all universities' e-business degrees are available over the web, the basis on which students select their institution will become ever more important. Why would a student select an online degree from a smallish, local university when she could enrol in one offered by a big-name, prestige institution? Clearly, service (in the sense of the quality of delivery and course content) will be crucial ingredients in this decision.

Other Attributes

Other attributes which were touched on earlier are just as relevant to e-commerce/e-business degree 'products':

(i)   accompanying goods and supplementary services – this is likely to relate to the quality of online facilities and course materials
(ii)   whether the product offers added value for customers – do students really believe that they have improved their employment prospects as a result of studying the program? And do they feel that they have learned useful information and gained a valuable network of contacts during the teaching process?
(iii)   the duration of ownership (the length of time over which the service is provided) – there is a conflict here between students' eagerness to complete their degree, and their desire for a high-quality outcome. Degree offerings vary widely in length and number of subjects across institutions
(iv)   the relationship between customers and the business – this tends to relate back to issues of perceived quality, both in terms of course content and in terms of management of students by teaching and administrative staff
(v)   whether the relationship continues after the service has been provided – this is not an area in which universities outside North America have tended to shine

in the past, but effective management of alumni programmes is crucial to long-term success of these degree products

(vi) delivery channels – whether the programs are delivered through the Web, electronic mall or e-mail.

Price and Payments Methods

Finally, the *price of the service product and the payment method(s) available* are an important differentiating factor for e-commerce/e-business degrees. Universities are, understandably, anxious to maximise income from these fashionable new degrees – but a trade-off must be made between the price the market will bear and the quality of facilities and staff expected in return for a high-priced, premium product. Universities which charge high fees without providing excellent facilities in return will tend to suffer long-term damage to reputation and student numbers.

Such an approach has both risks and returns – and these are significantly increased for those universities delivering their new programs not only within the country of origin of the degree, but offshore as well (as many of the universities in our sample are doing). Offshore programs and online delivery of programs and courses can place the offering institution in the role of intermediary (in the latter case, indeed, potentially in the role of cybermediary). Such a strategy is not dissimilar to those adopted by 'dotcoms' (both the 'clicks and mortar' variety which combine online access with a physical distribution network, as well as the 'pure play' online-only companies). Universities and other educational institutions which enter the cybermediary business without awareness of its risks may well not reap the benefits available to more Internet-aware organisations.

This brief introduction to the issues underpinning the offering of e-commerce/e-business degree products can be highlighted by some 'real' data illustrating the activities in at least part of the world. In the next section of this chapter, we briefly present the results of a survey of new e-commerce/e-business programs developed in four countries within the Asia-Pacific region – Australia, New Zealand, Hong Kong and Singapore – which casts some light on the service product approach to e-commerce/e-business education development.

6. E-Commerce/E-Business Academic Programs in the Asia-Pacific Region

Surprisingly little research has been undertaken into online e-commerce/e-business education. The first survey of e-commerce/e-business education programs was carried out by Davis, Hajnal, de Matteis and Henderson (see Davis et al., 1999) and investigated nearly 50 US and Canadian university-based electronic commerce courses for which syllabi are available on the world wide web between 1995–1998. The survey results suggested that early electronic commerce subjects, developed around 1995, were designed to provide instruction in the use of Web technologies. But, as the technology itself progressed, by 1998 most universities were routinely offering technical or remedial courses in web skills to students, thus relieving electronic commerce courses from the task of diffusing web skills. The authors also found that electronic commerce courses make abundant use of on-line resources, although a few of the subjects in their sample were still using a combination of online resources and paper handouts. Many of the electronic commerce courses originated in the IS department, where instructors possessed a greater degree of technological literacy than the average university educator – suggesting that lack of confidence with the technology was a hurdle to subject development as recently as 1998 in North America.

E-commerce/e-business academic programs have grown so quickly over such a short period of time that the lack of theory underpinning the development process in many of the examples seen on web sites such AACSB (1999) or Chan (2000) is hardly surprising. Our survey of e-commerce/e-business programs covered the period 1998–2000 and focused on the Asia Pacific region countries of Australia, New Zealand, Hong Kong and Singapore. Our intention has been to identify all academic e-commerce/e-business offerings in these institutions – full degree programs at any level, major streams, minor streams and single subjects.

Survey Methodology

We used a combination of email and web pages to obtain the data for the survey (the interested reader may refer to Smith (1997) or Comley (1996) for a more thorough discussion of the use of the Internet for survey data collection). Smith points out that *persuasive arguments for using e-mail include extreme cost reduction and quick turnaround time, facilitative interaction between survey authors and respondents, collapsed geographic boundaries, user-convenience and, arguably, more candid and extensive response quality'* (Smith, 1997). All these arguments applied to our own research design and intentions – and we used email to invite participants to fill in the actual survey form, which was available through a web site and made as user-friendly as possible.

Beginning in November, 1998, we sent out letters to the course coordinators of electronic commerce and Heads of Information Systems, Management, Business Computing, Marketing, and Accounting/Finance Departments within the Business Faculty or Business School of all the universities in Australia, Hong Kong and many other countries. They were requested to fill in our questionnaire on the web at URL http://www.businessit.bf.rmit.edu.au/elsieEC/survey1.htm. At the same time, the universities' web pages were surfed to identify any materials which might have been omitted from the survey responses. 'Electronic Commerce' or 'Electronic Business' were used as key words in our search, with the result that we have gathered only those subjects or courses/programs which are called e-commerce/e-business by their offering institutions. We have further restricted our search of e-commerce/e-business subjects/programs to those where information is available on-line:

- for the survey of Australian universities, we included all Australian universities which are members of the Australian Vice-Chancellor's Committee (AVCC), i.e. 39 universities
- in New Zealand, we included all New Zealand universities which are members of the New Zealand Vice-Chancellor's Committee (NZVCC), i.e. 8 universities
- in Hong Kong, we surveyed all 8 universities and
- in Singapore, we surveyed all 3 universities and ignored the polytechnics and institutes of technical education.

A list of the universities surveyed can be found in Appendix 1.

To avoid the almost inevitable confusion which cross-cultural academic curriculum discussion generates, we define the terms 'subject' and 'course/program' used in this paper:

- A 'subject' in this paper is the smallest object which contributes to a course / program – it cannot be further divided. The term 'course' adopted in North American universities, the expression 'unit' or 'module' used in some Australian universities and the term 'paper' used in some New Zealand universities, are equivalent to the term 'subject' we have used here;
- The terms 'course/program' we use in this paper refer to the gathering of several study objects (subjects) into a complete qualification, e.g. the course/program of a Bachelor's degree, a Graduate Diploma or a Master's degree etc. These terms are therefore equivalent to the term 'program' used in the US and Canada.

The following example illustrates our use of these terms: 20345 electronic commerce is a core *subject* for the *course / program* (degree) of Bachelor of Business.

Asia-Pacific E-Commerce/E-Business Program Survey Results

A market segment in this field may be composed of courses with common characteristics, catering for similar purchasing behaviour (needs), and consumption patterns. Effective segmentation means grouping all these courses into segments of high similarity in terms of their relevant characteristics. This was the approach adopted in the present survey. E-commerce/e-business programs ranged from, at the lower end, half day courses targeted for business professionals to, at the higher end, 3–5 year PhD research projects. The short courses are offered by TAFE (Australia's Tertiary and Further Education vocational training sector), the private sector, or universities. Since the majority of the short courses are *ad hoc* and thus fairly dynamic in terms of content, they were difficult to include in our survey. The Masters by research and PhD courses are, of course, specifically designed by supervisor and student for that particular student's needs – and we have therefore excluded them from our survey as well.

19 Australian universities out of 39 (48.7%) were offering e-commerce/e-business undergraduate and postgraduate programs at the time the data were collected. At a slightly lower level, 3 out of 8 universities in New Zealand (37.5%) were offering e-commerce/e-business undergraduate and postgraduate programs at the time of data collection. The similarity of these proportions suggests that levels of interest in e-commerce/e-business are also similar in the two countries, although New Zealand appears to be at a slightly earlier stage in new degree development.

In Hong Kong, Kwok (2000) stated that *"the first ever degree programme in e-commerce was started less than a year ago (1999) in Hong Kong. By this September (2000), nearly all the universities in Hong Kong will offer some form of e-commerce degree or diploma programme"*. In fact, Kwok's findings matched very closely with our own survey results, i.e., 6 out of 8 universities (75%) in Hong Kong offered e-commerce/e-business programs at the time we were gathering our data. Clearly, development time is an important criterion in what might be described as the more 'fashionable' end of the education spectrum – if it takes a long time to develop a service product, the result may already be out of date when the product is launched onto the market. Products that are designed closer to the time they are introduced are, naturally, less subject to technological and market changes (Moore and Pessemier, 1993).

Singapore, by contrast with the other three countries surveyed, shows a very different pattern. Although the Singapore government is a most enthusiastic sponsor and promoter of e-commerce, there has been very little interest in offering e-business/e-commerce educational programs by Singaporean universities and institutes of technology. Singapore has, for example, a number of government-run e-commerce programs, including:

– the central e-commerce web site (www.ec.gov.sg);
– the e-citizen program (www.ecitizen.gov.sg);
– the e-card with Singaporean photos for web visitors to send to their friends (www.gov.sg/sgip/ecards).

and yet only a few technical institutions offer e-commerce/e-business short courses or diplomas/certificates in e-commerce/e-business (Electronic Commerce Singapore, 1999). One university began to offer an e-commerce degree during the 2000 academic year; and a number of overseas universities are now offering bachelors and masters degree to local students (Management Development Institute of Singapore, 2000a, b). This apparently contradictory result is difficult to explain on the basis of the survey results alone. The enthusiasm with which offshore e-commerce/e-business degrees are being taken up in Singapore suggests that demand there is similar to that in the rest of Asia – clearly, more detailed investigation is required to clarify the issues in Singapore.

Appendix 2 summarises the results of the survey, and includes the details of New Zealand and Singaporean universities.

Segmentation of Programs

The 29 universities listed in Appendix 2 were offering 81 e-commerce/e-business programs (or something very similar). We have classified these into 7 segments:

Type	Description
Undergraduate degree with e-commerce major concentration	Students are required to finish a certain number of core subjects and, in addition, to take a 'stream' of e-commerce subjects. In terms of level of innovation this is comparatively low, because it adapts some/many existing subjects. However, in terms of resources, this degree type is fully utilised – it shares resources with other degree programs. For details, refer to Appendix 3.A.
E-commerce as a joint undergraduate degree with other disciplines	Only one university appears to provide this type of program. Monash University offers a Bachelor of Business and Electronic Commerce – both on campus and by distance education. For details, refer to Appendix 3.B.
Bachelor of e-commerce	A number of universities have chosen not to offer this degree, which differs from one offering institution to another, on the assumption that potential employers will not understand what it means in terms of skills provided. Its distinguishing characteristics need to be made explicit if it is to succeed. For details, refer to Appendix 3.C.
Graduate / Postgraduate Certificate / Diploma in e-commerce/e-business	These programs are primarily designed for those who wish to move into a new area, i.e. potential students may already have a degree in some other area(s). Undertaking a full degree will take too long, so this shorter program, which effectively offers the core of a degree without the electives, fills a market niche. For details, refer to Appendix 3.D.
Masters degree with e-commerce/e-business as a specialisation	These programs aim to provide students with advanced knowledge and skills in contemporary electronic commerce technologies and their applications within business, as part of a lifelong learning or professional development program. For details, refer to Appendix 3.E.
Master of e-commerce/ e-business	Usually offered by Information Systems Departments/ Schools, although increasingly being whole-of-Business-Faculty offerings, the technical foundations, strategic and management issues, development, information management issues in electronic commerce are studied in these programs. For details, refer to Appendix 3.F.
Master of e-commerce/ e-business and other discipline joint degrees	Only Bond University provides this type of program. It offers candidates the opportunity to gain a double masters degree. For details, refer to Appendix 3.G.

The majority of universities world-wide initially offered e-commerce/e-business content in the form of a single subject(s). Subject titles commonly found included 'Electronic Commerce' and 'Introduction to Electronic Commerce'. For details, refer to Appendix 4.

Distinguishing Characteristics of the E-Commerce/ E-Business Programs

How do e-commerce/e-business academic programs distinguish themselves from other, apparently similar degrees? We drew up these lists on the basis of an analysis of 33 Bachelors' degree programs in 22 universities and 29 Masters degree programs in 18 universities. We categorised subjects on the basis of our electronic commerce component model (Chan and Swatman, 1999) into 3 major components: infrastructure, services and legal (see Appendices 5 and 6 for the full analysis). For Bachelors degrees, students usually complete about 24 subjects over 3 years' full time study. The subjects listed in Appendix 5 may be studied as elective or core subjects for the degree. For Masters degrees, students usually complete about 12–16 postgraduate level subjects with/without an e-commerce or e-business project in 3 to 4 semesters' full-time study. The subjects listed in Appendix 6 may be studied as elective or core subjects for the Masters degree.

The subjects listed in Appendices 5 and 6 provide some idea of the scope covered by e-commerce/e-business programs. It is clear that there is considerable overlap among the subjects currently on offer (for example, there are many variations on the theme of e-marketing), and a number of areas are not yet being covered (for example, areas such as mobile commerce or e-health do not yet appear to be included in the material on offer). We currently anticipate that there will be some rationalisation of these subject offerings over time – there is presently too much redundancy and not enough focus on each university's area(s) of specialisation and expertise. In addition, the similarity of many of the programs listed will make it difficult for students to select their preferred university – successful new product developers understand the importance of targeting their market niche, a skill universities will also need to learn.

Discussion of Findings

It is important to reiterate that this survey represents one of the only two investigations of e-commerce/e-business teaching currently available (we briefly discuss the other such survey – Davis et al., 1999 – in the introduction to section 6 of this chapter). Findings are thus indicative, rather than providing a firm, generalisable basis for extrapolation. With that in mind, however, a number of interesting facts emerge from the data. We begin by discussing the results which emerge directly from the data – and then consider the broader issue of tertiary education in e-commerce/e-business as potential service product offerings.

1. The first point we noted was that our market segmentation of 7 types, while useful in categorising types of e-commerce/e-business programs available, did not provide mutually exclusive or orthogonal findings. Our survey results indicated a number of what appeared to be anomalies in the pattern:

   – E-commerce/e-business can be offered by a number of different departments within a single university. They may not necessarily work together to provide a unified program, e.g. the University of Wollongong, Monash University and the Open University of Hong Kong, in all of which several departments offer similar (and, it would appear, competing) programs. From the organisation (university) point of view, as long as their school/department can fulfil the market demand, this may still be feasible, although companies producing physical products which appear to compete are usually targeting specified market segments very carefully.
   – E-commerce/e-business programs are normally offered by Information Systems Schools/Departments, Business Schools, or Computer Science Departments. In fact, electronic commerce is/should be a cross-discipline area (since it combines materials from Information Technology, Information Systems, Law, Computer Science, Business, Marketing, Management, Accounting, Logistics, Finance, Economics and many other disciplines). In terms of service product offerings, it is clear that the producers/developers of these programs have not yet resolved many of the issues involved in new product development (such as identifying target markets, identifying the most appropriate providers, or identifying market requirements).
   – With the exception of Monash University, which has two separate teaching units with electronic commerce in their title across two faculties, the universities in the sample have not chosen to develop a teaching unit specifically for delivering e-commerce/e-business subjects and programs, preferring to run both e-commerce teaching and research centres/units within existing schools/faculties. The new product implications of this very general decision would seem to be that the e-commerce/e-business service product is seen as an extension of existing service product offerings, rather than as an entirely new service product, by almost all developers.

2. The number of courses/programs being offered has grown significantly over the past twelve months. This phenomenon replicates the North American experience (Tabor, 1999; Moran, 1999), but is built on a far smaller population base – and leads to a very important issue, that of availability of staff with sufficient expertise to teach the very challenging e-commerce/e-business programs which business and students alike are demanding.

A combination of the 'newness' of the discipline and the high salaries currently being offered to e-commerce professionals in the private sector has meant that some universities find it difficult to staff their academic programs in this area. Jackson (1999), writing in 'The Australian' newspaper in October 1999, stated that Australian universities are offering innovative e-commerce and Internet courses, but their capacity to staff them is in question. This issue raises the question of just how many new e-commerce/e-business courses/programs can be staffed effectively in the Asia-Pacific region – and places an equivalent question mark over the introduction of e-commerce degrees in other nations.

3. The variety of the offerings which this preliminary survey has elicited also raises the question of whether there is such a thing as an 'ideal' program in e-commerce/e-business. The differing needs of the institutions themselves, their varying levels of staff expertise, the type(s) of students attracted to any particular tertiary institution, and the delivery modes which may be required all combine to suggest that what may form an ideal program in Institution A may not necessarily be equally 'ideal' in Institution B. What should an e-commerce/e-business program focus upon? In terms of new product development, it is clear that considerably more work is required to identify market needs and target markets for these programs.

It is clear from the fairly raw data presented in the appendices that there are a myriad of degrees, courses and individual subjects being offered by the universities in our sample. It is equally clear, from even a cursory glance at the subject and degree titles, that offering institutions appear to be taking a 'scattergun' approach to e-commerce/e-business in which they endeavour to cover all bases, rather than attempting to specialise and/or play to the institution's particular strengths or expertise. As a long-term strategy for product development (whether of physical or service product) this approach is not an effective one. With so few staff having expertise in this field at all (although this problem may diminish somewhat as new, younger academics with recent degrees come 'on stream' to assist with the teaching) attempting to cover all subjects and all areas must surely be seen as a dangerous strategy. In terms of product differentiation, it is clear that this is still in its infancy – with only a few institutions targeting particular niche student groups.

While more (and more detailed) data are clearly required before authoritative statements can be made about the service product development strategies under-way, these preliminary data do suggest that the developers of many, if not most, of the degrees shown in the appendices are likely to have been motivated more by the need to produce programs quickly than by the desire to match as many as possible of the criteria for a successful new service product launch. A cursory glance at the e-commerce/e-business offerings in North America (the richest field for degrees in this field) suggests that these results may well hold true in that continent too.

7. Conclusions

As the popularity of e-commerce/e-business continues apparently unabated, universities are tending to compete in offering such programs – possibly without spending as long in development as they would for a new offering in a more established discipline such as, say, Accounting or Computer Science. The combination of multiple offerings, limited staff with expert knowledge, and intense student and industry demand may well lead to serious quality issues in the creation of courses/programs.

Our findings to date suggest that new courses are likely to appear in even greater numbers over the next 18–24 months – and that these new courses may well offer greater variety than the programs we have seen to date, possibly including a multidisciplinary focus, multiple delivery modes, or collaborative efforts in terms of curriculum development. Further research into B2C new service product development and services marketing, particularly based around electronic delivery, is clearly needed in this area.

One of the problems for academics striving to put together new degree programs and individual courses in the e-commerce/e-business field is that the majority of them do not have a background in marketing of any sort – let alone the specific field of service marketing. It is one of the difficulties of managing higher education at this time that, just as new courses and programs are most urgently needed, academic staff in many parts of the world are under greater pressure to achieve more and more than they have ever been (in terms of program/course development, publishing and other scholarly activity, and the obtaining of external funding from the private sector). Such pressure makes it both more difficult and, at the same time, more urgent than ever to develop degree programs in a sustainable way. We believe that a conscious awareness of the issues involved in new service product development would add to the quality of many of the degrees currently available (or under development); and that attention to market needs and target markets might well add further value to the new programs appearing with such incredibly rapidity around the world.

One aspect of the e-commerce/e-business program development process which we did not investigate is the offering of such degrees in locations other than their geographic 'home' – this applies both to online offerings and to offshore presentation of the degrees/programs by the developing institution. Both these approaches are gaining considerable popularity as the demand for e-commerce education in the Asian market grows to ever higher levels. Both these approaches also affect the new product development strategy which should be adopted by offering institutions. A number of considerations should be borne in mind when creating these new programs, for example:

– Subjects offered online need to be designed in formats which permit ready redevelopment for the requirements of Internet-based presentation and study

– Subjects offered offshore may need to be taught many times each year (depending on the number of locations at which they are offered and the frequency with which they are offered in each location). If the principal lecturer (lecturer-in-charge) of that subject cannot teach at all locations, adequate substitutes must be available and prepared to travel as required
– Multiple assessment methods may need to be developed for each subject, to cater for varying needs in different locations
– Additional subjects may need to be developed to cater for the lack of availability of pre-requisite subjects which are taken for granted in the 'home' country's institution.

Even this very brief summary of considerations shows that the new product development process for would-be education cybermediaries is considerably more complex than it might at first sight appear – particularly for those which are universities and thus comparatively inexperienced in aggressive consumer product marketing. Teams developing education programs which must be brought to market rapidly, and which are likely to require constant updating to retain their currency, need to consider the benefits which new product development techniques and theories can offer their endeavours. Merely getting a degree offered or, more particularly, getting an online degree onto the word wide web, provides no guarantee of success in an increasingly sophisticated market-space. If potential 'customers' can choose between e-commerce/e-business degrees offered around the world, they are likely to choose the best-designed – or even to choose the degree(s) offered by the most prestigious university. Only the quality of the service product offering can affect such an outcome.

References

AACSB (1999) E-Business Education. The International Association for Management Education Products and Services Web page. <http://www.aacsb.edu/e-business/>, (Accessed 25 Nov 2000)

AACSB (2000a) E-Business Education Bachelor's Degree Majors. <http://www.aacsb.edu/e-business/bachelors.html>last modified 7 Nov 2000 (Accessed 25 Nov 2000)

AACSB (2000b) E-Business Education Master's Degree Program. <http://www.aacsb.edu/e-business/msdgrprogram.html>last modified 7 Nov 2000 (Accessed 25 Nov 2000)

AACSB (2000c) E-Business Education Master's Degree Concentration. < http://www.aacsb.edu/e-business/msdgrconcent.html>last modified 19 Sep 2000 (Accessed 25 Nov 2000)

AIIA (1999) Career Tracking Research Project Final Report. <http://www.aiia.com.au/publications/Career%20Tracking%20Report%200299.pdf> (Assessed 25 Nov 2000)

Aptech (2000) ApTech Online Varsity. <http://www.onlinevarsity.com/ovc/ovdbhome.nsf/homepage/openform?openform> (Accessed 7 Dec 2000)

Australian Chinese Daily (2000) City University of Hong Kong will offer E-Business Program. 15 Nov, p. 27 (Chinese version)

Bebko, C. P. (2000) Service Intangibility and its Impact on Consumer Expectations of Service Quality. J Service Marketing 14 (1): 9–26

Berst, J. (2000) B2B: Why it's the Buzz and How to Cash. ZDNet, 21 Feb < http://www.zdnet.
    com/anchordesk/story/story_4487.html> (Accessed 25 Nov 2000)
Castleman, T., Coulthard, D. (1999) Not Just a Job: Preparing Graduates for Careers in the IS
    Workforce. ACIS'99 – Proceedings of the 10th Australasian Conference on Information
    Systems. Wellington, New Zealand, 1–3 Dec, 171–182 <http://www.vuw.ac.nz/acis99/
    Papers/PaperCastleman-097.pdf> (Accessed 25 Nov 2000)
Chan, E. S. K. (2000) Electronic Commerce Course/Program. < http://www.businessit.bf.
    rmit.edu.au/elsieEC/uni.htm > last modified 20 Nov 2000 (Accessed 25 Nov 2000)
Chan, E. S. K., Swatman, P. M. C. (1999) Electronic Commerce: A Component Model.
    Proceedings of the 3rd Annual CollECTeR Conference on Electronic Commerce,
    Wellington, New Zealand. 29 Nov. <http://www.businessit.bf.rmit.edu.au/elsieEC/pdf/
    1999-1.pdf > (Accessed 25 Nov 2000)
Chan, E. S. K., Swatman, P. M. C. (2000) Electronic Commerce Careers: A Preliminary Survey
    of the Online Marketplace. Proceedings of the 13th Bled Electronic Commerce
    Conference, 19–21 June, Bled, Slovenia. <http://www.businessit.bf.rmit.edu.au/elsieEC/
    pdf/2000-1.pdf > (Accessed 25 Nov 2000)
Clarke, R. (1993) EDI is But One Element of Electronic Commerce. Proceedings of the Sixth
    International EDI Conference, Bled, Slovenia 88–98 <http://www.anu.edu.au/people/
    Roger.Clarke/EC/Bled93.html> (Accessed 25 Nov 2000)
Clarke, R. (2000) e-Business Technology and Education: Virtual Universities, Virtual
    Professors' Johannes-Kepler-University Seminar. Linz, Austria, 30 June 2000 <http://
    www.anu.edu.au/people/Roger.Clarke/EC/VirtualUniProf.ppt> (Access 25 Nov 2000)
Comley, P. (1996) The Use of the Internet as a Data Collection Method. <http://www.sga.
    co.uk/esomar.html> (Accessed 21 Sep 2000)
Corkindale, D., Balan, P., Rowe, C. (1989) Marketing Making the Future Happen. Thomas
    Nelson, Melbourne, pp. 209–216
Davenport, T. (1996) Seven Syllables of Salience. CIO Magazine, 1 Feb. <http://www.cio.
    com/archive/020196_dave.html> (Accessed 25 Nov 2000)
Davis, C., Hajnal, C., de Matteis, D., Henderson, M. (1999) Management Skill Requirements
    for Electronic Commerce. 74-85. <http://business.unbsj.ca/users/cdavis/papers/
    Ecomm_mgt_skills_IC_report.pdf > (Accessed 25 Nov 2000)
Democker J. (2000) B-To-B Aggregators: Vertical Domination. Internetweek Online, 2 Feb.
    <http://www.internetwk.com/lead/lead020200.htm> (Accessed 25 Nov 2000)
EdSurf (2000) EdSurf: the Online Distance Education Learning Resource for Adult Students.
    <http://www.edsurf.net/> (Accessed 7 Dec 2000)
Electronic Commerce Singapore (1999) Courses/Relevant Modules on E-Commerce. <http:/
    /www.ec.gov.sg/24071999/24071999_1.html> last modified 21 Sep 1999 (accessed 25
    Nov 2000)
FACTOTUM Research (1996) Demand for skilled people in the IT&T industry toward the
    year 2000. <http://www.aiia.com.au/publications/Demand%20Survey%200496.pdf>
    (Accessed 25 Nov 2000)
GEM (2000) Gem Program. <http://www.heltrun.aueb.gr/gem/gem.htm> last modified 7
    Nov 2000 (Accessed 25 Nov 2000)
Gruenwald, G. (1992) New Product Development: responding to Market Demand. NTC
    Business Books, Illinois, pp. 31–48
Hampe, J. F. (1998) Electronic Commerce in Universities: A Case Study Report from the
    University of Koblenz, Germany. Proceedings of the Eleventh International Bled
    Electronic Commerce Conference, Bled, Slovenia, June 8–10, p. 128
Hart, S. (1999) New product Development. In: Baker, M. J. (ed.) The Marketing Book. The
    Bath Press, Great Britain, pp. 314–336

Hecht, I. (2000) 'e': The Millennial Reality for Business and Education. Proceedings of New Zealand Diploma of Business Conference, Christchurch, New Zealand, 5–7 Jul

Hicks M. (1999) B2B Goes Boom. PCWeek, 25 Oct. <http://www.zdnet.com/pcweek/stories/news/0%2C4153%2C2376988%2C00.html> (Accessed 25 Nov 2000)

Jackson, D. (1999) Staff Crisis in High-tech Uni. Courses. The Australian, 19 Oct. <http://technology.news.com.au/news/4237258.htm> (Accessed 21 Sep 2000)

Kwok, P. (2000) Artificial Intelligence for E-commerce. Open Link, The Open University of Hong Kong, 9 (2): 11

Langford, B. E., Cosenza, R. M. (1998) What is service/good analysis? J Marketing Theory and Practice 6 (1): 16–26

Lovelock, C. H. (1991) Services Marketing. Prentice Hall, New Jersey, pp. 24–38

Lovelock, C. H., Patterson, P. G., Walker, R. H. (1998) Services Marketing Australia and New Zealand. Prentice Hall, Sydney, pp.16–17, 232–236

Mahajan, V., Wind, J. (1991) New Product Models: Practice, Shortcomings, and Desired Improvements. Report No. 91–125, Marketing Science Institute

Management Development Institute of Singapore (2000a) Bachelor's Degree. <http://203.126.201.193/frame_master_body_bac_6.htm> last modified 25 Sep 2000 (Accessed 25 Nov 2000)

Management Development Institute of Singapore (2000b) Master's Degree. <http://203.126.201.193/frame_master_info_2.htm> last modified 16 Aug 2000 (Accessed 25 Nov 2000)

McCarthy, E. J., Perreault, W. D., Quester, P. G. (1997) Basic Marketing: A Managerial Approach. Irwin, Sydney, pp. 273–342

McCubbrey, D. (1999) Designing an Electronic Commerce Curriculum. Communications of the Association for Information Systems 1(2) <http://cais.aisnet.org/articles/default.asp?vol=1&art=2_> (Accessed 25 Nov 2000)

McKeown, P. G., Watson R. T. (1997) Metamorphosis: A Guide to the World Wide World & Electronic Commerce. John Wiley & Sons, New York

Mesenbourg, T. L. (1999) Measuring Electronic Business Definitions, Underlying Concepts and Measurement Plans <http://www.ecommerce.gov/ecomnews/e-def.html> (Accessed 25 Nov 2000) and <http://www.census.gov/epcd/www/ebusines.htm> (Accessed 25 Nov 2000)

Moore, W. L, Pessemier, E. A. (1993) Product Planning and Management: Designing and Delivering Value. McGraw-Hill, New York, pp. 89–116

Moran, S. (1999) B-Schools, New Rules. Business 2.0, Oct. 124–129

Nickell, J. (1999) Biz Schools Get an Update. Wired Magazine, 3 Apr. <http://www.wired.com/news/culture/0,1284,18839,00.html> (Accessed 25 Nov 2000)

NOIE (2000) IT and T skills. The National Office of the Information Economy website. <http://www.noie.gov.au/projects/ecommerce/skills/index.htm> (Accessed 25 Nov 2000)

Nunes, P. F., Papas B. C. (1998) Seeking Your Fortune in the Middle Kingdom. Outlook Magazine Andersen Consulting 10 (1) <http://www.ac.com/ideas/Outlook/6.98/over_currente3.html> (Accessed 25 Nov 2000)

OnlineEd (2000) Welcome to Online Education: Your Future of Learning, <http://www.online.edu/> (Accessed 7 Dec 2000)

Poon, S., Swatman, P. M. C. (1999) A Longitudinal Study of Expectations in Small Business Internet Commerce. Int J Electronic Commerce 3 (3): 21–33

Rao, M. (1999) EM-Wire: Internet Explosion Spurs Market in Training, Education. < http://www.electronicmarkets.org/electronicmarkets/electronicmarkets.nsf/pages/emw_9910_pabrai.html> (Accessed 25 Nov 2000)

Rao, V. R. (1997) Resources for Research and Pedagogy on New Product Development Processes. J Marketing Research XXXIV (Feb 97): 185–192

Ries, A., Ries, L. (2000) The Eleven Immutable Laws of Internet Branding. Harper Business Publications, New York < http://www.ries.com/11laws/11laws_toc.html> (Accessed 25 Nov 2000)

Snoke, R., Underwood, A. (1988) Generic Attributes of IS Graduates – A Queensland Study. Proceedings of the 9th Australasian Conference on Information Systems, Sydney, Australia, 29 Sep – 2 Oct, pp. 615–623

Smith, C. B. (1997) Casting the Net: Surveying an Internet Population. Journal of Computer Mediated Communication 3 (1) <http://www.ascusc.org/jcmc/vol3/issue1/smith.html> (Accessed 25 Nov 2000)

Songini, M. L. (2000) IT Changes Hit Supply Chains. Computerworld, Framingham, Oct 16. <http://www.computerworld.com/cwi/story/0,1199,NAV47_STO52455,00.html> (Accessed 25 Nov 2000)

Tabor, M. B. W. (1999) Latest Hit on Campus: Crescendo in E-Major. New York Times Special Section on E-Commerce, 22 Sep. <http://www.nytimes.com/library/tech/99/09/biztech/technology/22tabo.html> (Accessed 25 Nov 2000)

Tillett, L. S. (2000) Auction Sites In Bind Trying To Attract Return Bidders. Internetweek, Manhasset, Oct 9

Turban, E., Lee, J., King, D., Chung H. M. (2000) Electronic Commerce A Managerial Perspective. Prentice-Hall, New Jersey, 11: 291–299

University of Texas (2000) Measuring the Internet Economy 6 June 2000. <http://www.InternetIndicators.com/june_full_report.PDF> (Accessed 25 Nov 2000)

Urban, G. L., Hauser, J. R. (1993) Design and Marketing of New Products. Prentice Hall, New Jersey, pp. 164–175

Wang, S., Williams, L. (1997) Business Education in Electronic Commerce: a Survey on the Internet. Working Paper Series No. Business 97-001, Faculty of Business, University of New Brunswick, Saint John

Wind, J., Mahajan, V. (1997) Issues and Opportunities in New Product Development: An Introduction to the Special Issues. J Marketing Research XXXIV (Feb 97): 1–12

Young, J., Keen. C. (1998) Potential Information System Professionals: Initial Post Graduation Appointment Experiences. Proceedings of the 9th Australasian Conference on Information Systems, Sydney, Australia, 29 Sep – 2 Oct, pp. 709–721

Paula M. C. Swatman

Worked in e-commerce (both in business and academia) since the mid-1980's. Her academic interests focus on e-business strategy and implementation, and the impact of e-commerce on organisations. She was appointed Australia's first Professor of e-commerce and, after three years at RMIT University in Melbourne, moved in 2001 to the University of Koblenz-Landau in Germany, where she is Professor of e-business.

Elsie S. K. Chan

Adjunct lecturer and PhD student under the supervision of Prof. Paula Swatman at Deakin University, Australia. She holds a BSc in Mathematics and Computing (UEA), a MSc in Computer Studies (AI) (Essex) and a GradDip. in Computer Education (Monash). Since 1989 she has lectured at universities in Hong Kong, Macau and Australia. Her research interests lie in e-commerce/e-business education.

Appendix 1. A list of universities in the survey

Australia	
Bond University	http://www.bond.edu.au/
Central Queensland University	http://www.cqu.edu.au/
Charles Sturt University	http://www.csu.edu.au/
Curtin University of Technology	http://www.curtin.edu.au/
Deakin University	http://www.deakin.edu.au/
Edith Cowan University	http://www.cowan.edu.au/
Griffith University	http://www.gu.edu.au/
James Cook University	http://www.jcu.edu.au/
La Trobe University	http://www.latrobe.edu.au/
Macquarie University	http://www.mq.edu.au/
Monash University	http://www.monash.edu.au/
Murdoch University	http://www.murdoch.edu.au/
Northern Territory University	http://www.ntu.edu.au/
Queensland University of Technology	http://www.qut.edu.au/
RMIT University	http://www.rmit.edu.au/
Southern Cross University	http://www.scu.edu.au/main.html
Swinburne University of Technology	http://www.swin.edu.au/
The Australian Catholic University	http://www.acu.edu.au/
The Australian National University	http://www.anu.edu.au/
The Flinders University of South Australia	http://www.flinders.edu.au/
The University of Adelaide	http://www.adelaide.edu.au/
The University of Melbourne	http://www.unimelb.edu.au/
The University of New England	http://www.une.edu.au/
The University of New South Wales	http://www.unsw.edu.au/
The University of Newcastle	http://www.newcastle.edu.au/
The University of Queensland	http://www.uq.edu.au/
The University of Sydney	http://www.usyd.edu.au/
The University of Western Australia	http://www.uwa.edu.au/
The University of Western Sydney	http://www.uws.edu.au/
University of Ballarat	http://www.ballarat.edu.au/
University of Canberra	http://www.canberra.edu.au/
University of Notre Dame Australia	http://www.nd.edu.au/

continued

Appendix 1. Continued

Australia	
University of South Australia	http://www.unisa.edu.au/
University of Southern Queensland	http://www.usq.edu.au/
University of Tasmania	http://www.utas.edu.au/
University of Technology, Sydney	http://www.uts.edu.au/
University of the Sunshine Coast	http://www.usc.edu.au/
University of Wollongong	http://www.uow.edu.au/
Victoria University of Technology	http://www.vut.edu.au/

New Zealand	
Auckland University of Technology	http://www.aut.ac.nz/external.shtml
Lincoln University	http://www.lincoln.ac.nz/
Massey University	http://www.massey.ac.nz/
The University of Auckland	http://www.auckland.ac.nz/
The University of Canterbury	http://www.canterbury.ac.nz/
The University of Waikato	http://www.waikato.ac.nz/
Victoria University of Wellington	http://www.vuw.ac.nz/index.shtml
University of Otago	http://www.otago.ac.nz/

Hong Kong	
City University of Hong Kong	http://www.cityu.edu.hk/
Hong Kong Baptist University	http://www.hkbu.edu.hk/
Hong Kong University of Science and Technology	http://www.ust.hk/
Lingnan University	http://www.ln.edu.hk/
The Chinese University of Hong Kong	http://www.cuhk.hk/
The Hong Kong Polytechnic University	http://www.polyu.edu.hk/
The Open University of Hong Kong	http://www.ouhk.edu.hk/
The University of Hong Kong	http://www.hku.hk/

Singapore	
Nanyang Technological University	http://www.ntu.edu.sg/index_lo.htm
National University of Singapore	http://www.nus.edu.sg/
Singapore Management University	http://www.smu.edu.sg/

Appendix 2. E-commerce programs offered by universities in Australia, New Zealand, Hong Kong and Singapore

Name of University	Dept/School/Faculty	(A)	(B)	(C)	(D)	(E)	(F)	(G)
	Australia							
Bond University	School of Law							√
Bond University	School of Business			√			√	√
Central Queensland University	Faculty of Informatics and Communication			√	√		√	
Charles Sturt University	Faculty of Commerce	√			√			
Curtin University of Technology	School of Information Systems	√			√	√	√	
Deakin University	School of Management Information Systems	√			√		√	
Edith Cowan University	School of Management Information Systems	√			√		√	
La Trobe University	School of Business			√	√			
Monash University	School of Business and Electronic Commerce		√		√			
Monash University	School of Electronic Commerce			√				
Murdoch University	Department of Commerce	√			√		√	
RMIT University	Faculty of Business				√		√	
Southern Cross University	School of Multimedia and Information Technology	√				√		
Swinburne University of Technology	School of Business				√			
The University of New England	Faculty of Economics Business & Law Faculty of the Sciences				√			
The University of Queensland	Department of Commerce			√		√		
The University of Western Australia	Department of Information Management and Marketing	√				√		
University of South Australia	School of Accounting and Information Systems				√	√		
University of Tasmania	School of Information Systems	√						
University of Wollongong	Faculty of Commerce	√						
University of Wollongong	School of IT and Computer Science	√						

continued

Appendix 2. Continued

Name of University	Dept/School/Faculty	(A)	(B)	(C)	(D)	(E)	(F)	(G)
Victoria University	School of Information Systems	√						
New Zealand								
Auckland University of Technology	Business Faculty	√						
The University of Waikato	Department of Management Systems			√				
Victoria University of Wellington	School of Communications and Information Management	√						
Hong Kong								
City University of Hong Kong	Faculty of Business Administration					√		
City University of Hong Kong	Faculty of Engineering					√		
Hong Kong University of Science and Technology	Department of Information and Systems Management					√		
The Chinese University of Hong Kong	Faculty of Business Administration					√		
The Chinese University of Hong Kong	Faculty of Engineering					√		
The Hong Kong Polytechnic University	Department of Computing						√	
The Open University of Hong Kong	School of Business and Administration				√			
The University of Hong Kong	Faculty of Engineering					√		
Singapore								
National University of Singapore	Business School School of Computing	√				√		

(A) Undergraduate degree with electronic commerce / business major concentration
(B) Electronic commerce as a joint under-graduate degree with other disciplines
(C) Bachelor of Electronic Commerce
(D) Graduate Certificate / Diploma in Electronic Commerce
(E) Master degree with Electronic Commerce/Business as a specialisation
(F) Master of Electronic Commerce / Business
(G) Master of Electronic Commerce / Business and other discipline joint degrees

Appendix 3. Different types of courses/programs related to e-commerce/e-business offered by universities in Australia, New Zealand Hong Kong and Singapore

Appendix 3.A Undergraduate degree with electronic commerce major concentration		
Name of University	Faculty/School/ Department	Name of Degrees
Auckland University of Technology http://www.aut.ac. nz/external.shtml	Business Faculty http://www.aut.ac.nz/ faculties/business/ structurebus.shtml	Bachelor of Business (eBusiness) http://www.aut.ac.nz/faculties/business/ undergraduate/diplomadegree/bbus.shtml
Charles Sturt University http://www.csu. edu.au/	Faculty of Commerce http://www.csu.edu.au/ faculty/commerce/	Bachelor of Business (Specialisation EC) http://wwwdb.csu.edu.au/division/ marketing/courses/undergrad/ug-comm/ bbcbusbbcbuscou.htm#ecomm
Curtin University of Technology http://www.curtin. edu.au/	School of Information Systems http://www.cbs.curtin. edu.au/is/	Bachelor of Commerce (Electronic Commerce Major) http://www.curtin.edu. au/curtin/handbook2000/courses/is/ 230205.HTM Bachelor of Commerce (Banking and Electronic Commerce Double Major) http://www.curtin.edu.au/curtin/handbook 2000/courses/ef/234804.HTM Bachelor of Commerce (Finance and Electronic Commerce Double Major) http://www.curtin.edu.au/curtin/handbook 2000/courses/ef/234811.HTM Bachelor of Commerce (Information Systems and Electronic Commerce Double Degree) http://www.curtin.edu.au/curtin/handbook 2000/courses/is/234809.HTM Bachelor of Commerce (Information Technology and Electronic Commerce Double Major) http://www.curtin.edu.au/ curtin/handbook2000/courses/is/ 234810.HTM Bachelor of Commerce (International Business and Electronic Commerce Double Major) http://www.curtin.edu.au/curtin/ handbook2000/courses/man/234814.HTM Bachelor of Commerce (Marketing and Electronic Commerce) http://www.curtin. edu.au/curtin/handbook2000/courses/mkt/ 234818.HTM
Deakin University http://www.deakin. edu.au/	School of Management Information Systems http://mis.deakin. edu.au/	Bachelor of Commerce (Electronic Commerce Major sequence) http://mis.deakin.edu.au/Course_info/ Under_grad/elec_comm.htm

continued

Appendix 3. Continued

Appendix 3.A Undergraduate degree with electronic commerce major concentration

Name of University	Faculty/School/ Department	Name of Degrees
Edith Cowan University http://www.cowan. edu.au	School of Management Information Systems http://www-business. ecu.edu.au/mis/	Bachelor of Business (Major Electronic Commerce) http://www-business.ecu.edu. au/mis/planners/ecomm.htm
Murdoch University http://www. murdoch.edu.au	Department of Commerce http://www business.murdoch.edu. au/commerce/index.htm	Bachelor of Commerce (Electronic Commerce Stream) http://wwwbusiness. murdoch.edu.au/commerce/undergrad/ electcom.html#primary
National University of Singapore http://www.nus. edu.sg/	Business School http://www.fba.nus.edu. sg/postgrad/gsb/ School of Computing http://www.comp.nus. edu.sg/	Bachelor of Business Administration (E-Business) http://www.fba.nus.edu.sg/ undergrad/BBA.htm
Southern Cross University http://www.scu. edu.au/	School of Multimedia and Information Technology http://www. scu.edu.au/schools/smit/	Bachelor of Information Technology (Electronic Commerce) Bachelor of Business (Electronic Commerce) (These programs will be offered in 2001)
The University of Western Australia http://www.uwa. edu.au	Department of Information Management and Marketing http://imm.uwa.edu.au	Bachelor of Commerce (Major in Electronic Commerce) http://www.imm.ecel.uwa.edu.au/imm/ major_in_electronic_commerce.htm
University of Tasmania http://www.utas. edu.au/	School of Information Systems http://www.infosys.utas. edu.au/	Bachelor of Information Systems (Electronic Commerce Program) http://www.infosys.utas.edu.au/courses/ BIS-EC.html
University of Western Sydney (Macarthur) http:// www.macarthur. uws.edu.au/	Department of Computing and Information Systems http://fistserv.macarthur. uws.edu.au/cis/	Bachelor of Business Computing (E-Business)
University of Western Sydney (Macarthur) http:// www.macarthur. uws.edu.au/	Department of Computing and Information Systems http://fistserv.macarthur. uws.edu.au/cis/ Faculty of Business http:// bus.macarthur.uws.edu.au/	Bachelor of Commerce (E-Business)

continued

Appendix 3. Continued

Appendix 3.A Undergraduate degree with electronic commerce major concentration

Name of University	Faculty/School/Department	Name of Degrees
University of Wollongong http://www.uow.edu.au/	Faculty of Commerce http://www.uow.edu.au/commerce/	Bachelor of Commerce (Combined specialisations with Electronic Commerce) Specialisations: Accounting, Business Information Systems, Economics, Finance, Marketing and Management http://www.uow.edu.au/commerce/ecommerce.html
University of Wollongong http://www.uow.edu.au/	School of IT and Computer Science http://www.itacs.uow.edu.au/	Bachelor of Information and Communication Technology (Combined Specialisations with Electronic Commerce) Specialisations: Software Development, Network Management, Telecommunications, Business Information Systemshttp://www.itacs.uow.edu.au/undergrad/iact/binfotechsch.html
Victoria University http://www.vu.edu.au/	School of Information Systems http://www.business.vu.edu.au/inform_systems_about_depart.htm	Bachelor of Business in Electronic Commerce Bachelor of Business in Accounting and Electronic Commerce http://www.vu.edu.au/handbook/fob/2000Bus-38.pdf
Victoria University of Wellington http://www.vuw.ac.nz/index.shtml	School of Communications and Information Management http://www.scim.vuw.ac.nz/	Bachelor of Commerce and Administration (Electronic Commerce and Multimedia) http://www.vuw.ac.nz/home/undergraduate/subjects/elcm.html

Appendix 3.B Electronic commerce and other disciplines as joint degree

Name of University	Faculty/School/Department	Name of Degree
Monash University http://www.monash.edu.au	Faculty of Business and Electronic Commerce http://www.buseco.monash.edu.au/Schools/SOBEC/	Bachelor of Business and Electronic Commerce http://www.monash.edu.au/pubs/handbooks/undergrad/ug0212.htm

Appendix 3.C Bachelor of Electronic Commerce

Name of University	Faculty/School/Department	Name of Degrees
Bond University http://www.bond.edu.au	School of Business http://www.bond.edu.au/bus/index.htm	Bachelor of Electronic Commerce http://www.bond.edu.au/bus/degrees/ugpro/Ug-becom.htm

continued

Appendix 3. Continued

Appendix 3.C Bachelor of Electronic Commerce		
Name of University	Faculty/School/ Department	Name of Degrees
Central Queensland University http:// www.cqu.edu.au/	Faculty of Informatics and Communications http://www.infocom.cqu. edu.au/	Bachelor of Electronic Commerce http://handbook.cqu.edu.au/2001pdf/ ugprograms.pdf
La Trobe University http://www.latrobe. edu.au/	School of Business http://www.business. latrobe.edu.au/	Bachelor of Electronic Commerce http://www.latrobe.edu.au/handbook/ wodonga/courses_aw.htm#P465_21894
Monash University http://www.monash. edu.au	School of Electronic Commerce http://www. ecom.monash.edu.au/ overview.html	Bachelor of Electronic Commerce http://www.ecom.monash.edu.au/ Course/
The Open University of Hong Kong http:// www.ouhk.edu.hk	School of Business and Administration http:// balinux.ouhk.edu.hk/~ school/bec/index1.htm	Bachelor of Electronic Commerce Bachelor of Electronic Commerce (Honours) http://balinux.ouhk.edu.hk/ ~school/bec/overview.htm
The University of Queensland http:// www.uq.edu.au/	Department of Commerce http://www.commerce.uq. edu.au/	Bachelor of Electronic Commerce http://www.commerce.uq.edu.au/ecom/ brochure.html#brochure
The University of Waikato http:// www.waikato.ac.nz/	Department of Manage- ment Systems http:// www.mngt.waikato.ac.nz/ depts/mnss/Home.htm	Bachelor of Electronic Commerce http://www.waikato.ac.nz/slice/ degrees/becomm.shtml

Appendix 3.D Graduate certificate / diploma in Electronic Commerce		
Name of University	Faculty/School/ Department	Name of Grad Certificate / Diploma
Central Queensland University http:// www.cqu.edu.au/	Faculty of Informatics and Communications http://www.infocom.cqu. edu.au/	Graduate Diploma in Electronic Commerce http://handbook.cqu.edu.au/2001pdf/ pgprograms.pdf
Charles Sturt University http:// www.csu.edu.au/	Faculty of Commerce http://www.csu.edu.au/ faculty/commerce/	Graduate Certificate in Electronic Commerce http://wwwdb.csu.edu.au/ division/marketing/courses/gradcert/gc- comm/egctqm/egctqmcou.htm
Curtin University of Technology http://www.curtin. edu.au/	School of Information Systems http://www.cbs. curtin.edu.au/is/	Graduate Certificate in Electronic Commerce http://www.cbs.curtin.edu.au/ UNITS/PDFliers/IS/GCert-El-Comm.pdf Postgraduate Diploma in Business (Electro- nic Commerce) http://www.cbs.curtin.edu. au/UNITS/PDFliers/IS/Pgd-EC.pdf

continued

Appendix 3. Continued

Appendix 3.D Graduate certificate / diploma in Electronic Commerce		
Name of University	Faculty/School/ Department	Name of Grad Certificate / Diploma
Deakin University http://www.deakin. edu.au/	School of Management Information Systems http://mis.deakin.edu.au/	Graduate Diploma of Electronic Commerce http://www.detc.deakin.edu. au/MECom/graddip.asp Commerce http://www.detc.deakin.edu. au/MECom/gradcert.asp
Edith Cowan University http://www. cowan.edu.au/	School of Management Information Systems http://www-business.ecu. edu.au/mis/	Graduate/Executive Certificate in Electronic Commerce http://www-business.ecu.edu.au/mis/ planners/ecertecom.htm Graduate/Executive Diploma in Business (Electronic Commerce)
La Trobe University http://www.latrobe. edu.au/	School of Business http://www.business. latrobe.edu.au/	Graduate Diploma in Electronic Commerce http://www.aw.latrobe.edu. au/depart/dbus/gdipec.htm
Monash University http://www. monash.edu.au	School of Business and Electronic Commerce http://www.buseco.monash. edu.au/Schools/SOBEC/	Graduate Certificate in Electronic Commerce http://www.monash.edu.au/ pubs/1999handbooks/buseco/be0210.htm Graduate Diploma in Electronic Commerce http://www.monash.edu.au/pubs/ 1999handbooks/distance/de0069.htm
Murdoch University http:// www.murdoch. edu.au/	Department of Commerce http://wwwbusiness. murdoch.edu.au/ commerce/index.htm	Postgraduate Certificate in Electronic Commerce http://wwwbusiness.murdoch. edu.au/commerce/degree/pcec.htm Postgraduate Diploma in Electronic Commerce http://wwwbusiness.murdoch. edu.au/commerce/degree/pdec.htm
The University of New England http: //www.une.edu.au/	Faculty of Economics Business & Law http:// www.une.edu.au/febl/ Faculty of the Sciences http://www.une.edu.au/ sciences/index.html	Graduate Certificate in E-Commerce http://www.une.edu.au/febl/awards/ ecom.htm
Swinburne University of Technology http://www.swin. edu.au	School of Business http://www.swin.edu.au/ business/	Grad Cert of Business (eBusiness and Communication) http://www.ld.swin. edu.au/ebusiness/html/subjects.htm#top
RMIT University http://www.rmit. edu.au	Faculty of Business http://www.bf.rmit.edu.au	Grad. Certificate in E-Business Grad. Diploma in E-Business http://www.bf.rmit.edu.au/e-commerce/ html/course_structure.html

continued

Appendix 3. Continued

Appendix 3.D Graduate certificate / diploma in Electronic Commerce

Name of University	Faculty/School/ Department	Name of Grad Certificate / Diploma
University of South Australia http:// www.unisa.edu.au/	School of Accounting and Information Systems http://business.unisa.edu. au/infosys/index.htm	Grad Cert and Grad Dip in Business (e-Business) http://business.unisa.edu.au/infosys/ courses/
University of Western Sydney (Macarthur) http:// www.macarthur. uws.edu.au/	Department of Computing and Information Systems http://fistserv.macarthur. uws.edu.au/cis/	Graduate Diploma in Information Technology (E-Business)

Appendix 3.E Master degree with Electronic Commerce/Business as specialisations

Name of University	Faculty/School/ Department	Name of Master Degrees
City University of Hong Kong http:// www.cityu.edu.hk/	Faculty of Business http://www.cityu.edu.hk/ fb/homepage/index.htm	Master of Science in Electronic Commerce http://www.cityu.edu.hk/fb/homepage/ CourseOfferings.htm Master of Arts in Electronic Business http:// www.is.cityu.edu.hk/maeb/rationale.html
Curtin University of Technology http://www.curtin. edu.au/	School of Information Systems http://www.cbs.curtin. edu.au/is/	Master of Commerce – Electronic Commerce http://www.cbs.curtin.edu.au/UNITS/ PDFliers/IS/MCom-EC.pdf
Hong Kong University of Science and Technology http://www.ust. edu.hk/	Department of Information and Systems Management http://www.ismt. ust.hk/	Master of Science in Information System Management (Electronic Commerce Concentration) http://www.bm.ust.hk/ mscis/curriculum.html
National University of Singapore http:// www.nus.edu.sg/	Business School http://www.fba.nus.edu. sg/postgrad/gsb/ School of Computing http://www.comp.nus. edu.sg/	Master of Science in e-Business http://www.fba.nus.edu.sg/postgrad/gsb/ eBusiness/master_of_science_in_e.htm
Southern Cross University http:// www.scu.edu.au/	School of Multimedia and Information Technology http://www.scu.edu. au/schools/smit/	Master of Information Systems (Electronic Commerce Stream) This program will be offered in 2001
The Chinese University of Hong Kong http://www. cuhk.hk/	Faculty of Business Administration http://www. cuhk.edu.hk/baf/	Master of Science in E-Commerce (Business Program) http://www.cuhk. edu.hk/msc-programs-in-ecommerce/ business_ecom.htm

continued

Appendix 3. Continued

Appendix 3.E *Master degree with Electronic Commerce/Business as specialisations*		
Name of University	Faculty/School/ Department	Name of Master Degrees
The Chinese University of Hong Kong http://www.cuhk.hk	Faculty of Engineering http://www.erg.cuhk.edu.hk/	Master of Science in E-Commerce (Technologies Program) http://www.cuhk.edu.hk/msc-programs-in-ecommerce/engine_ecom.htm
The Hong Kong Polytechnic University http://www.polyu.edu.hk/	Department of Computing http://www.comp.polyu.edu.hk/ Faculty of Business and Information System http://www.polyu.edu.hk/fbis/	MSc in E-Commerce MSc in E-Commerce (Executive Stream) http://www.comp.polyu.edu.hk/mscec/content.htm
The University of Hong Kong http://www.hku.hk/	Faculty of Engineering http://engg.hku.hk/	Master of Science (Engineering)in Electronic Commerce http://aajc.hku.hk/ecomprogram.html
The University of Queensland http://www.uq.edu.au/	Department of Commerce http://www.commerce.uq.edu.au/	Master of Commerce Concentration in Electronic Commerce http://www.commerce.uq.edu.au/ecom/master_of_commerce.htm
The University of Western Australia http://www.uwa.edu.au	Department of Information Management and Marketing http://imm.uwa.edu.au/	Master of Electronic Marketing and Information Management http://www.imm.ecel.uwa.edu.au/imm/M_in_EC.htm
University of South Australia http://www.unisa.edu.au/	School of Accounting and Information Systems http://business.unisa.edu.au/infosys/index.htm	Master of Business (e-Business) http://business.unisa.edu.au/infosys/courses/mbebu.html

Appendix 3.F *Master of Electronic Commerce/Business*		
Name of University	Faculty/School/ Department	Name of Master Degrees
Bond University http://www.bond.edu.au/	School of Business http://www.bond.edu.au/bus/index.htm	Master of Electronic Commerce http://www.bond.edu.au/bus/degrees/pgpro/pg-mEcomm.htm
Central Queensland University http://www.cqu.edu.au/	Faculty of Informatics and Communications http://www.infocom.cqu.edu.au/	Master of Electronic Commerce http://handbook.cqu.edu.au/2001pdf/pgprograms.pdf
Curtin University of Technology http://www.curtin.edu.au/	School of Information Systems http://www.cbs.curtin.edu.au/is/	Master of Electronic Commerce http://www.curtin.edu.au/curtin/handbook2000/courses/is/296515.HTM

continued

Appendix 3. Continued

Appendix 3.F Master of Electronic Commerce/Business

Name of University	Faculty/School/Department	Name of Master Degrees
Deakin University http://www.deakin.edu.au/	School of Management Information Systems http://mis.deakin.edu.au/	Master of Electronic Commerce http://www.detc.deakin.edu.au/MECom/mec.asp
Edith Cowan University http://www.cowan.edu.au	School of Management Information Systems http://www-business.ecu.edu.au/mis/	Master in Electronic Commerce (will change to Master of E-Business in 2001) http://www-business.ecu.edu.au/mis/planners/MEC.htm
Murdoch University http://www.murdoch.edu.au/	Department of Commerce http:// wwwbusiness.murdoch.edu.au/commerce/index.htm	Master of Electronic Commerce http://wwwbusiness.murdoch.edu.au/commerce/degree/mec.htm
RMIT University http://www.rmit.edu.au/	Faculty of Business http://www.bf.rmit.edu.au/	Master of E-Business (Research) http://www.bf.rmit.edu.au/e-commerce/html/course_structure.html

Appendix 3.G Master of Electronic Commerce and other disciplines joint degrees

Name of University	Faculty/School/Department	Name of Master Degrees (Joint)
Bond University http://www.bond.edu.au/	School of Law http://www.bond.edu.au/law/	Master of Electronic Commerce / Master of Laws Master of Electronic Commerce / Master of Jurisprudence Master of Electronic Commerce / Master of Business Law http://www.bond.edu.au/law/degrees/pg/Combined.htm
Bond University http://www.bond.edu.au/	School of Business http://www.bond.edu.au/bus/index.htm	MBA / Master of Electronic Commerce MIT / Master of Electronic Commerce Master of Finance / Master of Electronic Commerce Master of Accounting / Master of Electronic Commerce http://www.bond.edu.au/bus/degrees/pgpro/pg-mEcomm.htm

Appendix 4. E-commerce/e-business offered as single subjects

Name of University	Faculty/School/Department	Name of Subject
Massey University http://www.massey.ac.nz/	Graduate School of Business http://ied.massey.ac.nz/mba.html	115.760 Electronic Commerce http://www.massey.ac.nz/~DViehlan/115760.html 157.754 Electronic Commerce Systems http://www.massey.ac.nz/~DViehlan/157754.html
The University of Melbourne http://www.unimelb.edu.	Department of Information Systems http://www.dis.unimelb.edu.au/	615655 Electronic Commerce http://www.dis.unimelb.edu.au/courses/subjects/pghandbook/615-655.htm
University of Canberra http://www.canberra.edu.au/	Division of Management and Technology http://www.canberra.edu.au/uc/faculties/div_man_tech.html	005456 Electronic Commerce: Technical Issues 005457 Electronic Commerce: Business Issues
University of Notre Dame Australia http://www.nd.edu.au/	College of Business http://www.nd.edu.au/colleges_departments/business/	CO225 Electronic Commerce http://www.nd.edu.au/colleges_departments/business/units/
University of Southern Queensland http://www.usq.edu.au/	Faulty of Commerce http://www.usq.edu.au/faculty/commerce/	51170 Introduction To Electronic Commerce http://www.usq.edu.au/unit/synopsis/51170.htm

Appendix 5. Subjects which may be studied as elective or core for an undergraduate e-commerce/e-business degree

Infrastructure		
Commerce and WWW Applications Systems	Data Communication	Developing Electronic Commerce
Electronic and Desktop Publishing	Electronic Commerce applications	Electronic Commerce Fundamental
Electronic Commerce Laboratory	Electronic Commerce Systems	Electronic Commerce Technologies
Electronic Document Design	Electronic Meeting System	Fundamentals of Computing and Electronic Commerce
Future Direction	Information Technology	Infrastructure for electronic commerce
Innovation and Electronic Commerce	Instruction to business on the Internet	Internet Function and Facilities

continued

Appendix 5. Continued

Infrastructure		
Introduction to Electronic Commerce	Introduction to the Internet	Java Programming and the Internet
Multimedia and Internet	Security Control	Supra-organisational Systems
Technology Infrastructure Management	Web Site Design and Management	Electronic Solutions

Services		
Business Applications	Business On-line	Commercial Aspects of Electronic Commerce
Decision Support	Electronic Commerce and Marketing	Electronic Commerce and the Economics of Information Electronic
Commerce Electronic Trading	Business Interfaces Global Electronic Finance	Electronic Marketing Information Systems and Electronic Commerce
Commerce Strategy Internet Commerce	Inter-organisational systems	Management and Electronic Business
Marketing on the Commercial Internet	Marketing on the Internet	Network applications and Electronic Commerce
Supply Chain management	Trading Systems	

Legal		
Commerce Law	Electronic Commerce and Law	Cyber Law
Management and Legal Implications of Electronic Commerce		
Legal Foundations of Electronic Commerce		

Appendix 6. Subjects which may be studied as elective or core for a masters degree in e-commerce/e-business

Infrastructure	
Advanced Electronic Business Application Development	Analysis and Design of Electronic Business Systems
Business Focused Electronic Commerce and Managing	
Electronic Commerce Systems Development	
Contemporary topics in Electronic Business	Cryptography, Information Security and Electronic Commerce
Electronic Business Software and Technology	Electronic Business Strategy
Electronic Commerce Data Mining Techniques	Electronic Business Resources
Foundations of Electronic Business Systems	Fundamentals of Electronic Commerce Technologies
Fundamentals of Electronic Commerce	Information Systems and Electronic Commerce Strategy
Infrastructure and security management for electronic commerce	Internet and Computer Communications
Internet and the World Wide Web	Internet Communications Campaigns
Internet for Business	Internet Programming
Issues in Electronic Business	Java and information technology for executives
Network and Web Programming	Open Systems for Electronic Commerce
Web Advertising and Web Publishing	Web-publishing: design and creation

Service	
Business transformation and process re-engineering	Business-to-business Electronic Commerce
Customer Focused Electronic Commerce	Cyber Marketing and Customer Relationship Management
Electronic Business Fulfilment	Electronic Business Supply Chains
Electronic Business Planing and Implementation	Economics of Electronic Commerce
Electronic Financing	Electronic Business Strategies and Management
Electronic C ommerce on the Internet	Electronic Payment Systems
Electronic Marketing	Information Technology Based Organization Transformation
Internet and Computer Communications	Internet and Electronic Commerce Marketing

continued

Appendix 6. Continued

	Service
Internet Computing for Managers	Internet Marketing
Logistics Management	Online Marketing
Supply Chain Management	The Electronic Business Regulatory Environment: An executive perspective
Underlying Technologies for Electronic Commerce – A managerial perspective	
Web Design and Management	

	Legal
Electronic Business Law	Legal Aspects of Electronic Commerce
Electronic Commerce Law	Legal Aspects of Information Technology and Electronic Commerce

Pauline J. Sheldon,
Karl W. Wöber,
SpringerComputerScience

Hannes Werthner, Stefan Klein

Information Technology and Tourism —Canada, 2001
A Challenging Relationship

2001. XII, 386 pages. 83 figures.
Softcover DM 138,–, öS 966,–, as of Jan. 2002 EUR 70,20
(Recommended retail prices)
All prices are net-prices subject to local VAT.
ISBN 3-211-83649-7

This collection comprises the papers presented at the International
Conference on Information and Communication Technologies in
Tourism held in Montreal, Canada. The role played by information and
communication technologies in the management and marketing of
destinations, the convergence of communication systems and the
integration of heterogeneous information systems, the designs of
intelligent recommendation systems, the use of destination web sites
by consumers, and the implementation of information and communication technologies in small and medium-sized tourism enterprises
are addressed.

SpringerComputerScience

Springer Wien New York

A-1201 Wien, Sachsenplatz 4–6, P.O. Box 89, Fax +43.1.330 24 26, e-mail: books@springer.at, Internet: www.springer.at
D-69126 Heidelberg, Haberstraße 7, Fax +49.6221.345-229, e-mail: orders@springer.de
USA, Secaucus, NJ 07096-2485, P.O. Box 2485, Fax +1.201.348-4505, e-mail: orders@springer-ny.com
Eastern Book Service, Japan, Tokyo 113, 3–13, Hongo 3-chome, Bunkyo-ku, Fax +81.3.38 18 08 64, e-mail: orders@svt-ebs.co.jp

SpringerComputerScience

Hannes Werthner, Stefan Klein

Information Technology and Tourism –
A Challenging Relationship

1999. XX, 323 pages. 134 figures.
Softcover DM 90,–, öS 629,–, as of Jan. 2002 EUR 45,–
(Recommended retail prices)
All prices are net-prices subject to local VAT.
ISBN 3-211-83274-2

Information systems in tourism, such as computer reservation systems, yield management systems, and tourism-marketing systems, have been among the pioneers of leading-edge technology applications and have driven the dynamics of development in tourism services. Tourism is regarded as one of the most successful applications of electronic commerce.

The book is synthesizing and analyzing the current situation, trying to set the stage and to show ways of future research. A common methodological approach and framework enables the analysis of the ongoing processes and the underlying trends. From both a technological and a management point of view, the work is focusing on interorganizational processes and information systems, it takes a network-oriented approach, corresponding with the fact that travel and tourism is an interorganizational business. In order to provide a coherent picture, the work is located within a triangle of tourism research, information technology and computer science, and management science.

SpringerWienNewYork

A-1201 Wien, Sachsenplatz 4–6, P.O. Box 89, Fax +43.1.330 24 26, e-mail: books@springer.at, Internet: www.springer.at
D-69126 Heidelberg, Haberstraße 7, Fax +49.6221.345-229, e-mail: orders@springer.de
USA, Secaucus, NJ 07096-2485, P.O. Box 2485, Fax +1.201.348-4505, e-mail: orders@springer-ny.com
Eastern Book Service, Japan, Tokyo 113, 3–13, Hongo 3-chome, Bunkyo-ku, Fax +81.3.38 18 08 64, e-mail: orders@svt-ebs.co.jp

Springer-Verlag
and the Environment

WE AT SPRINGER-VERLAG FIRMLY BELIEVE THAT AN international science publisher has a special obligation to the environment, and our corporate policies consistently reflect this conviction.

WE ALSO EXPECT OUR BUSINESS PARTNERS – PRINTERS, paper mills, packaging manufacturers, etc. – to commit themselves to using environmentally friendly materials and production processes.

THE PAPER IN THIS BOOK IS MADE FROM NO-CHLORINE pulp and is acid free, in conformance with international standards for paper permanency.